W0038426

THE GUIDE TO
GOOD CHEAP
HUNTING

THE GUIDE TO
GOOD CHEAP
HUNTING

Bob Gilsvik

Illustrations by David Gilsvik

A Scarborough Book
STEIN AND DAY / *Publishers* / New York

FIRST SCARBOROUGH BOOKS EDITION 1979.
The Guide to Good Cheap Hunting was originally published in hardcover by
Stein and Day/*Publishers* in 1978.

Copyright © 1978 by Bob Gilsvik
All rights reserved.
Printed in the United States of America
Stein and Day/*Publishers*/Scarborough House
Briarcliff Manor, N.Y. 10510

Library of Congress Cataloging in Publication Data
Gilsvik, Bob.
    The guide to good cheap hunting.
    Includes index.
    1. Hunting—Handbooks, manuals, etc.   I. Title.
SK33.G55   799.2   77-22744
ISBN 0-8128-6031-4

*To my brothers, Jim, Ken,
and Rich Gilsvik.*

CONTENTS

CONTENTS

INTRODUCTION

In the last few years the price of just about everything has doubled, and in some cases even tripled. *The Guide to Good Cheap Hunting* was written to help you lower the high price tag on hunting; to show you how to enjoy more and better hunting.

This manual contains many drawings and photos which illustrate how to make hunting gear and how to utilize items that cost little or nothing. It tells you what you need to know about such often overlooked weapons as pellet guns, slingshots, and blowguns. It points out the advantages of camping while on hunting trips, and includes information on winter camping and backpack hunting. It explains how to save money by handloading and by making your own hunting clothes. A chapter on hunting and trapping tells how you can return from a hunting trip money ahead. There is information on cabin building, dog handling, rifles, shotguns, and bows and arrows. There are individual chapters that tell you how to hunt waterfowl, upland birds, squirrels, doves, deer, and bears. Winter hunting for rabbits and predators are covered in special detail.

The book has one continuous theme: how to enjoy *good cheap hunting*.

1
RIFLES AND SHOTGUNS

The purchase of a rifle or shotgun is a major expense. But a moderately priced firearm can last a lifetime. Resale value may equal, or even surpass, your original investment. Inflation does play a role. A well-cared-for pre-1964 Winchester Model 70, for example, is worth almost triple its original price tag. Just like old cars, certain rifles and shotguns remain popular over the years. Some hunters have found buying and selling guns a profitable sideline.

But that's not for everyone. To keep your firearm purchases to a minimum, and to get to know each one well, think in terms of rifles and shotguns with all-around capability. You can buy a light, fast-swinging 20-gauge side-by-side double for grouse and a heavy 12-gauge magnum autoloader for geese, but it's cheaper to buy one gun that will be adequate, if not ideal, for both grouse and geese and many other species as well.

CHOOSING YOUR SHOTGUN

Although shotguns are made in six different gauges, just two—12 and 20 —are the most popular and useful. Of the two, the 12-gauge will do what the 20-gauge can do, and sometimes do it better. If you plan to use your shotgun for hunting deer with slug or buckshot, there is no question that the 12 will prove more satisfactory. More 12-gauge shotguns are sold each year than any other size. Its advantage is the large variety of loads it handles. You can load it as light or as heavy as you wish. More different kinds of shells are produced in 12-gauge than in any other gauge; more sizes of shot pellets are used in 12-gauge ammunition. This gives you the adaptability to meet different hunting demands. You can buy a light 12-gauge load that duplicates the power of a medium 20-gauge shell and the cost will be less. At the other end of the power range, you can choose heavy 12-gauge charges that shoot almost as hard and as far as a 10-gauge.

Adapters are made which fit a single- or double-barrel 12-gauge and let you fire .410 loads with patterns very much like those of a regular .410. This permits short-range target practice and shots at small pests for a smaller cost per shell.

The pump repeating shotgun is the most popular type with American shooters. Pump-operated shotguns are rugged and strong. They handle heavy loads with ease. Current models are made with a short slide action; just a flick of the wrist ejects the empty shell and shoves a loaded one into place. They are lighter than older models, usually weighing 6½ to 7½ pounds. Grade for grade, pump repeating shotguns cost less than double-barrel and autoloading models. It's a fact that a working man can still buy a good pump shotgun for quite a bit less than one week's pay.

For true all-round capability, the pump repeating shotgun should have an adjustable choke installed. Cost-minded shooters usually choose the adjustable choke over an extra barrel because it costs less, especially when the factory offers a package deal of gun and choke.

The big advantage of the adjustable choke is the large number of adjustments it allows. You're set for everything from geese to quail. And you get another advantage when you have the device installed to your order. Depending on your instructions, the gunsmith can change the original barrel length by 1 or 2 inches either way by cutting a little extra off the barrel for a shorter dimension or leaving it all on for a longer dimension. An overall barrel length of 26 inches is all that's needed for any type of upland game gun. You may want a longer sighting plane for waterfowl, but this is not as necessary with a repeater because its front sight is 4 or 5 inches farther from the breach or stock comb than is the front sight of a double-barrel gun.

The average hunter can get by without an automatic since he rarely gets the chance to cut loose with more than one or two shots at a rabbit or pheasant. The waterfowler and skeet shooter, however, may prefer the autoloader. They have become increasingly popular in recent years. The autoloading, or automatic, shotgun works on one of two principles—recoil or gas. Both types work well and both are equally acceptable in the field. Remington uses gas-operation in its Model 1100, while Browning's well-known automatic is recoil-operated.

The autoloading shotgun has all the advantages and disadvantages of the pump. The only difference is that manual operation after each shot is eliminated with the autoloader, which means faster shooting.

The double-barrel is another choice for all-round gunning. If your main targets are grouse and woodcock, you can choose a lightweight model with barrels bored improved cylinder and modified. The same light double can be used for close-range shooting of waterfowl over decoys and pheasant at moderate ranges. Many who use the double prefer barrels bored modified and full, for tighter patterns at longer ranges.

The big drawback to the double-barrel, aside from its being a poor choice for deer hunting with slugs (accuracy is terrible), is the high price tag. Cheap ones are available, but their quality is usually poor. Exceptions are the moderately priced Fox and Stevens models sold by Savage Arms Co. They do run a little heavy in weight but the 24-inch Fox B Lightweight is a fast-handling gun. The Ithaca Model 100 costs more, but in 12 gauge is lighter and faster-handling than some 20-gauge shotguns. It has a single trigger and is available in three barrel lengths.

A CHEAP SHOTGUN TARGET

A cheap target for shotgun shooting is a Frisbee—the saucer-shaped plastic toy that flies like a clay target when thrown. About 9 inches in diameter, it's larger than a clay target, and tougher. The Frisbee will still fly flawlessly at the end of the day with light streaming through countless shot holes. And it's considerably easier to hit than conventional clay targets. That can be a blessing for the beginning shooter who needs an easier target to gain confidence.

Of course it doesn't fly to pieces when it's hit, and thus is not as spectacular as a clay target, that is a small disadvantage. Also, a good hit will cause the Frisbee to change its trajectory without knocking it down, so a shooter can sometimes score two or three hits on the target while it's still in the air.

Added realism can be achieved if several throwers conceal themselves in a gully. The man on top with the shotgun walks parallel to the gully and about 12 yards from its edge. He never knows for sure when the "birds" will fly.

CHOOSING YOUR HIGH-POWERED RIFLE

In choosing an all-round caliber of rifle, consider its uses. Will it be used for varmint as well as big-game hunting? Is your big-game hunting confined to deer and black bear, or do you plan to hunt larger animals such as moose and elk? Actually, you can't go wrong with either of the two calibers popularly considered to be all-round—the .30-06 and the .270 Winchester. The .270 gets the edge for accuracy on hard-to-hit varmints. The .30-06, with its variety of bullet weights, including the 220-grain and 180-grain, gets the

Hunting with a muzzleloader is fun and challenging. Cut costs by building your own from a kit.

edge on heavy-boned big game. The heaviest factory load for the .270 has a 150-grain bullet, which, for practical purposes, has no real advantage over the excellent 130-grain bullet, which will handle anything from woodchuck to bull moose.

A new development is Remington's "Accelerator" cartridge which converts the .30-06 rifle to a flat-shooting varmint gun. This became available in January 1977. The "Accelerator" cartridge involves the use of a .22-caliber 55-grain pointed softpoint bullet inside a .30-caliber sabot casing. The sabot-encased .22-caliber bullet is loaded in a standard .30-06 case and fired in a regular .30-06 rifle. Muzzle velocity from a 24-inch barrel is 4080 fps. Once the sabot-encased bullet leaves the muzzle, air resistance peels open the sabot, causing it to drop off the bullet.

The Accelerator cartridge gives the shooter two advantages. First, the varmint hunter gets the highest velocity he has ever had available, along with remarkably flat trajectory. Second, it enables the owner of a manually operated (bolt-, pump-, or lever-action) .30-06 rifle to convert that rifle to a tight-grouping long-range varmint gun by simply switching ammunition. Accelerator cartridges do not operate the action of autoloading rifles but will function in them on a single-shot basis.

The .243 Winchester is another choice for an all-round rifle if you hunt varmints and big game no larger than deer and black bear. It has far less recoil than either the .270 or .30-06 and sounds a great deal less like a cannon. Other choices include 6mm Remington, .25-06 Remington, .250 Savage, and .257 Roberts.

The lever action rifle has won a place for itself in American history and has earned continuing popularity with the hunting clan. The Winchester Model 94 is the most familiar to hunters. It's chambered for the 30/30 Winchester and the .32 Winchester Special, two fine medium-class deer cartridges which can generally be expected to group at about 3½ inches at 100 yards. There are disadvantages; they are not particularly accurate at long range and, for a number of reasons, are a poor choice for handloaders. Where most shots are within 100 yards, both the .30/30 and .32 are adequate for medium-size game. They are very popular and relatively inexpensive.

A bolt-action rifle is the first consideration for an all-round caliber such as the .270. More bolt-action rifles are made and used in this country than

The .243 will handle anything from crows to deer, but the .270 or .30-06 is a better choice for an all-round rifle if you plan to hunt bigger game.

any other type. Bolt-action rifles can be highly accurate. One reason is the strong close support given the cartridge head; another is that they have a one-piece stock. All the highly developed special target rifles used in match and bench shooting have bolt breeches. The bolt-action is the first choice of the handloader.

Finding a suitable bolt-action rifle should be easy, since all U.S. firearm factories make them and many foreign brands are imported. Two very popular models are the Remington Model 700 and the Winchester Model 70.

CHOOSING YOUR .22 RIMFIRE

You can limit your basic battery to shotgun and high-powered rifle, but you'll be missing some fun. American shooters fire 3 billion rounds of .22 ammunition every year. The .22 cartridge is inexpensive and produces little noticeable recoil. People have killed Alaskan grizzlies and African lions with .22 rifles, but the usual game is rabbits, squirrels, and small pests of all kinds. The .22 rifle is handy on the trapline, will give pinpoint accuracy on the target range, and is a never-ending source of economical fun with tin cans and swinging bottles.

Most .22 rifles are chambered for .22 Short, Long, and Long Rifle ammunition. The Long Rifle cartridge is the best all-round load. The Long is an intermediate load of little practical value. The .22 Long Rifle cartridge in Super-X and Super-Speed has a 40-grain bullet that leaves the muzzle at 1365 fps.

Generally, it pays to buy an at least moderately priced .22 rifle. The cheapies usually have birch stocks rather than walnut, and there is the strong possibility that small parts will break. Usually the trigger pull is rough and the sights crude, and the action may jam or otherwise malfunction. Take care of a fine .22 rifle and you'll get good resale value.

If you've used bolt-actions all your life and have wanted to try a lever-action or autoloader, or vice-versa, consider doing so when you purchase a .22. Most of the good ones will deliver plenty of accuracy at normal .22 ranges. A scope sight will add to the rifle's accuracy and help you spot squirrels and rabbits in shaded nooks. If you've never used a scope sight for big-game hunting, you can first mount a scope designed for high-powered rifles on your .22. It's a fine way to familiarize yourself with a scope, and the additional clarity and light-gathering power of scopes made for high-powered rifles make them far superior to scopes made expressly for .22s.

SCOPES

If you're going to use your rifle for varmint hunting or long-range shooting of any kind, a scope sight is a must. A good all-round choice for scope power is 4×. (Power is expressed by ×). This is a compromise between 1.5×, which is sometimes recommended for close-range timber shooting because of its wide field of view, and 6× to 12×, which is recommended for long-range varmint shooting. The shooter who is familiar with scopes could probably use 6× even for close-range timber shooting, particularly with a wide-angle scope such as the moderately priced Weaver K6-W.

SCOPE MOUNTING AND BORE-SIGHTING

Most centerfire rifles come from the factory already drilled and tapped for scope-mount bases. Bases and mounts are easily attached, using the instructions included with them. No need to pay a gunsmith for that job. Most .22s have the male portion of a dovetail machined into the top of the receiver. Scopes designed for .22s such as the Bushnell Custom, come equipped with an attached mount that fits into factory-grooved .22 receivers.

Before tightening scope mounting rings, use the following method to ensure that cross hairs are properly aligned. Set the rifle across a wooden or cardboard box in which two V-shaped grooves have been cut. Align the rifle in the grooves as level as is possible. Then place a water glass containing water and food coloring on another box 12 feet away. While looking through the scope, rotate the scope until the horizontal cross hair is parallel to the surface of the water in the glass. Then tighten the scope mounting rings.

To bore-sight the rifle—in other words, to align the rifle bore and scope cross hairs on the same aiming point—set the rifle in position across a box with V-shaped grooves as described above. Now set a target 25 yards distant. Any kind of target will do. Remove the bolt from the rifle. Now look through the rifle bore and adjust the rifle until you see the target through the center of the bore. Once the target and rifle bore are aligned, the next

CROSS-HAIR ALIGNMENT
USING COLORED WATER

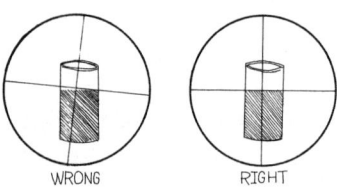

WRONG   RIGHT

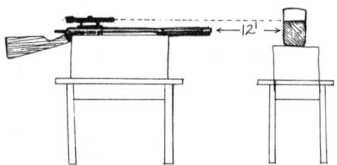

step is to adjust the scope windage and elevation adjustments until the scope
cross hairs are centered on the target. Check occasionally to make sure that
the target is still aligned with the bore. When bore and scope cross hairs are
both aligned on the target, the rifle is bore-sighted. (To finish sighting in,
you will have to actually fire at a target, but bore-sighting will ensure that
the first few shots land close to the actual target point.)

If you have a lever-action, pump-action, or autoloading rifle that has no
bolt you can remove to allow easy sighting down the bore, use a piece of
mirror to align the bore with the target. Any fragment of mirror small
enough to fit into the open breech will do.

Remember that the slightest movement of the scope or mount will result
in inaccurate fire. Everything must be tight, including the base screws and
scope clamping screws. All screws are hardened; turn them tight with
a screwdriver that has a medium-large handle and a well-fitting hardened
blade. If necessary, grind the blade to fit the screws. *Don't* use a screwdriver on any large knurled screwheads designed to be tightened by hand.

SIGHTING IN YOUR SCOPE

Don't attempt to sight in a rifle unless you have a solid rest from which
to shoot. A heavy bench is best, but you can use the hood of your car. Place

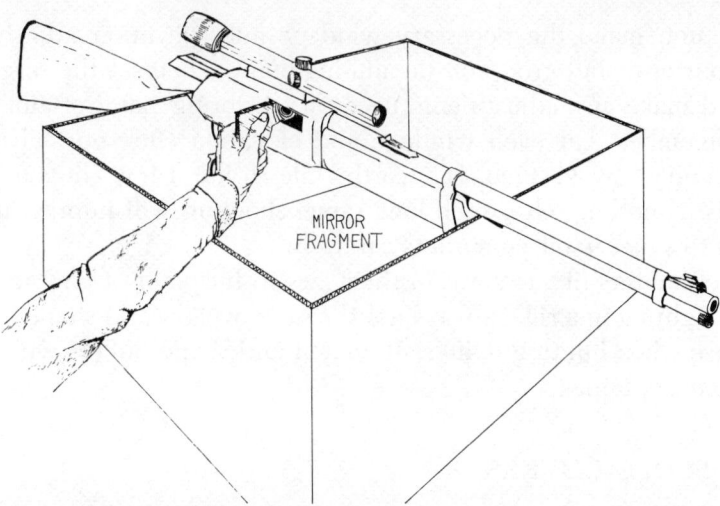

MIRROR
FRAGMENT

padding under the fore-end of the rifle stock and near the butt. Do not rest the rifle barrel or fore-end on anything hard. That would cause shots to strike high. Sandbags can be used. However, if the rifle has considerable recoil, your shots may still be high. Avoid that by resting your hand between the sandbag and the fore-end. Only when you fire from an absolutely solid rest can you expect to sight in a rifle accurately.

The all-round high-powered rifle in the .30-06/.270 class should be sighted in to hit 3 inches high at 100 yards. This setting will allow the shooter to hold on the center of the chest cavity on any big-game animal from 25 to 300 yards distant and score a killing shot. This is also a good setting for long-range varmint shooting. The actual sighting in—particularly if a scope has just been mounted on the rifle—should start with the target set at 25 yards. That will ensure hitting somewhere on the paper. A sheet of paper tacked to a cardboard box with a 2-inch bull's-eye inked in the center of the paper will do for a target.

Now fire a three-shot group. If the center of the group is, say, 2 inches high and 2 inches to the right at 25 yards, and your scope has "clicks" or graduations that make ½ inch change at 100 yards, you need 16 clicks down and 16 clicks to the left. (Note that at 25 yards, each click changes the aiming point only ⅛ inch.) Scope sights are clearly marked for windage and elevation adjustments. Your next group should then blanket the aiming point. If not, make the necessary windage and elevation adjustments to center your next shot group on the aiming point. Then set the target at 100 yards and make any adjustments necessary to bring point-of-aim 3 inches high. Remember that each windage and elevation click now changes the point of impact by ½ inch. It's worthwhile to fire a few shots at 200 and 300 yards. If nothing else, such long-range shooting will impress upon you the need to *squeeze* off your shots carefully.

Squirrel hunters like to sight in their .22s to hit point-of-aim at 20 yards.

When sighting in a rifle, always use the same weight and shape bullet you plan to use when hunting. Different weight and shape bullets will have different points of impact.

CHEAP SCOPE COVERS

You can cut your own scope covers from used inner tubes. The fit of a pickup-truck tube is about right for most big-game scopes. For small scopes, use a smaller tube. Simply lay the inner tube on its side and trace the shape of the capital letter "I" across the tube from the inner circumference to the outer. Be sure to round off all corners. Next hold the tube tightly and cut through both sides simultaneously with shears or heavy scissors. This results in a rubber band with enlarged circular areas on both ends. Slip it over the scope so the enlarged sections cover the lenses. This is excellent protection when hunting in inclement weather, which might otherwise cause wet and fogged scope lenses. It's also worthwhile if you store your guns in a dusty area. A flip of the thumb and the cover snaps off.

PATTERNING YOUR SHOTGUN

Shotguns are pointed at the target rather than truly aimed, so you don't normally use a scope. But to find out what your shotgun will do at different ranges and with different loads, you should pattern it on paper. A barrel stamped "modified" is no guarantee that's what you've got. Individual barrels vary, even from the same manufacturer. Any 4×4-foot sheet of paper will do for patterning. Make a frame for the paper. Pine furring strips 6 feet long work well. Sharpen the ends of two of them and drive them into the ground. Then use three 45-inch crosspieces. Tack the 4×4-foot sheet in place.

To pattern your shotgun, you must know the approximate number of pellets in the shotshells. You should always pattern your gun with the hunting loads you usually use. You can determine the number of pellets from gun books and catalogs, or cut open several shells, count the pellets in each, and average the results. For example, 12-gauge shells loaded with 1¼ ounces of No. 6 shot contain about 276 pellets, and 12-gauge low-base shells loaded with 1 ounce of No. 8 shot contain about 410 pellets. There are approximately 350 pellets in each ounce of No. 7½ shot. There are only 90 pellets in each ounce of No. 2 shot. The magnum load in 12-gauge No. 2 shot weighs 1½ ounces, giving a count of 135 pellets.

The degree of choke is determined by the percentage of pellets in a shell that hit within a 30-inch circle at 40 yards.

CHOKE	PERCENT OF SHOT IN 30-INCH CIRCLE AT 40 YARDS
Full	70–80
Modified	55–60
Improved Cylinder	45–50
Cylinder	35–40

Fire a shot at the center of the paper. Then pick the approximate center of the pattern—the densest area of holes—and draw a 30-inch circle around it. Then count the number of holes within the circle. Mark the holes with a felt pen as you count them. It's not necessary to count the holes outside the circle. Multiply the number of holes within the circle by 100, and divide by the number of pellets in the shot charge. That's your percentage.

This is a good time to find out where your shotgun is hitting in relation to where you're pointing it. Before firing the patterning shot, mark a indicate you're seeing too much or too little barrel. Shots that consistently bull's-eye on the paper and aim for that. Shots that hit always high or low hit to the left or right can indicate that the stock is too long or too short for you.

If you have a good pump, autoloader, or single-barrel shotgun, don't shy off trying slugs with it; the slugs won't hurt the choke and your barrel may group just as well as a special slug barrel. The best sighting arrangement is to mount an inexpensive, low power, scope on your gun and just remove it for bird hunting. The least expensive route is to acquire a device called Slug Site, which is a one-piece strip of metal with its own adhesive backing that sticks to the receiver or rib of your regular shotgun barrel. It is a front and rear sight all in one, and it works.

The factory sends instructions on mounting and removal with the kit, which costs only a few dollars. You can get more information from Slug Site, 3835 University Ave., Des Moines, Iowa 50311.

GUN CARE

It is nearly impossible to wear out a .22 rimfire barrel in a lifetime. About the only way to hurt the barrel is through excessive cleaning. Cleaning rods do more damage to a .22 rimfire barrel than anything else; in fact, you can usually get by without cleaning the barrel, unless you live in a very damp climate. The .22 rimfire cartridges do not generate the hot gases that centerfire cartridges do. Modern rimfire bullets leave a coating of lubricant in the bore that actually prevents rust. So when in doubt, don't clean.

A centerfire rifle requires more care, but don't overdo it. If you've fired a rifle during the course of the day and have access to a cleaning rod that evening, run a patch through the bore moistened with solvent such as Hoppe's No. 9. Clean the barrel more thoroughly when it's convenient. The solvent, having soaked in for several days, will have loosened any residue. You'll want to clean rifle or shotgun thoroughly after an extended hunt. Centerfire rifles require a soft metal bore brush to loosen caked residue, bullet wash, and lead.

Shotguns require less attention than do centerfire rifles, but that's no reason to leave them uncleaned for weeks or months at a time. Aluminum rods are good for shotguns because they're strong enough to withstand all the strain you should put on a cleaning tool and they require only a moderate-size patch. Two sizes of cleaning rod are available, one for .410 bore and 28 gauge, the other for 20, 16, and 12 gauge. Systematic cleaning of rifles and shotguns is worthwhile. A satisfactory gun-cleaning kit includes rod, soft metal brush, cloth patches, and a solvent.

When you run out of patches, make your own. An old flannel shirt is tops. What about making your own oil and solvent?

"There are indeed some formulas for making cleaning solvents for guns," reports *Outdoor Life* Shooting Editor Jim Carmichel. "You can even get along in high fashion simply lubricating your guns with a lightweight motor oil. Some of the new motor oils have a very broad temperature range and I presume allow a gun to operate smoothly at subfreezing temperatures.

"The military used to use a solvent, which they made themselves in large batches, for removing metal fouling from rifle barrels. It was commonly referred to as 'ammonia dope.' The formula is as follows: ammonia persulphate 1 ounce, ammonium carbonate 200 grains, stronger ammonia water 6 ounces, and water 4 ounces.

"The ammonia is the 28 percent variety which can be purchased at drug stores. By comparison, household ammonia is only a 5 to 10 percent solution. Don't get your nose too close or you'll wish you hadn't. Actually, a pretty good solution can probably be made by simply mixing stronger ammonia with light oil—about a 50-50 mix. Ammonia can be used straight to remove copper fouling, but it is a pretty ticklish business and unless done carefully can harm a rifle barrel."

A-FRAME GUN RACK

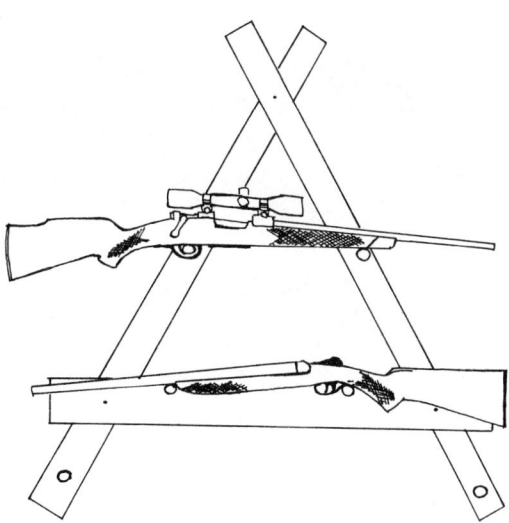

A-FRAME GUN RACK

If you plan to build a gun cabinet or gun rack in a basement recreation room, a good location is close to a gas furnace. The flow of warm air in winter will help keep your firearms from rusting. In summer, the slight heat from the pilot light will help keep the weapons dry in what might otherwise be a damp environment.

An easy-to-build, low-cost gun rack can be made from only three boards fitted together to form the letter "A." See the illustration. Boards are 1 × 2½ × 32 inches. Wooden pegs or dowels support the firearms. Shotgun shell casings covering the dowels make a nice added touch. To accommodate more than three firearms, increase the size of the rack and add an extra cross arm for each firearm.

2
HANDLOADING

With the tools and detailed information available today, anyone who can work carefully and follow directions is qualified to take up reloading. None of the steps is complicated or unsafe when accomplished intelligently. And, of course, there are advantages—like saving money and having a good time.

RIFLE HANDLOADS

If you are enthusiastic enough about rifle shooting and hunting to fire 100 or more rounds of centerfire ammunition a year, reloading is economically worthwhile. Those who don't reload are sometimes reluctant to even sight in their rifles at the beginning of the hunting season because ammunition is costly and it may require several boxes of ammo to sight in. You can save one-half to two-thirds of your ammunition expense by recharging your fired cases, shoot two to three times as much as you do now, and be a better shooter . . . and a better hunter.

There are more reasons. A varmint shooter may want to use a bullet of different weight from the single one available in factory ammunition for certain calibers. You may prefer a less "hot" load with less than factory velocity. Or you can load to the maximum. You may want a specially constructed bullet for use on predators whose fur is valuable if not badly damaged. Many of the biggest problems of rifle shooting can be solved by reloading.

There are five operations in cartridge reloading. The case is decapped, reprimed, and resized, the powder is added, and finally the bullet is seated. That's less involved than you might think, because some steps are performed simultaneously. Of the components of a cartridge, the case is the most expensive and accounts for the greatest saving through reloading. Actual case life depends on the caliber and powder charge used. Many can be reloaded 10 or 12 times, some as often as 15, and a few survive 20.

Probably the most confusing problem facing the beginning reloader is learning which powders go with which cartridges and how much powder to use. Powders are identified by both a brand name and a number, but these numbers do not tell you which powder goes with which caliber. Thus a reloader must have a handloading manual. Good manuals are sold by Hodgdon, Hornady, Lyman, Sierra, and Speer. Winchester and Du Pont also supply excellent loading data.

Handloading manuals often name one or two particular powders that have been found especially suitable for your combination of rifle and bullet. If this is not the case, a workable rule of thumb is to select the powder that gives the highest velocity listing for a specific bullet weight. That powder is usually the most efficient for that bullet weight and caliber. Most manuals, for example, list No. 4831 powder as giving the top velocity for the .270 with the 130-grain bullet. Some reloaders try two or three different powder and bullet combinations. These are then test-fired and the combination that proves most accurate is used from then on.

The least-expensive loading tools, such as the Lee Loader, sell for about $12. You can also reload without special tools, as explained later in this chapter. If you want a first-class setup complete with scale, adjustable powder measure, case trimmer, loading press, and die, plan on spending $70 to $160. Even at this price, you break even long before you shoot up your first 1,000 rounds.

A reloading press will constitute your largest cash investment. However, it can be used for virtually all rifle and pistol calibers. In order to change from one caliber to another, all you need is another set of dies and possibly

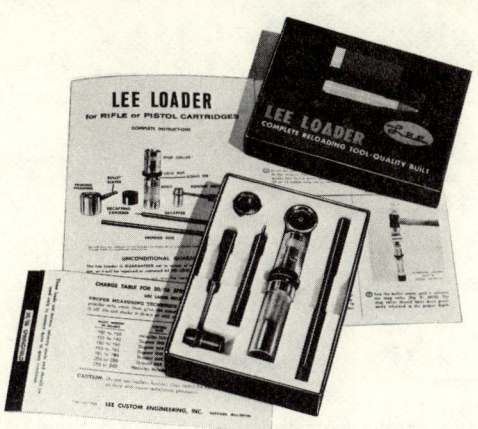

This reloading set includes everything needed for decapping, repriming, neck sizing, charging, and bullet seating. It sells for about $12. *(Photo courtesy Lee Custom Engineering, Inc.)*

another shell (case) holder. These will cost $10 to $20.

Reloading tools come with instructions for their use. Handloading manuals detail reloading procedures. Yet either can seem a little confusing at first because of unfamiliar terms such as "full-length sizing" and "neck sizing."

Rifle chambers vary somewhat in size and shape, even those of the same caliber, make, and model of rifle. Ammunition makers take this into account and produce cartridges that will fit and fire in all of these thousands of chambers. When the round is fired, the internal forces expand the case and mold it to the shape of the chamber in which it was fired. It now fits the chamber of the rifle perfectly. To ensure reliable feeding and chambering of the load, however, and particularly if you are loading for a lever-action, a pump-action, or an autoloader, the cartridge should be returned to its original shape. In other words, it should be full-length-sized. Any ammo to be used for serious hunting, even with bolt rifles, should be full-length sized.

For plinking, target shooting, or varmint shooting, neck sizing is all that is necessary. If you use neck-sized ammo for hunting, be sure first to cycle it through the action to see if it feeds and chambers freely. For small-caliber centerfire rounds such as the centerfire .22s, you'll need to size only the top of the neck, just enough to hold the bullet. With each firing the case gets a little bigger, and eventually the chamber fit gets too tight. When

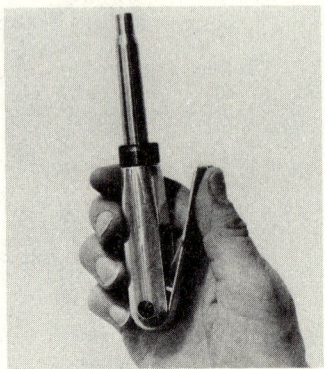

This tool accurately and safely seats the primer with a "feel" that is appreciated by the experienced reloader. *(Photo courtesy Lee Engineering, Inc.)*

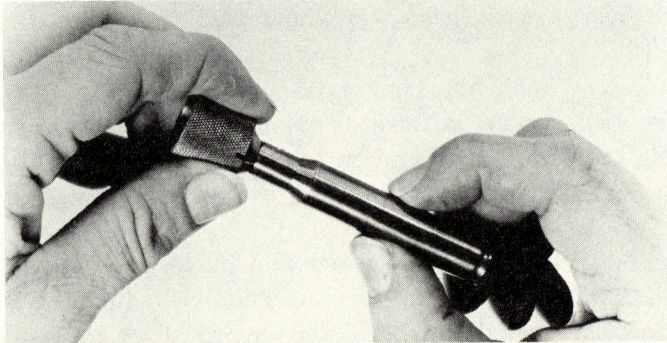

This tool chamfers and deburs inside and outside of case necks. One turn does the job. *(Photo courtesy Lee Engineering, Inc.)*

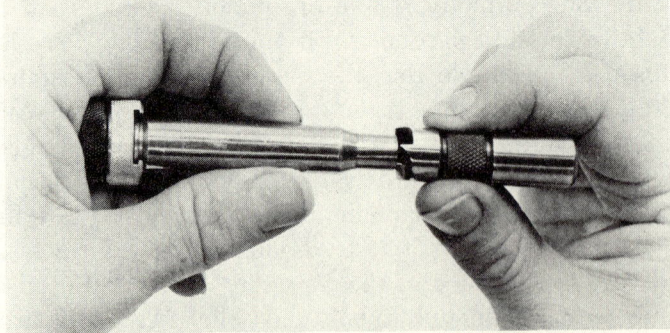

Factory-set case trimmer ensures that the case will be trimmed to the maximum length the standard chamber will accept. *(Photo courtesy Lee Engineering, Inc.)*

this happens, full-length resizing is necessary. Full-length resizing is also necessary if you're using cases fired in another rifle (reloaders love to pick up empty cases at target ranges).

Full-length resizing is done with a reloading press. The press forces the case into the sizing die, which squeezes it back down to its original shape. While the case is being resized a pin in the center of the die punches out the old primer. Now it's ready for a new primer.

The primer is the heart of the cartridge and comes, fortunately, in only two sizes: large and small. The small sizes are pretty much limited to such small cases as the .22 Hornet, .218 Bee, .25/20, .222, .223, and .222 Remington Magnum. Most of the rest use the large primer. A properly seated primer will be slightly deeper than flush with the base of the case. If the primer becomes flattened or deformed in any way, it is likely that too much pressure has been applied. It's okay if the primer is perfectly flush with the base. If it protrudes even slightly it must be seated deeper. Be sure to use a primer of the correct flash strength.

Resizing and hot powder loads cause metal flow forward to thicken and lengthen the case neck until it must be trimmed. After a few reloadings the neck will be so long that it jams against the step at the front of the chamber. This ruins accuracy and causes pressures to rise dangerously. That is why cases must be trimmed from time to time. Prices for trimmers range from about $5 for simple trimmers to $25 for adjustable models.

Some reloaders weigh every powder charge before pouring it into the waiting case. This can be rather time-consuming. The alternative is to use a powder measure. These are very accurate, but don't try to get by with just a powder measure. The accuracy of your measure must first be tested with a scale. Despite their sensitivity, most of these scales are simple to use and easy to read.

Seating the bullet is the last step in reloading, and once the seating die is properly adjusted for the bullet used, it is a largely automatic one. Manuals give the permissible overall length of the complete cartridge, but since you're not likely to have equipment to measure hundredths of an inch, you'll want to adjust the tool to fit a similar factory round.

SHOTSHELL HANDLOADS

Shotshell-reloading tools vary enough in price to suit a great many shooters. If you desire the use of sophisticated and costly equipment, consider sharing the cost with two or more shooters. Some shooters load their friends' empties along with their own to help pay for tools and earn a little cash. There are some who custom-load for pay. Their workshops are only moderate in size but their income from sales and loading is impressive.

Using the simplest models that cost least, you can turn out some 60 loads an hour. The bench-press type turns out up to 150 an hour, and power-driven models turn out 750. If your needs are modest, you can do your reloading in your home kitchen, since no special support is necessary for hand rammer tools. Lever tools, of course, must be clamped to a firm surface.

Manuals are available that tell the kind and quantity of powder, the correct primer identified by the manufacturer's number, the type and number of wads, and the proper case to use when assembling any of the loads listed. There are a sufficient variety of loads listed to handle all kinds of shotgun shooting.

Loading tools come with directions, and the labels on powder containers carry instructions for use. But a handloading manual is a must. These man-

Here's a loading press with more features than you would expect to find on a tool costing several times as much. *(Photo courtesy Lee Precision, Inc.)*

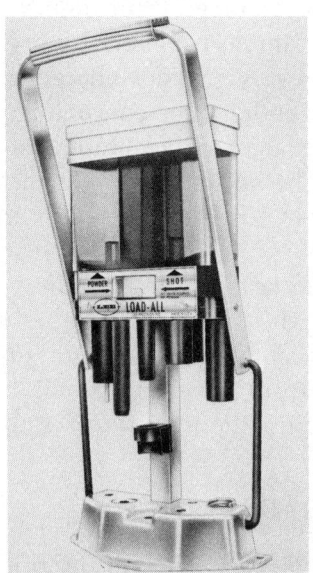

uals cost little. The one published by Lee Engineering Co. sells for $1, and that issued by the Lyman Gun Sight Co. costs $3.50 as of this writing. By following their directions, handloaders can avoid slight errors that waste materials or cause ·incorrect crimping space, as well as more serious ones that could spell danger.

The first step in shotshell reloading is decapping—punching out the fired primer. Next a new one is pressed in place. The powder charge is loaded next. Seating wads is the next step. Pour in the shot and you are ready for crimping. At some point in the reloading cycle the shell is resized to fit smoothly in your shotgun chamber. Just when this occurs varies with different tools. Sometimes it is part of the primer-seating operation, sometimes it's done when the shell is being crimped.

CHEAP RIFLE HANDLOADS

To show how basic, how cheap, and how productive reloading can be, the following method of reloading fired cases requires no special tools other than those commonly found in the home. Here's the recipe for 100 rounds of light loads to be used strictly for target shooting.

Items to buy: one can of Hercules Unique Powder, one box of 100 large rifle primers (not magnum), and one box of jacketed bullets, the lightest available, of your caliber. For the .30-06 owner this would probably mean Speer or Hornady 100-grain bullets. Total cost about $15.

The reloaded cartridges must be fired singly in a bolt-action or lever-action rifle. No automatics. They must be single-loaded because this low-cost method of reloading does not include crimping. It would be dangerous to run an uncrimped reload through a tube magazine because the bullet could be pushed back into the powder area and increase pressure. The finger-loaded bullets might stay in place if loaded into a box, clip, or rotary magazine, but play it safe and load and fire singly.

A large nail or spike is used as a depriming punch. You will have to file the last ½ inch of it down all around until it is small enough to slide into the cartridge flash hole.

To hold in place the cartridge case to be deprimed, use a 2 × 4-inch block. Drill a ½-inch hole, ¾ inch deep; now drill a ¼-inch hole in the center of the first hole. Set the case in the large hole (see illustration). Feel around with the tip of your depriming punch until the tip of it enters the flash hole, and tap the punch lightly with a hammer. The fired primer will drop into the ¼-inch hole. Do this with all the cases you plan to reload.

You can use the same block of wood for installing new primers or, as seen in the photo, a separate block of wood. Drill a hole just large enough to force a ¼-inch bolt through the block from the underside. A metal plate can be bolted to the bottom of the block for greater stability. The bolt supports the case when a new primer is tapped into place.

Warning: Primers are the dangerous component of reloading; an exploding primer can blind or injure you. Do not use the old-style convex-head type of primer. Use flat-head primers only.

A primer, surprisingly, will not explode as long as you do not dent the center or flatten the primer at all. Nevertheless, use a putty knife as an intervening shield. With an empty unprimed case over the vertical bolt, lay a primer on the pocket, hold the flat surface of the putty knife over the primer, then sink it flush with gentle taps. General Hatcher, a popular gun authority of the 1950s and 1960s, primed thousands of cases in this manner. My own nephew has primed several hundred.

Probably the safest method of priming empty cases without a special tool is to use a vise. Get a ¼-inch bolt 3 or 4 inches long, slide an empty unprimed case over it, hold a primer to the pocket with your finger, and slip the whole horizontally into a vise opened just wide enough. Tighten the jaws and the primer will slide into place.

Handloading reduced to its simplest form with homemade and common household tools.

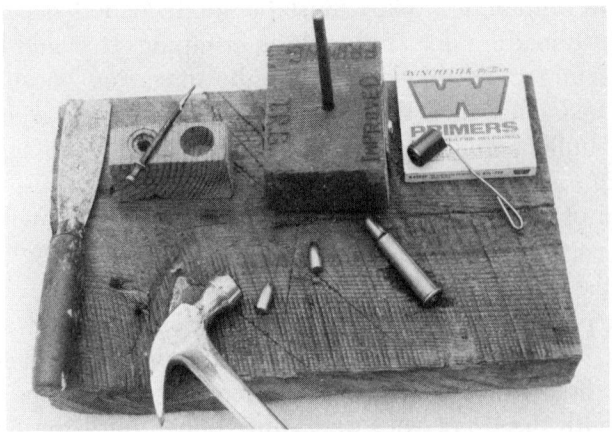

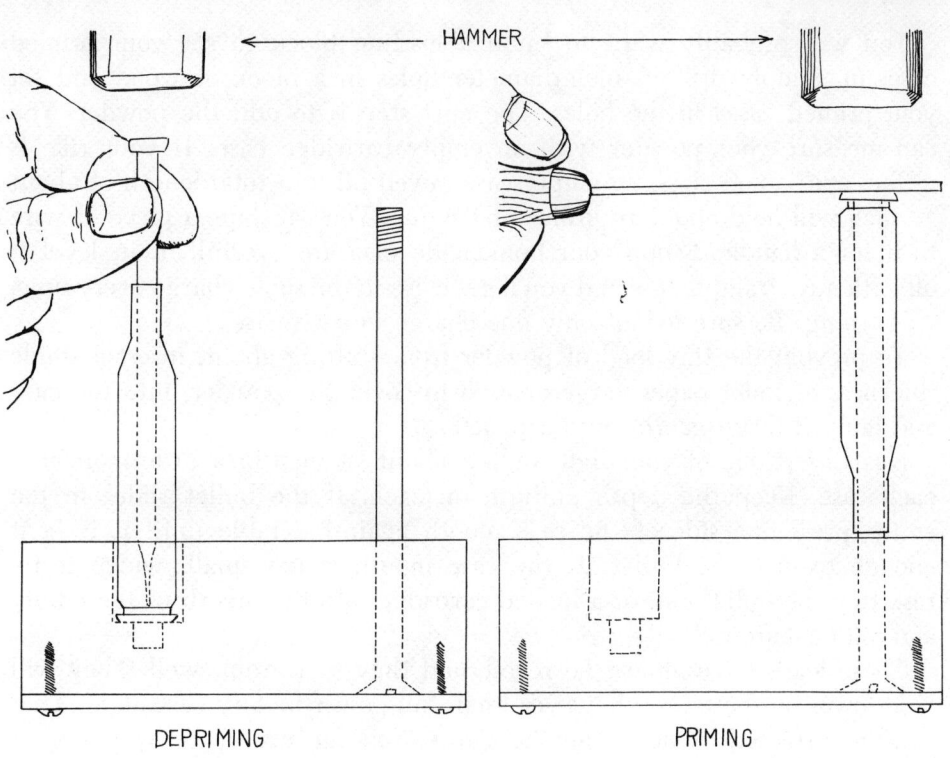

HAMMER

DEPRIMING

PRIMING

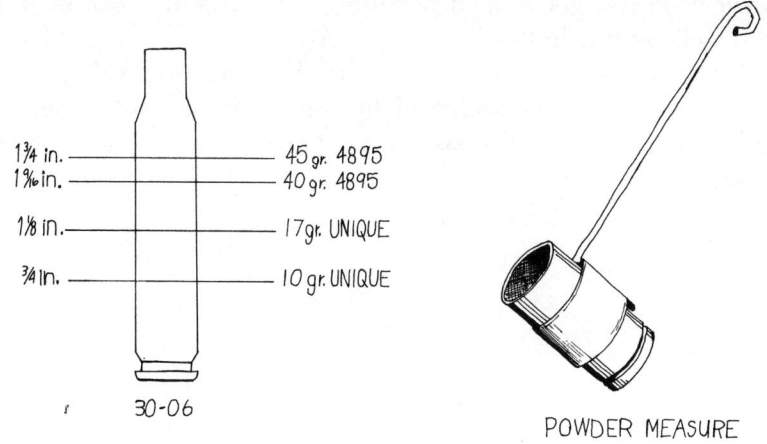

1¾ in. ——————— 45 gr. 4895
1⅜ in. ——————— 40 gr. 4895

1⅛ in. ——————— 17 gr. UNIQUE

¾ in. ——————— 10 gr. UNIQUE

30-06

POWDER MEASURE

You will probably want to build a loading block to set your primed cases in. Simply drill ½-inch-diameter holes in a block of wood and set your primed cases in the holes. The next step is to add the powder. You can measure your powder with an empty cartridge case. If your rifle is in the .270/.30-06 class, an empty case sawed off to a total length of about ¾ inch will hold about 10 grains of Unique. You can tape a piece of wire to it for a handle. Scoop your homemade measure overfull of it, level it off with any straightedge, and you'll get close to the same charge every time.

Warning: Be sure to put only one charge in each case.

To prevent the tiny load of powder from shifting about, insert a single thickness of toilet paper, large enough to cover the powder, into the case and tamp it down *gently* with a pencil.

Next insert one of your light bullets about ⅛ inch or a little more into each case. Keep the depth uniform on each. If the bullet slides in too easily, press one side of the case mouth against a table until it is bent enough to grip the bullet. If the case mouth is too small, widen it by inserting the bullet end of a loaded cartridge into the mouth of the empty and rolling it around.

These loads have almost no recoil, and they will group well. They will land lower on the target, however, than full-power factory cartridges. That can be corrected by adjusting the sights. You can use up to 17 grains of Unique with light bullets, but don't try too much with Unique. It's a very fast-burning powder. If you're interested in medium to heavy bullets, or speeds over 2000 fps, get a good reloading manual and a can of different powder, as well as other bullets.

For informative articles that deal with handloading, rifles, shotguns, handguns, and a complete catalog of loading tools and components, read *Handloader's Digest*, Digest Books, Inc., 540 Frontage Road, Northfield, Illinois 60093.

3
AIR GUNS, BLOWGUNS, BOOMERANGS, SLINGS, SLINGSHOTS, AND CROSSBOWS

Most of the weapons in this chapter have one thing in common: you don't become proficient with them overnight. It takes years of practice to become a reasonably good bowman, let alone achieve proficiency with a blowgun or boomerang. Yet an increasing number of people seem willing to make the effort to learn old, almost forgotten skills. The cost is low, the rewards high.

AIR GUNS

While the common BB gun is not a serious contender for any kind of hunting, the air rifle, or pellet gun, is. It is also safe enough and quiet enough to use indoors in a game room, den, or basement. And it provides precision accuracy. It is particularly suitable for lawn and garden pest control. It's a weapon that can actually pay for itself in ammunition savings. Nor is it subject to the Gun Control Act of 1968. An air rifle may freely be transported interstate while camping and on vacations and outings.

A quality air arm in your hands can instantly convert almost any wooded area, field, or suitable lot into a shooter's paradise. An air rifle also gives you shooting flexibility. Since the energy of a pellet is minimal beyond 100 yards, and carrying range is limited, you'll find it *relatively* safe to plink away at elevated targets such as squirrels or offending pigeons. Nothing, however, relieves you of the responsibility of taking care where your pellets land. The biggest advantage is being able to shoot closer to home in semi-populated areas unsuitable for conventional firearm use. You won't have to worry about gasoline and traffic.

There are many models from which to choose, including a large number from Europe. Almost all the European makes are spring-operated rather than powered by CO_2 gas. As a result, they say, complex valves aren't required and reliability is vastly improved. In addition, the use of a consistent power source has resulted in an accuracy level much superior to any other system; CO_2 cartridges, of course, lose a little pressure each time a pellet is fired, and thus the power varies. Most of these are rifles chambered for the .177-caliber pellet.

There is little doubt that Europeans take their air rifles seriously. Economy models in the catalog of a major importer sell from $58.50 to $89.95. Intermediate all-purpose arms representing a hybrid design suitable for both target and outdoor field activity run from approximately $100 to $160. Sporters, designed primarily for field use, run from $150 to $375. Match rifles can cost $500 and more. For detailed information on European air rifles write: Robert Law's Air Rifle Headquarters, Inc., 247 Court St., Box 327, Grantsville, W.Va. 26147.

American air rifles generally represent one of two different principles in air-gun design. One is the pneumatic (pump) air rifle as typified by the Crossman Model 1400 Pumpmaster rifle, powered by compressed air. The

The Crossman Company calls this the most powerful pellet gun made. It's the Model 1400 Pumpmaster, powered by compressed air. Scope is optional. *(Photo courtesy The Crossman Co.)*

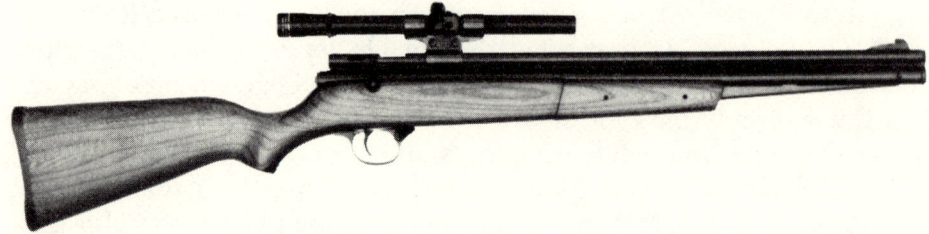

company calls it the most powerful pellet gun made. The shooter determines the amount of power by the number of pumps. Each pump boosts the energy, to a maximum sufficient to achieve a muzzle velocity of over 600 fps, shooting .22-caliber super pellets. Because the barrel in pneumatic air rifles is sandwiched over rear cylinder components, the overall size and weight are reduced and less cost is involved.

CO_2-operated arms were introduced in the United States to overcome objections to the physical effort pump models require and their slow rate of fire. Most models use a 12.5-gram disposable gas bulb. The bulb is pierced on insertion and meters out an appropriate amount of gas on each shot by use of a valve system. The number of rounds fired from one bulb vary from 30 to as high as 220, depending upon model and power setting. An example is the Crossman Model 70 .177-caliber single-shot CO_2 pellet rifle. For more information contact: The Crossman Co., Inc., Fairport, N. Y. 14450.

Model 70 .177-caliber single-shot CO_2 pellet rifle. Scope is optional. *(Photo courtesy The Crossman Co.)*

BLOWGUNS

Absolutely noiseless, deadly accurate up to 40 yards, and more lethal than a rifle if poisoned darts are used, the blowgun is an extremely dangerous weapon.

"The Yaqua Blowgun is not a toy," stress the manufacturers (Mar-Vac, Inc.). "A 3-inch dart will kill rabbit and similar-size animals. Darts up to 8-inches in length have been used and taken javelina and puma. Longer darts have more impact, and less range."

The Yaqua Blowgun is made of hard-drawn aluminum in lengths of 4½, 5½, and 6½ feet. Darts come in kit form and will assemble to 50 darts of 3-inch length. Making the darts is easy:

1. Using either wire cutters or snips (not pliers, because they crimp wire), cut a number of pieces of wire to 3-inch lengths.
2. Next, using either your hands or a pair of pliers, pull an equal number of beads from the string of beads in your dart kit.
3. Then light a candle or cigarette lighter, and hold the very tip of one of the 3-inch wires you have cut in the flame for 30 seconds.
4. Then insert the hot tip into the same hole in the plastic bead that the string was through. Push the hot tip of wire about two-thirds of the way through the plastic bead.
5. The plastic bead will melt to the wire, and you'll have a dart. If you want to sharpen your darts, you may do so on a knife sharpener or a grinding wheel.

Blowguns are "fired" by filling your lungs with air, putting your mouth to the mouthpiece, and giving a quick, hard puff.

Warning: Do not inhale the dart! Always turn your head away from the mouthpiece of a blowgun to fill your lungs with air, then blow *through* the mouthpiece.

Poison, the Mar-Vac people say, is recommended for use only by responsible persons at least 18 years of age, and knowledgeable hunters. The poison does not affect the meat; it is nicotine sulfate, which works on the nervous system. Check local laws and regulations before you acquire or use it. *And handle it with care.*

Mar-Vac's suggested retail prices as of this writing are: 4½-foot gun,

$18.95; 5½-foot gun, $19.95; 6½-foot gun, $21.95; kit of 50 darts, $3.95; 1/32 ounce of poison (on special request), $7.95. For more information write: Mar-Vac, Inc., P.O. Box 35157, Tulsa, Okla. 74135.

A HOMEMADE BLOWGUN

A blowgun works exactly like a kid's peashooter. A 6-foot length of ½-inch aluminum conduit makes a good blowgun. Conduit is available at hardware and electrical stores. Darts can be of almost any length, although the lighter they are, the farther they will fly. Darts can be made from clothespins and armed with nails or steel knitting needles cut in half. The clothespin should be of the one-piece style with a slightly rounded head. Only the head end of the clothespin is used. Cut off the remainder of the clothespin about 1 inch down (see the illustration). The clothespin may have to be sanded slightly to fit. The snugger the fit, without sticking, the better. At the end of the dart, where feathering would be on an arrow, there should be some sort of "stopper." The stopper should fit snugly inside the barrel of the blowgun but not so snugly that it makes the dart stick. A twist of cotton glued to the end of the dart will act as a stopper. The fit of the stopper is important because it is the force of the blower's breath against it that shoots out the dart.

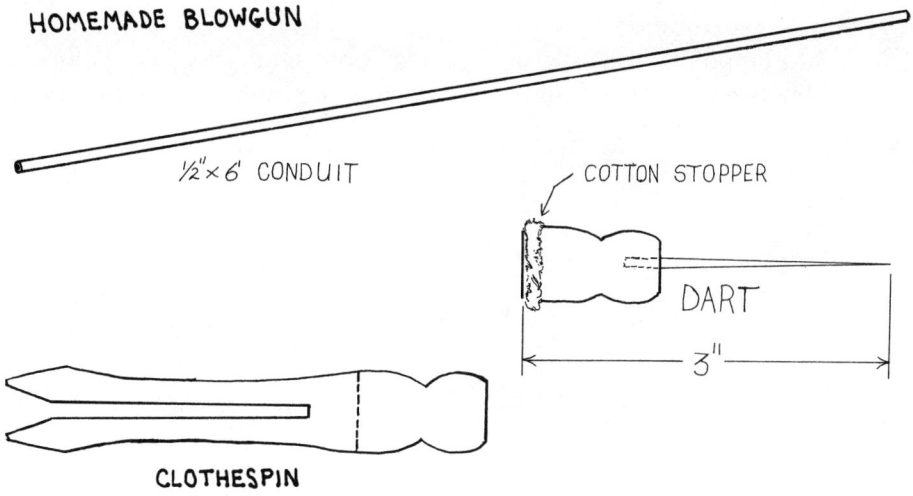

HOMEMADE BLOWGUN

½"×6' CONDUIT

COTTON STOPPER

DART

3"

CLOTHESPIN

You'll find it easier to recover your darts if you coat them with brightly colored paint.

BOOMERANGS

If you have ever tried throwing a stone at a quarry you know how ineffective it is. Even a pro ball player cannot throw a stone more than 200 feet, and even then the stone will have lost so much power it won't hurt the quarry. A curved stick, or boomerang, is far more effective.

A hunting boomerang is about a yard long and usually only slightly curved. One side of the boomerang is flat. The other side is curved to form an airfoil. In a way it resembles the wing of a plane. The boomerang speeds toward the target, spinning sideways. It not only can fly farther than any other hand-projected missile, it will also hit harder. It is said an Australian expert can throw one with deadly effect at 700 feet. Horses have been reported knocked down by boomerangs. Persons have received ugly wounds over 1½ inches deep.

A boomerang has deadly effect when thrown into a flock of birds. It whirls through the flock like a buzzsaw and often knocks down two or three birds. It is not as effective if the birds are in full flight because they can see it coming and avoid it. It works very well on a flock of ducks just as they are rising from the water, when unable to maneuver effectively because they are trying to gain altitude.

It should be pointed out that a "hunting" boomerang does not return. A "return" boomerang is basically a toy. Boomerang clubs are quite popular

BOOMERANG IN ACTION

in Australia. Contests are held and the contestants compete for accuracy; they stand within a small circle and the thrown boomerang must return and land within the circle. It is very difficult to hit anything with a return boomerang. Also, a return boomerang has to be light enough to "soar" easily, and will not deliver a strong blow.

MAKING A BOOMERANG

"A hunting boom," says Daniel P. Mannix in his book *A Sporting Chance*, published by E. P. Dutton, "should be made of the heaviest and toughest wood available—hickory or oak being probably the best. Simply outlining the shape of the boom on a plank and then cutting it out is useless; the boom will break the first time it hits against the grain. A round of the proper wood has to be bent so the grain follows the bend." Mannix was able to get his wood bent by a barrel stave maker who had a special apparatus for steaming the material to make it pliable. Australian aborigines, he says, "simply keep looking until they find a crooked branch in the right shape." No matter how long it takes.

"I found the best-sized boom for me was 24 inches from wingtip to wingtip, with the top of the curve 14 inches high. The widest part of the boom (at the apex of the curve) should be about 2½ inches across, and the arms gradually taper down to about 1½ inches. The length of an arm should be about six times the width of the boom at the center. The airfoil has to be whittled out with a knife and then worked down with sandpaper. It rises fairly abruptly from the outer edge of the boom to a ridge running the length of the boom (and naturally following its curve). The top of this ridge, the thickest part of the boom, should not be more than ½ inch. The airfoil then tapers more gradually down to the inside curve. There is no airfoil on the reverse side of the boom; it is perfectly flat."

SLINGS

The common sling (the kind David used to slay Goliath) is said to be superior to the bow. A good bowman can shoot a 1-ounce arrow about 300 yards, though it can be made to go much farther with special equipment. With regular equipment the arrow travels at about 150 feet per second and has an energy of about 25 foot-pounds.

A good slinger, however, can cast a 1-ounce pellet nearly 400 yards. The pellet travels at about 190 fps and with an energy of nearly 36 foot-pounds.

The sling is basically a pouch with two cords attached. The sling is swung around and around to build up momentum and then one cord end is released and the pebble or steel pellet is propelled forward. The faster you can swing it the faster the pellet goes.

There is no standard cord length or pouch size. But the pouch should be of fairly soft leather or rubber and large enough to hold an irregularly shaped stone without its falling out. Be very careful the first few times you try a sling. Until you get the hang of it the projectile may fly in any direction. It's a good idea to have the end of one cord wrapped around your finger or hand. That way you can simply open your hand at the release and the other cord end will fly free and release the projectile. The disadvantage of the sling is that it is pretty well restricted to open terrain.

SLINGSHOTS

A slingshot is a forked stick with an elastic band attached which shoots small pellets. Though it is usually associated with small boys, there are sophisticated commercial forms. The Saunders U.S. Open Slingshot Tournament is held each January in Las Vegas, and slingshot clubs are springing up across the country. Slingshot small-game hunting is attracting fans of all ages.

"Drop rabbits, rats and other vermin as well as small game and birds with rifle precision," say the manufacturers of the Saunders Wrist-Rocket Slingshot. The Saunders commercial slingshot features the surgical-tube type of strap which is so difficult to stretch that the slingshot is designed to fit around the user's wrist to provide extra leverage. Many consider the tube type to be the most powerful slingshot. Accessories include a lead-pellet mold for slingshot ammo and replacement power bands with pouch. These slingshots cost as little as $3.50. For more information write: Saunders Archery Co., Columbus, Nebr. 68601.

HOMEMADE SLINGSHOTS

A forked limb from a cherry, plum, or similar hardwood tree makes the best slingshot framework. The pouch can be cut from the leather of a dis-

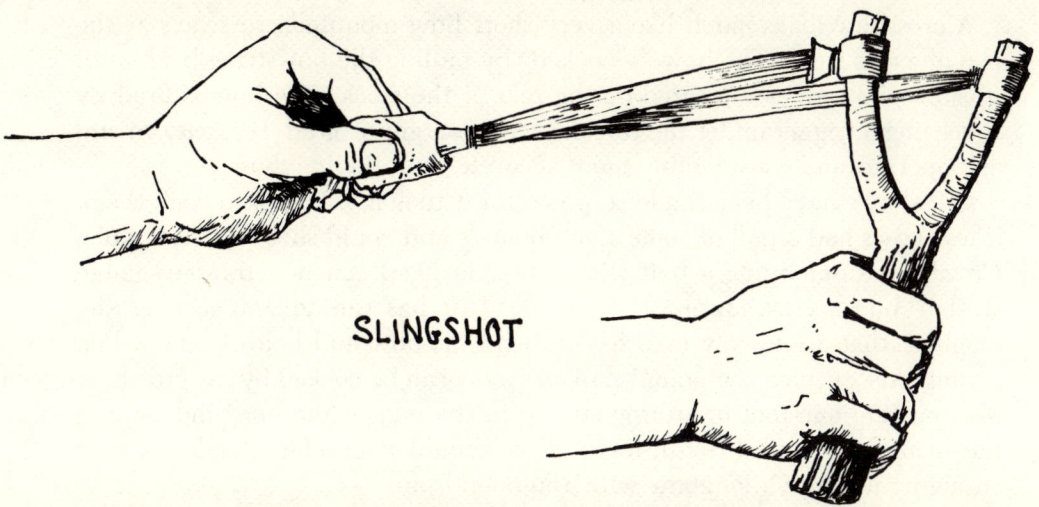

SLINGSHOT

carded hunting boot. The important element is the bands. One of the best types of band, in terms of ease of pull and powerful delivery of the projectile, is a flat rubber strap of vulcanized pure natural rubber. Unfortunately, vulcanized rubber is not as easy to come by as it was before World War II. Since then, synthetic rubber has come out of the laboratory and into mass production. When compared to all other types of synthetic rubber (of which there are many), neoprene is the most like natural rubber in both its elastic properties and its physical appearance.

Considered to be even better than the vulcanized-rubber strap is the band made of eight B. F. Goodrich rubber bands tied two long and two wide on each side of the pouch. Besides being the most powerful, this is the easiest slingshot to repair. The rubber on any slingshot is going to tear sooner or later. When you have a slingshot that uses the combination bands, if one band breaks, you just cut it out and tie in a new one.

CROSSBOWS

Richard the Lion-Hearted was killed by a short steel bolt that penetrated his heavy armor and buried itself in his neck. That happened even though Richard was well out of bowshot range of the castle his troops were besieging. The bolt was fired by the most deadly of primitive weapons, the crossbow.

A crossbow looks much like a very short bow mounted crossways at the end of a rifle stock. The bow is "cocked" by pulling the bowstring back until it catches in a release located on the rear of the stock. The bow is fired by squeezing a trigger under the stock exactly as a gun is fired. It is easy to aim and operate, and considerably more accurate than the longbow.

Crossbows have been made so powerful it took a windlass to cock them. These bows had a pull of some 1,200 pounds and could shoot nearly a mile. Crossbows discharging a bolt with a bodkin head can penetrate 19-gauge steel. While a crossbow is slow to reload, it has the advantage over the longbow that a longbow man has to bend his bow and hold it bent while aiming. Also, even a 200-pound-pull crossbow can be cocked by the crossbow man putting one foot in an iron stirrup in the end of the bow and pulling the string back with the full force of his shoulder muscles. It takes a very strong man to use a longbow with 100-pound pull.

Commercial models are available. The Jayhawk crossbow is one. The bow is made from 7075 T-6 aluminum alloy. The bowstring is made of 49-strand galvanized-steel cable and has a spring-steel center bearing for smooth release from the trigger. The Jayhawk crossbow comes completely finished except for a light sanding and application of the finish of your choice. It is available in 40-pound and 75-pound weights. The factory-direct price is $24.95.

The Jayhawk is also available in kit form for $10.50. The kit consists of an aluminum-alloy bow, one steel-cable bowstring, one trigger assembly, one hanger-bolt assembly, two aluminum-alloy strips, one peep sight, and a complete set of plans for making the crossbow stock. Arrows are also available in kit form. Write: Jayhawk Archery Inc., Afton, Okla. 74331.

Because they are silent, crossbows make perfect poaching weapons, and are outlawed in several states. Check your local regulations if you plan to hunt with a crossbow.

HUNTING WITH AIR GUNS AND PRIMITIVE ARMS

Summer and early fall are good times to explore, experiment, and generally utilize air guns, blowguns, boomerangs, slings, slingshots, and crossbows.

Many small creatures become pests or nuisances when their numbers increase, and these make excellent practice targets for the beginning primitive-arms enthusiast. There are, for example, dozens of forms of ground squirrels, living all the way from the Alaskan tundra through the heartland of both Canada and the United States. The 13-lined ground squirrel, more commonly known as a gopher to Midwesterners, is very active from daylight to dusk. It favors short-cropped fields, cow pastures, even golf courses. Because of the silence and general unobtrusiveness of primitive weapons, gophers can sometimes be hunted in suburbs and even within city limits, if local laws permit.

It doesn't take much to send a gopher scurrying for its hole. The hunter should move in close with his blowgun, pellet gun, or slingshot and wait for the gopher to get curious and pop its head out for another look.

Patience is necessary for any kind of hunting; it is doubly so when hunting with a primitive weapon. As the fall hunting season approaches, consider duck hunting with a boomerang. One way is to walk along a winding creek and hurl a boomerang into flocks of ducks as they flush from the water. It's nice to have two boomerangs because you'll often have a chance for a second throw. And two boomerangs with the same flight characteristics are ideal. Easy? This kind of hunting never is. And that's where the fascination lies.

Many members of the grouse family are fine targets and excellent eating as well. The ruffed, spruce, and blue grouse will sometimes offer close-range ground shots or will sit, more obligingly at times, on a tree limb. Gray and fox squirrels are great targets for the more powerful models of air gun. But confine your shots to within 30 yards, and take head shots only. Cottontail rabbits and snowshoe hares provide close-range shooting opportunities for many weapons. Black bear have been killed with the powerful crossbow, and all manner of large game treed by trailing hounds have been killed with blowguns and poisoned darts. Mannix's book *A Sporting Chance* is definitely recommended reading for anyone considering hunting with a primitive arm.

4
BOWS AND ARROWS

Hunting with bow and arrow is good hunting and, relatively speaking, cheap hunting. Practice shooting with rifle and shotgun will cost you. With archery tackle you can shoot to your heart's content for free, unless you miss the target and lose some arrows or smash shafts against rocks or trees. And you can do it in your own back yard.

Taking advantage of the archery season means that in most states you can spend considerably more time in the woods. In a few states it is legal to bag a deer in both the archery and the gunning season (check with local authorities). It usually means early-season hunting, before snow and cold. Even the bowhunter who fails to tag a deer benefits—if he's a two-season hunter. Archery season helps him to sharpen his basic hunting skills and to locate the best deer spots so he knows where to go during gun season.

Sharpening your basic hunting skills deserves attention. Frankly, you have to be a better hunter to get a deer with a bow than with a gun. A good rifleman with a flat-shooting scoped rifle can take deer out to 250 yards. There is little chance of that for the bowman. Few bowmen will consider taking a shot at much over 35 yards. Some of the best bowmen get their trophies at ranges of under 20 yards.

At such close ranges, the bowman's body movement, the wind, and noise all become vitally important. A smothered cough might not bother a deer 75 yards upwind, but at 25 yards the deer would certainly hear and instantly leap away. For the hunting archer the wind is a vital element. At 25 yards it is almost certain that a downwind deer will pick up a bowman's scent and explode into flight.

But the archer has some advantages too. His bow produces no loud report. Deer are not usually as alarmed as they are during gun season. In fact, if a bowhunter is properly concealed and quiet, he can miss a shot at a deer without the deer realizing that it is a target. It's not unusual for an archer to get a second or even a third shot at a feeding deer. Because of the lack of noise and because the bowhunter is not likely to present any potential danger to livestock or buildings, it is usually not difficult to get permission to hunt. Urban sprawl and the tendency of city dwellers to move back to the country and commute to their city jobs have divided much good deer-hunting woodland into small parcels that contain residences. Bowhunting is often the only safe hunting in such circumstances.

If you're anxious to get started with a bow, first seek advice from a veteran bowhunter. If you don't know any hunting archers, ask your state game agency for information about field-archery clubs or bowhunting groups in your area. Other good sources of information are indoor archery ranges and shops that specialize in archery tackle.

The market is flooded with a variety of bows, arrows, and accessories. Most will do the job. Stick with reputable manufacturers, and don't buy a bow drawing less than 45 pounds. Get the best arrows you can afford, and keep the broadheads shaving-sharp. Then practice. No matter how good your archery equipment is, you must practice. Do most of your practice shooting with arrows tipped with field points. But well before the deer season begins you should familiarize yourself with the flight characteristics of your broadheads.

Since you generally have to get very close to the game to be a successful bowhunter, you may want to use camouflage, if your state regulations permit it. Chapter 6 includes instructions for tie-dyeing your own camouflage clothes.

One of the cheapest aids to camouflaging your face, hands, bow, or any other shiny item that could betray your presence is cork. Simply burn one end of the cork until it turns deep black, then apply where needed. It's easily removed with soap and water.

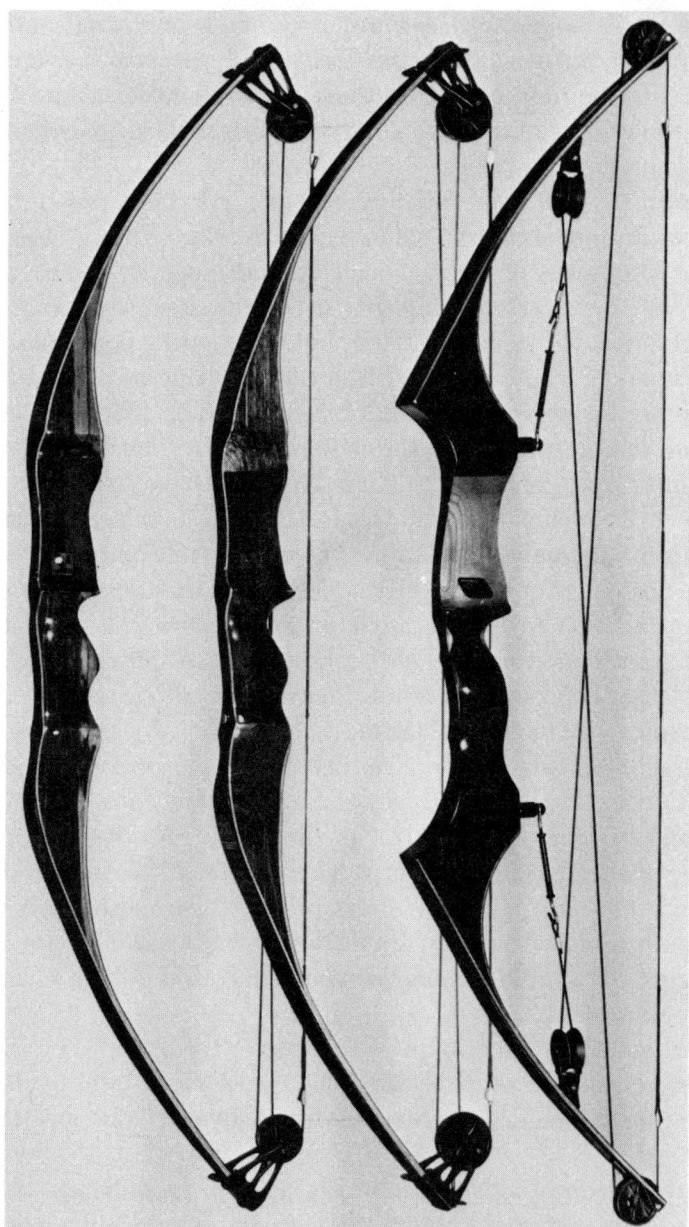

Compound bows that retain all the beauty and feel of a traditional one-piece bow.
(Photo courtesy Ben Pearson Archery)

48

There are three basic bow types, the straight bow, recurve bow, and compound bow. The recurve and compound are the most popular; both give greater arrow speed and superior all-round performance.

THE COMPOUND BOW

The main thing that sets a compound apart from a conventional bow (aside from its Rube Goldberg arrangement of pulleys and cables) is that during the draw, roughly halfway back, a pair of eccentric cams turn over in the bow's tips. The turnover reduces the energy required to complete the draw and then to hold at full draw while aiming. The compound bow is set for two draw weights. The heavier weight applies to the initial portion of the draw; the lighter weight is the effective poundage for the hold.

For example, you can order a compound bow set at 45-60 pounds. That means you pull 60 pounds until the cam flips over; thereafter you are working with a force of 45 pounds. Most important, when the arrow leaves the bow, it is propelled by the 60-pound force. The reduced draw weight after the eccentric cams turn over permits a longer, more careful aim.

The limiting factor is the price tag, which is usually more than $200. This is considerable when you consider that a really good standard hunting bow can be bought for considerably less than $100. Many veteran bowhunters who have been taking deer regularly over the years with the standard recurve have no inclination to switch to the compound.

THE RECURVE BOW

Recurve bows are constructed from wood, solid fiberglass, light metals, or a combination of woods and fiberglass in laminated form. The laminated wood-and-fiberglass bow is called a composite bow and is by far the best type. It weighs less, is stronger, and can cast an arrow faster and more accurately than the others.

Generally speaking, a shorter bow will produce greater arrow speed, is lighter, and is more convenient to handle. Bows between 50 and 60 inches long are normally preferred for hunting.

In most states, a hunting bow must be no less than 40-pound draw weight. When a bow is used entirely for hunting, the only limitations on draw weight need be the hunter's strength and ability. For the average

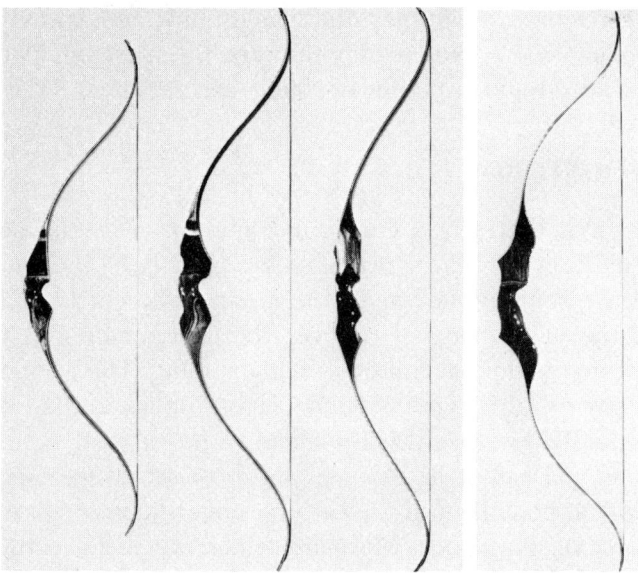

The conventional recurve bow is still a favorite. *(Photo courtesy Ben Pearson Archery)*

archer, a bow in the 45-to-50-pound range is recommended. Don't make the common mistake of selecting a bow that's too heavy.

ARROWS

"Spine" is the characteristic of an arrow which allows it to flex around a bow in such a way that it travels straight instead of being deflected to the side as it passes the bow. There is a recommended spine for each bow weight, and it is fundamental to achieving good accuracy to use arrows that have the correct spine. The spine of an arrow is designated by the draw weight of the appropriate bow so that the two may be more easily matched by the archer. Arrows are usually spined in increments of 5 pounds. Thus for a bow with a draw weight of 42 pounds, arrows should be selected which have been spined in the 40-to-45-pound classification.

Arrow weight an arrow spine are closely related, and variations in either can cause considerable flight inconsistency. Hence, it is also important that each set of arrows match in weight. All better makes of arrows are closely matched to weigh within a few grains of one another.

50

All components of your archery tackle should be balanced both with one another and with the game you're after. Any good archery shop can explain the variations in arrow construction and design, bow weight, etc., and help you select a proper outfit.

Two popular names in archery gear are Bear and Ben Pearson. Both offer catalogs. At Ben Pearson, talk's not cheap—it's free. Call on them 24 hours a day on their toll-free hot line, 1-800-331-4661. Ben Pearson Archery, P.O. Box 270, Tulsa, Okla. 74101. Bear Archery, Grayling, Mich. 49738.

BOWHUNTING FOR DEER

"Working your muscles into shape for that heavy bow should be done slowly," says Doug Kittredge, a famed bowhunter who holds the world record for the largest mountain lion ever taken by an archer. "Don't overdo shooting sessions at first," cautions Kittredge, "just shoot for 15 or 20 minutes a day for the first week or so, and pull the bow a few times in the morning before work, just for exercise."

George Wright, an eight-year member of the Ben Pearson Bowhunting Advisory Staff, suggests that bowhunters should get away from shooting at targets. "I believe that we get too bull's-eye-oriented" says Wright. "There's no spot on that big buck—just one you imagine."

Wright practices on an empty hay bale, just one bale, which he states is about the size of a big deer's body. His practice method involves putting one arrow in a specific spot on the bale, shooting at an imaginary aiming point from all distances and positions. It pays off for George Wright, who collects several trophy bucks a year in the Western states.

John Lamicq, another Pearson staff member who is a professional guide in Colorado, feels that the most important element is to shoot a lot, with broadheads.

John shoots into old bales and does a lot of roving around the country of his native Colorado scouting out the game haunts. He takes his bow and shoots at spots in soft dirt banks, pine cones on grassy hillsides, and similar marks. "I may wreck a Switchblade broadhead or two, but when the season rolls around I'm ready and I know where those broadheads are going to go."

That's good advice. Seasoned bowhunters agree that broadheads have their own flight characteristics; nothing beats practice with the real thing.

"There are a lot of ways a bowhunter can practice," says Jim Dougherty, director of the Ben Pearson Advisory Staff. "It really doesn't matter what he does as long as he gets out in plenty of time before the season and does it. Each bowhunter will figure out what's best for him. Doing it is the important thing when the time for that shot comes along."

Most successful bowhunters share the same secret for consistently taking whitetails: they are trail watchers—dogged, persistent, seemingly oblivious to cold, doubt, or boredom.

Don't overlook comfort when building a tree stand or selecting a ground location for a stand. A narrow tree limb or log is comfortable for a few minutes, but you'll soon grow cold or cramped.

Doubt is an attitude the successful bowhunter does without; *he knows* he is going to tag a deer. Anyone can develop this attitude. Start by scouting your proposed hunting site before the season. Know exactly where you are going to be waiting for deer, and then, on opening morning, stick it out. Deer have a small home range, but it is not so small that they return to any given spot every 20 minutes. The most well trodden of trails may be used only once during daylight. To score, you have to be there when that happens. Pack a lunch and stick it out from dawn to dusk if necessary.

A big buck can suddenly materialize at any time. The middle of the day, when other hunters are heading out of the woods for snacks, is a prime time for deer to be pushed past your stand. Or that fat buck may simply rise from its bed at 3:00 p.m. and amble by, or maybe it will be at 7:10 a.m., or maybe . . .

Tales about the bow being an inhumane weapon are mainly fiction. A sharp, well-placed arrow is just as lethal as a rifle slug and more lethal than most buckshot loads. Studies in several states, including New York and Wisconsin, show that cripple losses by bowhunters are no greater than those by gun hunters.

BOWHUNTING FOR SMALL GAME

Don't overlook small-game hunting. It's the best practice you can get for bigger game. And it's plenty exciting. Rabbits and hares are prime targets. You'll lose some arrows, so use low-priced target models. Blunt points work well for small game. A common rubber eraser fitted on the end of an

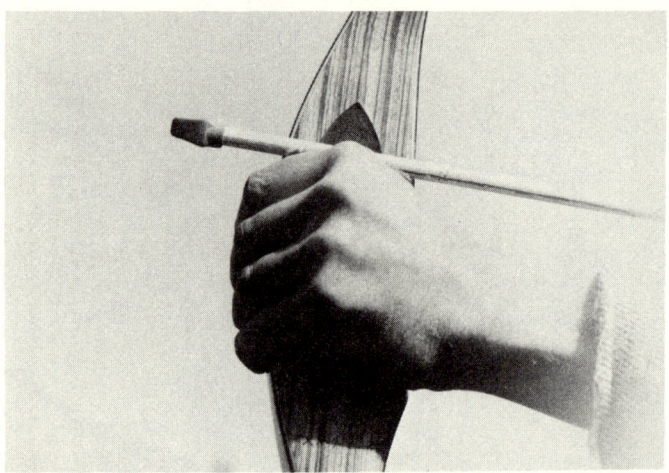

A rubber eraser makes an effective tip for hunting small game; it kills squirrels without sticking in tree limbs.

arrow shaft will kill most small game, yet not stick in tree limbs when used for squirrels, or a barn roof when ridding the place of pesty pigeons.

Rabbits are very adaptable, especially the common Eastern cottontail. It can find shelter in an overgrown city dump almost as well as in brushy forest areas, and is especially fond of "edges" or border area, such as weed-choked ditches, brushy fencerows, and hedges. Warm, sunny days are particularly good for hunting cottontails with bow and arrow. The rabbits will be sitting along the edge of cover sunning themselves.

Snowshoe hares are super targets. In soft snow the hunter can sometimes walk within 2 or 3 feet of a snowshoe. But what it lacks in brainpower the hare more than makes up for in being a tough bunny to see. Look for them in thickets. When the going gets tough and you have to thread your way through junglelike tangles, you're in snowshoe country.

Flu-flu arrows can be used for wing shooting of upland birds. Smart feather design permits fast flight at release, but slows the arrow quickly to limit distance.

Bowhunting takes on another season with the addition of a bowfishing rig. Bowfishing for rough fish in either fresh or salt water is fun and a good way to improve your aim. Carp, gar, shark, and many other species are exciting quarry.

54

5
DOGS

The easiest way to save money on hunting dogs is not to own any. It may, in fact, be the only way. And *every species of game bird and animal can be successfully hunted without one.*

Yet, for some, hunting without a dog is not really hunting. You won't understand why they feel this way until you've experienced for yourself the satisfactions that come with molding a hunting dog. A good hunting dog virtually guarantees more game for the hunter. This is especially true when the quarry you seek is the cagey rooster pheasant. Sharptail grouse are far easier to locate in vast areas of grassland when a wide-ranging pointing dog is doing the looking. And what a sight it is when the retriever that *you* trained brings in his first duck.

Can you get one cheap?

"People sometimes luck out and get something good free or cheap," says *Outdoor Life* Dog Editor Dave Duffey. "But the chances of getting a dog free or cheap—a good one—aren't good, and there is no free or cheap way to properly train a dog, other than doing the training yourself. And that, in terms of time, investment in necessary gear, birds, shells, etc., isn't free.

"There are cut-rate trainers, but even they aren't cheap and they certainly aren't free—and usually you get a cut-rate dog back. Occasionally guys luck out and get a dog that's so naturally good he virtually learns his trade just by being taken out hunting, but that usually is the result of good breeding, and dogs of good breeding aren't given away.

Maybe the initial cost of the dog shouldn't even be considered. It's the upkeep that kills you, and a bargain dog and an expensive dog cost the same to keep, properly."

It follows that money spent on a dog with good potential is money saved in the long run. By getting a potentially good dog off to a good start, you may be pleasantly surprised to discover that your dog responds by going on to "train himself." Nevertheless, you don't have to spend much time afield to discover that many a hunter has failed in this respect.

So what is the big secret?

Presuming that you're working with a young dog who's been born with the instincts, desires, and potential to be a satisfactory hunting dog, the answer is proper introduction to every aspect of its training. For example, a

dog may hunt and retrieve beautifully but be unsatisfactory because he brings in birds badly chewed and mutilated. Proper introduction to bird handling could have prevented this bad habit. It's far easier to establish a good habit by sound training than to break a dog of a bad habit. That's one of the biggest drawbacks of buying an older dog. Breaking its bad habits may be virtually impossible.

Training includes obedience commands like "Sit," "Come," and "Stay" which are applicable to both hunting and nonhunting dogs. Yet if your early training in obedience is too rigorous, your dog may be unable to develop its natural hunting instincts. So restraint is very important in proper training.

Avoid making long-distance trips to the country for some aspect of training. If the dog does not respond well, you may lash out at it because of time and expense you've wasted. This results not in proper introduction but in fear of that aspect of training. There is less at stake with a back-yard training session. When actual field conditions are needed, you can work a 10-minute training session in with a fishing trip or hike.

If you plan to work your dog from a duck boat, for example, first encourage the dog to join you on a summer boat ride. Throw a training dummy and encourage the dog to jump from the boat. Don't be surprised if a dog that normally loves the water is frightened at first about jumping from a boat. Don't force it if the dog is frightened. Row back to shore and let him jump from there to make the retrieve. Then take him out in deep water again. If he's still frightened, don't push it; go fishing instead! Take it easy on your dog. Make the training sessions short and fun. It's so much easier to quit and try another day. Don't make an ego trip out of training your dog.

It's important to know that the learning process for a dog is rarely gradual. They learn in spurts. You can work your dog 20 minutes every day for a week and each time the dog may fail to respond, usually because he really doesn't know what you want. So you put the mutt back in its pen and practically ignore it for a week. Then one morning you let the dog out and halfheartedly encourage it to do the desired action and, suddenly, the dog does it. And with style! This can be the result of the dog suddenly realizing what it is you want. But sometimes a long stint in the kennel gets a pooch to thinking that you mean business.

Occasionally you will have to punish your dog. Don't do it unless you are sure the dog understands what the punishment is for. Punish only when a dog has learned a command and defies you. More important, praise lavishly when a dog does right. A dog delights in pleasing his master. Make it easy for him.

Be consistent. Give a command only when you are prepared to enforce it. Don't make the dog obey sometimes and let him get away with it at other times. Too often dog owners alternate between spoiling the dog and being brutally harsh. This is pretty confusing for the dog.

The key to proper training is repetition. Some dogs learn faster than others, but all benefit from repetition whether in introducing a new idea or reinforcing something already learned.

Before any training session, let the dog run off a little pent-up energy and relieve himself. Then keep training sessions short. Pups are especially apt to lose interest.

To put you both in a good mood, begin each lesson with a review of one or more previous lessons so that the dog can earn praise right from the start.

When possible, conduct lessons in privacy, without distractions. Always try to end each session with the dog accomplishing some goal no matter how slowly and clumsily. Ending on a note of success, accompanied by profuse praise, does wonders for the dog's morale.

It would be wonderful to own a dog who did everything. Unfortunately, such an animal does not exist. Some versatile hunting breeds, such as the German shorthaired pointer and the Brittany spaniel, will handle a lot of bird-hunting situations from woodcock to sage grouse, but you can't expect them to compete with Labrador in retrieving waterfowl or with a hound in trailing furred game such as rabbit and raccoon. Your choice of dog should depend on the hunting you do the most. If you do a lot of upland-game hunting you will want to select one of the pointing dogs or spaniels. Pointers are generally expected to hunt well beyond gun range and, upon locating birds, to freeze on point, waiting for the hunter to come up and put the birds into flight. Spaniels, on the other hand, must restrict their search to gun range, indicating the presence of game by their animation and accelerated tail action before driving in to flush the game.

Retrievers can be used solely to retrieve game, either walking at the hunter's side or crouched in a blind. But most hunters also want them to work ahead of the gun in the manner of spaniels to produce game as well as to recover it after the shot.

Hounds trail their quarry either by working out a cold track or following a hot line or scent until the game is brought around to the gun, cornered, treed, or holed up.

Whatever breed of dog you decide on, the pup must possess the potential to be a hunter and to accept training. The closest you can come to assuring this is to buy a pup that comes from proved hunting or field-trial stock. The pup should be registered with the American Kennel Club. However, this only guarantees that the dog is of purebred strain; it does not guarantee hunting potential. Then get a good book on dog training. Get out regularly with your dog for training and workouts, doing the things you've read about. And don't fail to take your dog hunting. No dog ever became great solely through training. He was hunted hard and often.

Books that are helpful in the training of hunting dogs:

American Beagling, by G. G. Black (Putnam).
Hunting Hounds, by David Michael Duffey (Winchester Press).
Hunting Dog Know How, by David Michael Duffey (Winchester Press).
Dave Duffey Trains Gun Dogs, by Dave Duffey (Sporting Dog Specialties).
Training Your Spaniel, by Clarence Pfaffenberger (Howell).
Bird Dogs, by Larry Mueller (Stoeger).

BUILDING A KENNEL

A kennel that is big enough for you to walk in and for your dog to move around in will make owning and caring for a hunting dog a breeze, even in the city. The best will have a poured cement floor. But if you can get them, old 2-foot-square sidewalk blocks will do very nicely. In a big city it is not hard to find where a sidewalk is being torn up. What makes this kind of floor ideal is that it can be hosed down and stools can be picked up easily. With occasional hosing and the hot summer sun shining on it at least part of the day, this kind of floor will be sanitary and free of obnoxious odor. And the dog cannot dig its way out.

A kennel makes owning a dog easy even in town.

The kennel should be roughly 4 feet wide by 6 feet high, and 20 feet in length. If appearance is not important, the kennel framework can be constructed of cedar posts with used 2×4-inch studs between the posts. The entire structure is then enclosed with 12-gauge 2×4-inch wire mesh. Old wire mesh found around the home or farm will do fine, but be sure it is strong enough; a big dog can eat right through chicken wire.

The kennel shown in the photo is neat in appearance, with a poured cement slab floor and 4×4-inch redwood posts. The owner saved money on pouring the floor by picking up the liquid cement himself, bringing it home in barrels, and pouring it into a framework he built himself. The wire mesh in the kennel is on the outside of the posts. It is better to have the mesh on the inside of the posts, because dogs are frequently habitual wood chewers and are very rough on wooden fence posts. The lower 2×4-inch studs that run between the posts should be several inches above the floor. That way water and debris can be hosed under the studs and out of the kennel. A simple door is made from 2×2-inch lumber and hinged and equipped with a lock. If you live in a heavy-snow area, it is wise to have the bottom of the door a foot above ground level.

The dimensions of this kennel, 24 feet long, 4 feet wide, and 6 feet high, make it a convenience for both dog and owner.

BUILDING A LOG DOGHOUSE

Building a doghouse is expensive at today's prices, especially if it is a double-wall doghouse complete with insulation, as is often recommended for cold climates. An easy solution is to build a log doghouse. Logs need only be 3 or 4 inches in diameter to provide the necessary insulation if closely fitted and well chinked. Logs can be cut from almost any kind of tree. Aspen is popular and very common in many areas of the United States and Canada and is of little commercial value. The easiest model to build is a simple rectangular shape with a flat piece of board for a roof. The logs can be notched as are toy Lincoln logs. A removable roof makes it easy to replenish the dog's straw bedding.

61

LOG DOGHOUSE

BUILDING A BARREL DOGHOUSE

The easiest doghouse to make is one from an old 55-gallon oil drum. With a metal chisel knock an opening in one end large enough for the dog to enter. The cut edges of the entrance will be sharp, so hammer them flat. With straw bedding, this doghouse is fairly comfortable in a moderate climate. Keep it out of the hot sun. It can get uncomfortable in extreme cold, too.

One use for the barrel doghouse even in the winter months is protection for your dog in the back of a hunting vehicle. It will provide *some* shelter in the back of an unheated vehicle. Should the dog become lost during the day's hunting, leave the barrel where you were parked and the dog will probably be found sleeping in it the following morning. This is especially useful if you hunt with a trailing hound—the kind that doesn't want to leave the trail even after dark.

A barrel filled with straw makes a cheap doghouse.

MAKING A PORTABLE DRINKING DISH

During warm-weather hunts, dogs can become desperately thirsty. There isn't always a river, stream, or pond nearby. A portable drinking dish that won't spill is a handy item to have along. Simply cut a 5-inch hole in the cover of an 8-inch or larger plastic dish. Many food items are sold in these kind of containers and housewives seldom throw them away. See the illustration. By making the hole only 5 inches in diameter, you leave a baffle that minimizes spilling.

PORTABLE DOG DISH

6
CLOTHING AND ACCESSORIES

More and more hunters are buying kits and stitching together their own gear these days. The savings, according to manufacturers of the kits, run from 30 to 50 percent of the ready-made price. The items include everything from coats, hoods, and vests that reverse to blaze orange to rain gear, sleeping bags, and tents.

Most kits contain everything needed to make the item, including precut material, zippers, snaps, prepackaged down or sheets of synthetic material, and even the thread. All that is needed is a sewing machine and time. Detailed instructions are designed so that even junior high school students, who have never sewn before, are making clothing and other items as classroom projects. In fact, instructions are written for the novice sewer, say the Frostline Kits people. Experienced sewers are warned that the construction of outdoor equipment and clothing is unlike ordinary sewing projects (such as shirts, tops, dresses, etc.) and are cautioned to follow instructions step by step. A beginner may actually have an easier time with these kits because he is willing to follow directions closely, while the experienced sewer may think he knows how to do it, and then do it wrong.

The down content of insulated items may vary from one manufacturer to another. It may be goose down or duck down. The quality of the down

Sew-it-yourself kits mean money saved, and you build in the quality. *(Photo courtesy Frostline Kits)*

can also vary. Some state laws allow up to 25 percent extraneous materials such as feathers or dirt in their down. It's difficult to know if you're getting quality down in either a manufactured product or a kit. One solution is to stick with brand-name goods.

Some kits feature popular synthetics such as Fiberfill II and Polar Guard. The biggest advantage of synthetics is price. Synthetics are generally much cheaper than real down. They are also easier to work with. Polar Guard comes in sheets and some find it easier to handle than packets of down. With the synthetics there is no need for the compartments or quilting lines that down items require.

If you've never used a sewing machine before, it is wise to seek the advice of someone who has. After a few pointers, you will soon be stitching away confidently. The kit offers you the chance to see that the sewing is done right. Stress areas can be reinforced if you do it yourself. Salesmen say that if you had to pay for the amount of time and quality you can build into the finished kit, the item would probably cost twice as much.

One final word: start small and take your time. A vest or mittens are usually recommended starters. Larger kits require a substantial investment

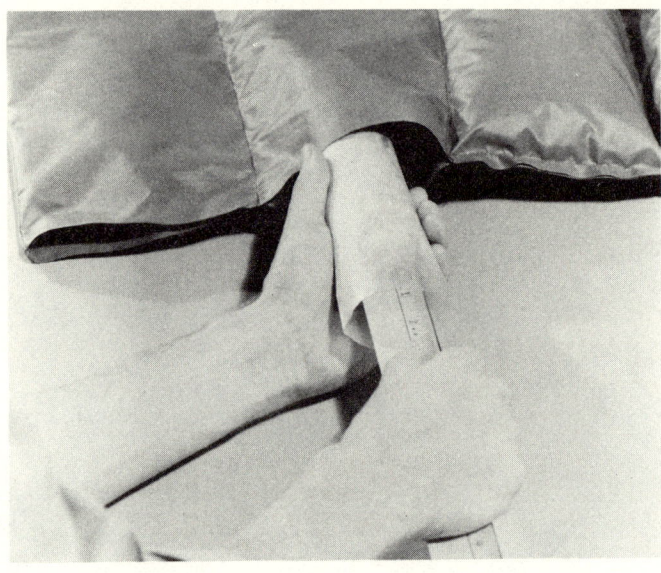

Filling a garment with prime northern goose down is made easy by the use of flip-top packets. *(Photo courtesy Frostline Kits)*

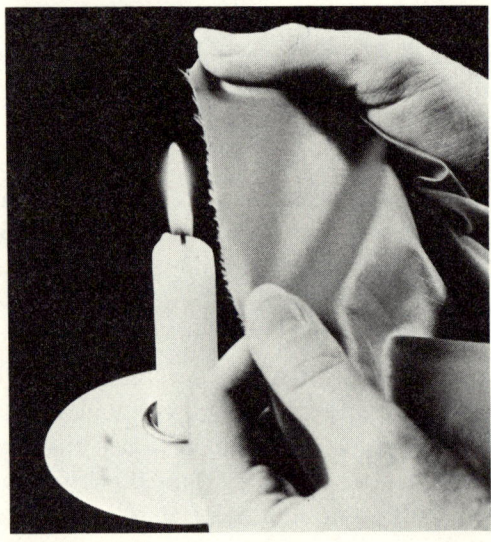

Edge searing is a good example of the kind of quality you build into your own gear. No factory can take the time to sear the edges of each piece of cloth. *(Photo courtesy Frostline Kits)*

in time. For example, one tent kit contains a step-by-step instruction booklet of 70 to 80 pages. A ski jacket may require about 30 pages. You may decide it's not worth the trouble to you. It certainly is easier to walk into a store and walk out with the equipment. On the other hand, you may find it worth the trouble to try to save money, build in extra quality, and have a finished product that will give you great personal satisfaction and pride.

KIT SUPPLIERS

Frostline Kits
Dept. C
452 Burbank
Broomfield, Colo. 80020

Sun Down
P.O. Box 1023
Burnsville, Minn. 55337

Holubar
P.O. Box 7
Boulder, Colo. 80302

Eastern Mountain Sports
1627 W. County Rd. B
St. Paul, Minn. 55113

Country Ways
3500 Hwy. 101 South
Minnetonka, Minn. 55343

One of the great joys of early-fall hunting for upland birds is its simplicity. Your basic needs are only a shotgun and a pocketful of shells. Old clothing, light field boots, and a visored cap to keep the sun out of your eyes will suffice. The only real extra you need is a vest-type game bag. This is preferable to a hunting coat with built-in gamebag because the vest style can be worn comfortably in warm weather.

You can get more use from leather hiking boots with the judicious use of rubbers. Carry a pair of rubbers in your car trunk or in a daypack and slip them on when your outdoor activities entail walking in light snow, mud, or swampy terrain. Nothing shortens the life of leather hiking boots more than many thorough soakings. The rubbers enable you to wear your hiking boots in conditions where you might otherwise have to wear uncomfortable knee-high rubber boots or cumbersome and heavy winter footwear.

The best rubbers are those that cover the whole of your foot. Get heavy-duty rubbers that won't tear under tough hiking conditions. Most have ribbed soles that provide traction on slippery rock and ice.

One of the best substitutes for a hunting coat, at least in mild weather, is a denim jacket. It's tough and resists snagging on limbs far better than one made of most other material, and it's trim, lightweight, and inexpensive.

Plastic bags have hundreds of uses. A couple of them will make it possible to start a new day with a dry pair of socks even if you have a not-so-dry pair of boots. A plastic bag slipped over your socks will keep away the dampness. They're also handy when starting out on a rainy day or when the woods are wet with early-morning dew. Most leather boots will quickly soak up moisture; plastic bags will keep your feet comfortable for a while. Remove the bags early, though, since feet perspire and need to "breathe."

A plastic garbage bag makes an economical, lightweight poncho. Simply cut a hole in the bottom of the bag. Then pull the bag over your head with the hole fitting around your head.

Rabbits bagged on winter hunts may freeze. It pays to clean them on the spot and keep the meat in plastic bags. This protects your coat pocket or game carrier from blood stains and the frozen meat can go directly into the freezer on arriving home, without the need to thaw first for cleaning.

It's easy and cheap to use tie-dyeing to make your own camouflage clothing for deer hunting with bow and arrow or fooling spring or fall turkeys. An old pair of tan or green work pants is a good start. Wrap rubber bands tightly around random parts of the pants, then dip the pants in colored dye. The parts of the pants compressed by the rubber bands will not be affected by the dye. Later, move the rubber bands to other parts of the pants and dip the pants into another color dye. Good combinations of color are green, yellow, and brown, or brown, yellow, and red, depending on area and season. The longer an article of clothing is left in the dye the darker will be the color.

It is desirable, if not essential, to have some special clothes for upland hunting. A pair of tough hunting pants is often the first choice for the grouse hunter, because in some areas the cover is so wicked that hunting pants of heavyweight canvas duck are a must. Another option is double-front pants, which are usually a blend of synthetics and cotton, with a second layer of fabric protecting the leg in front.

You can make a comfortable pair of upland hunting pants by facing an old pair of flannel pants or Levis—any comfortable pair of casual pants will

HOMEMADE HUNTING PANTS

do—with heavy duck. You can do it yourself or have a tailor do it. The heavy duck material should be sewn across the front of the pant legs from a point just below the pocket to the foot. No cuffs are needed; they are just a catchall for weeds and debris. It is a great way to recycle your old pants into well-fitting, comfortable hunting pants.

Clothing is more complicated for the deer hunter. Cold weather is a part of deer hunting throughout most of the animal's range, whether whitetail or mule deer. It can be the raw cold of a Kansas river bottom, the subzero cold of Michigan's Upper Peninsula, or the cutting cold of Montana's high country.

It may seem old-fashioned to speak of wool in this day of super-light goose down and synthetic products, but wool is great for deer hunting, especially for one's outer garments. Down garments have synthetic coverings which are noisy in brush or even when shifting position in a tree stand. Wool is silent. When it is wet, it still offers some insulation. A goose-down vest (made from a kit, of course) under a wool shirt or jacket-shirt (wool coats are too heavy, and too warm in mild weather) is a happy combination of the old and the new. Wool pants are always a good bet in wet and snow. Wear them over long underwear.

69

Rubber-bottomed pacs with felt liners will keep your feet warm and dry, but only if the liners are dried out nightly, or if you have an extra pair to wear every other day. An old method of keeping feet warm and dry is to wear an ordinary pair of socks inside a pair of work shoes or old dress shoes. Pull a large pair of wool socks over the outside of the shoes. Then step into a pair of roomy galoshes. If the snow is deep, tie the bottoms of your trouser legs snugly around the tops of the galoshes to prevent snow from entering.

Most gloves are not warm enough nor do they stay dry enough for cold and wet weather. Buckskin chopper mitts with wool inserts are better. It takes only a moment to slip one off your trigger hand.

For headwear the fur-lined hats with "retractable" ear muffs are nearly perfect. A wool face mask like those worn by skiers is just right for severe wind and cold.

A turtleneck dickey or sweater will retain body heat around your head and open coat top, and you'll want to consider such accessories as hand and seat warmers. Burlap bags filled with straw make good warm seat cushions. In severe cold, a snowmobile suit is hard to beat. You can perspire excessively walking any distance in a snowmobile suit, so it's a good idea to carry one to your stand in a daypack, or tied with twine and slung over your shoulder, and put it on once you're settled.

MAKING YOUR OWN KNIFE

You can make a simple but useful knife with a blade about 4 inches long, thin and light, ground to a double taper with the point in line with the handle. This makes a good skinning knife. The blade is ground from a power-hacksaw blade and fitted with a hardwood handle.

Best-quality power-hacksaw blades are tough, hard, and resilient, and they hold an edge well. Any grinder will shape them if the work is done slowly, dipping the blade in cold water frequently to cool it. Grind for brief periods to keep the steel from heating enough to destroy its temper. A lapidary-type grinder which plays water over the stone makes the work far easier, and the danger of destroying the temper is lessened.

Metal files are another source of knifemaking material. The essentials needed for home knifemaking are available commercially. You can obtain blade blanks or blades in various stages of development, up to the fully

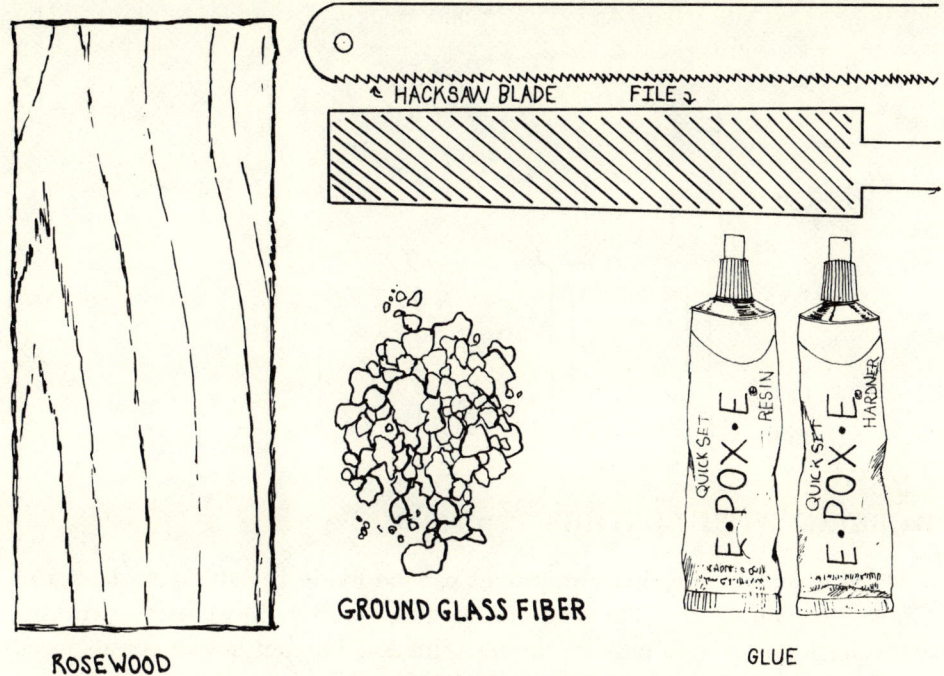

HACKSAW BLADE   FILE

GROUND GLASS FIBER

GLUE

ROSEWOOD

ground, sharpened, and polished steel, all ready for hilt and handle. You can also secure, for a nominal price, knife steel of the proper length for forging.

For catalogs of knife blades and parts ($1 is the customary catalog fee) contact the following:

Custom Knifemakers Supply
Box 11448
Dallas, Texas 75223

Indian Ridge Traders
Box X-50
Ferndale, Mich. 48220

Atlanta Cutlery Corp.
Box 33266
Decatur, Ga. 30033

Dick Van Sickle
Dwr. 3688
San Angelo, Texas 76901

Morseth Knives
1705 Hwy. 71 N
Springdale, Ark. 72764

KNIFEMAKING STEPS

WORKING WITH LEATHER

Durable leather hunting equipment can be made for about a quarter of the cost of commercial items of comparable quality. Most leatherworking enthusiasts start with a patent stitcher. This is a wooden holder for a special needle with its eye near the point. The hollow handle contains a bobbin of thread. Start with easy projects such as a moccasin kit sold at leather stores. You can make even more moccasins for other members of your family by tracing the pieces of precut leather. Then buy scrap leather and make more moccasins at a fraction of the cost of either kits or finished moccasins.

As your enthusiasm advances, so will your need for more tools. You won't need many:

> A card each of harness needles and glover's needles
> A spool each of Size 6 and Fine waxed nylon thread
> An awl
> A carpenter's utility knife and spare blades
> An adjustable stitching groover
> A common edge beveler
> A revolving leather punch
> A circle edge slicker
> A pair of 2-inch dividers with legs ground to square points
> Snaps, rivets

A punch and anvil for installing snaps
Beeswax, neat's-foot compound

MAKING A CARTRIDGE CARRIER

A cartridge carrier is a leatherworking project that should be of interest to hunters. Materials needed: sufficient 5-6 ounce leather, No. 2 round punch, two Baby Dot Fasteners, anvil and setter, 2½ feet waxed thread, needles, knife or leather shears, and 3/32-inch thonging chisel.

In a book of this size it is not possible to use patterns large enough to trace, and the precise pattern you want will depend on the size cartridges you intend to carry. However, the pattern illustrated will give you a start in making your own. Follow these steps:

1. Cut out parts A, B, and C.
2. Punch holes for Baby Dot Fasteners.
3. Install snaps. Position the button on the flesh side and the stud on the grain side in holes 1 and 4. In holes 2 and 3 position the eyelet on the flesh side and the stud on the grain side.
4. Punch the lacing holes.
5. Assemble and lace.

The magazine *Make It with Leather* features many leatherworking features each month. Write: *Make It with Leather*, P.O. Box 1386, Fort Worth, Texas 76101.

REPAIRING BOOTS

By using two needles (harness needles, sail needles, or darning needles) threaded endlessly as shown in the illustration, you can repair broken stitching in moccasin-toed footwear. The best thread to use is waxed nylon twine available at marine-supply stores. In a pinch you can use monofilament fishing line.

Remove all of the old broken stitching. Start stitching at the forward end of the broken seam. Tie in the last of the still-sound stitches there by pushing one needle through its front pair of holes and pulling through half your length of twine. Then tackle the next pair of holes. Pass the first needle

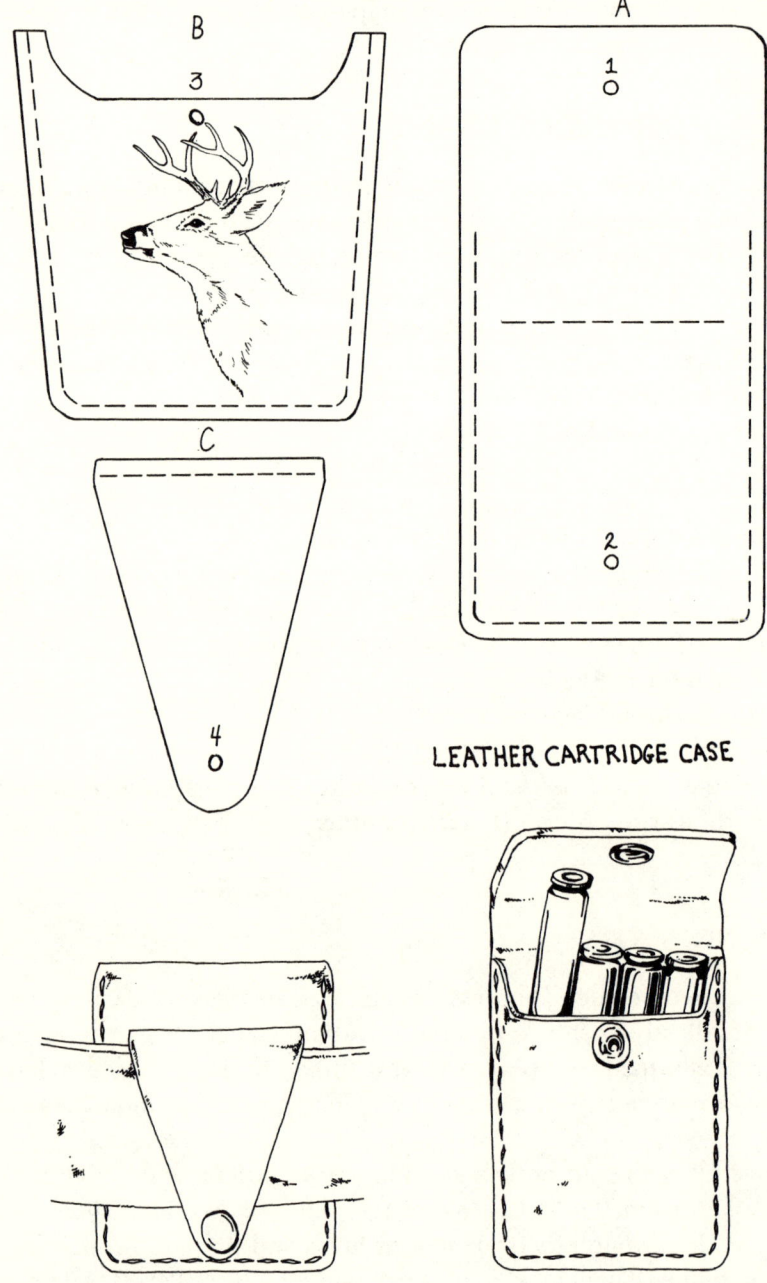

LEATHER CARTRIDGE CASE

74

through, then the second needle, and pull threads tight, leaving a needle and its length of twine on each side of the seam. Do the same for the next pair of holes, etc.

Very serviceable bootlaces can be made from an old automobile-tire inner tube provided that it has not dried out and still has live rubber. Cut around the tube with scissors, making narrow strips the same thickness and length as ordinary bootlaces. These laces even "give" with the movement of your feet.

BOOT REPAIR

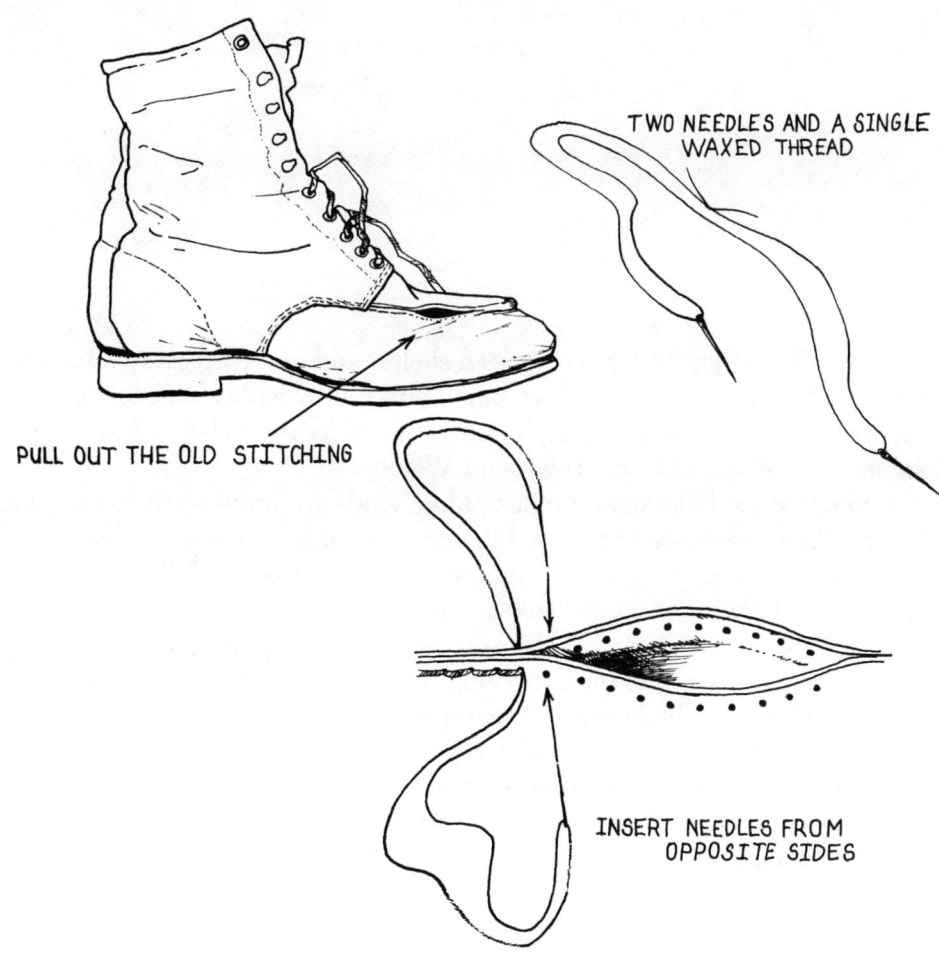

PULL OUT THE OLD STITCHING

TWO NEEDLES AND A SINGLE WAXED THREAD

INSERT NEEDLES FROM OPPOSITE SIDES

7
CAMPING AND TRAVEL

Camping offers low-priced shelter and ready access to a hunting area. Early fall is prime camping time, with mild weather and few insects. Hunters can use a tarp or simple lean-to such as the Whelen lean-to, designed by the late Colonel Townsend Whelen.

County, state, federal, and other public lands are often open to camping during the deer season. Many public campgrounds which normally charge a fee for summer camping are unattended and free in fall and winter. Private land can often be utilized for the asking.

An important point in tent, lean-to, and tarp camping is never to sleep on the ground if you can help it. The ground will be cold in the North, and in the desert it will be hotter at ground level than slightly above. Put down boughs or grass—anything available—to make space between your body and the ground. You can make a cheap camp bed by sewing together a heavy-canvas sling 7 feet long and 4 feet wide, with a 4-inch tubular seam running along each long side. Then cut two smooth poles to insert into these tubes. To keep your body and bedding off the ground, set the pole ends on a log or stone at each end of the camp bed.

76

TARPS

Tarps are the cheapest, lightest, and simplest of all shelters. They can be pitched in half a dozen different ways to provide shelter for the hunter in warm and moderate weather. Drape it over a pole to form a simple pup tent. Hunting from a canoe? Tip the canoe on its side, pinch one end of the tarp under the side of the canoe, bring the other end over the canoe, and stake it to the ground—or use rocks, or roll the end of the tarp around a log.

Heavy canvas tarps when properly waterproofed by the manufacturer will hold pools of water without leaking a drop. They are excellent when camping near your car or boat. But nylon is a lot easier to carry around. The Browning Company offers a 10×6-foot tarp of tough urethane-coated 1.9-ounce nylon that weighs only 1 pound. An aluminum tent pole, seven stakes, lots of metal grommets for tie ropes, and a 9-foot draw cord with fix lock come with it.

Another choice is the light, thin plastic sheeting now available everywhere. It weighs next to nothing, is completely waterproof, and is so inexpensive that a ripped sheet is a trifling loss. It does puncture or tear easily, though, and wilts or burns if too near the fire.

MAKING A WHELEN LEAN-TO

The Whelen lean-to will reflect and bounce a fire's warmth much like a reflector oven. Add to this the cheery atmosphere of an open fire and you have the ingredients for memorable camping. For cooking purposes, an overhang wards off rain. During dry weather it can be thrown back over the main panel.

The easiest fabric to work with is 6-ounce poplin. It will take 12 yards of material 40-45 inches wide. The finished tent should weigh about 7 pounds.

Make three patterns from newspapers, one for the back panel, one for the hood, and one for an end panel. The end panel can be turned over and used for the opposite end. When making patterns, allow an extra inch over the diagram dimensions for seams. You can reinforce the seams with

77

TARP SHELTERS

PATTERN FOR TWO-MAN WHELEN LEAN-TO

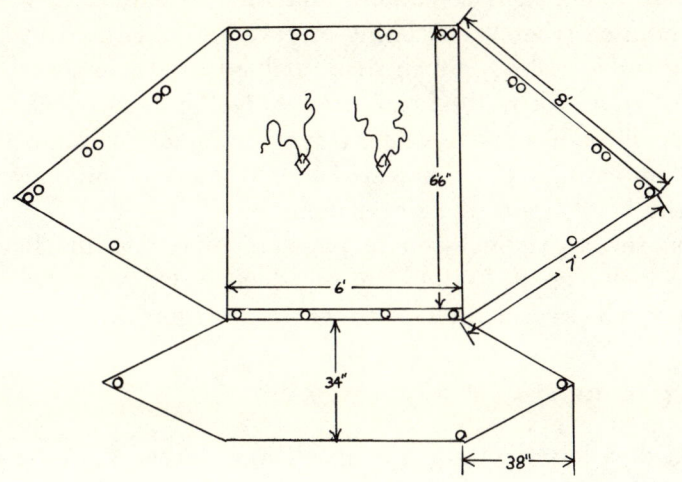

ROPES TIED TO TREES

LEAN-TO ERECTED

¾-inch webbing or cotton tape. For hems you should allow 2 inches. Outside seams are hems. Then place on fabric, trace, and cut the material.

Sew the four panels separately and then assemble. A ¾-inch overlap should be used wherever webbing or cotton tape is used in hems. Double stitching is desirable. A 5-inch strip doubled to 2½ inches should be used for a tape ridge where the hood attaches to the main panel. Grommets for hanging will be used in this tape ridge. Grommets will also be inserted in the bottom hems, and, as indicated by the diagram, grommets are needed where the hood ties to the side panels.

If you sew two 5-inch-square panels centered in the back panel and about 18 inches apart, D-rings can be attached. By tying guy ropes to these D-rings, you'll prevent the rear panel from sagging when you use the tent.

MAKING A BLANKET BAG

If you do a lot of camping, you will want either to invest in a sleeping bag or to make one yourself. But for moderate weather, wool blankets will serve. Most Boy Scouts know how to fold one or two blankets into a makeshift sleeping bag. They are also aware of its limitations. If the temperature is near freezing, more substantial bedding is needed. Start with a waterproof ground cloth between you and the ground. For more comfort, put a layer of straw, dry grass, dry leaves, or ferns under your ground cloth. You can convert a raincoat or poncho into a mattress by stuffing it with straw. If you have no mattress or other padding under you, fold clothing into pads and place them under you where you need support: the small of your back, your neck, and your knees.

With two blankets, place the left half of one overlapping the right half of the other. Then fold the other halves on top. Tuck the bottoms underneath. Hold in place with large safety pins—blanket pins. L. L. Bean Company sells economically priced camp blankets tightly woven from 85 percent reprocessed wool, with 15 percent nylon added for strength. These can be washed in lukewarm water with mild soap. Write: L. L. Bean, Inc., Freeport, Maine 04032.

BLANKET BAG

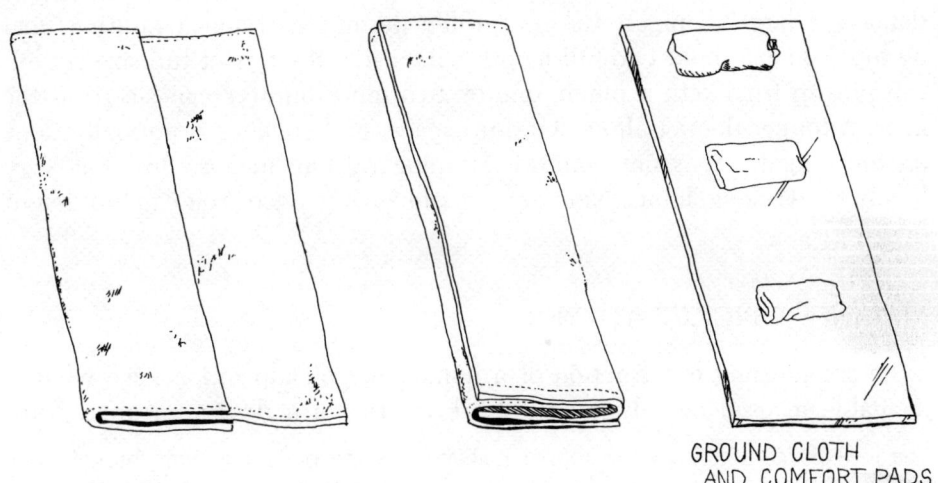

GROUND CLOTH
AND COMFORT PADS

PICKUP TOPPERS

A versatile vehicle for the hunter/camper is a pickup truck with a simple shell canopy, called a topper, over the truck box. While it lacks the comforts of a big camper, a topper does not prevent the vehicle from tackling rough backcountry logging trails with overhead tree limbs that could damage a larger camper. Its low profile permits carrying a hunting boat on top. You can build two full-length cots inside the box of full-size American pickup trucks. In a pinch, one or two more hunters can sleep on the floor. A topper doesn't allow stand-up space, and cooking is normally done on the tailgate. It is not comfort camping by any means. But it is very handy for weekend hunts. New toppers run $250 to $500. You can build your own for less.

MAKING A PICKUP TOPPER

Before tackling construction of a homemade pickup topper, see what is available in used models, especially if you're not a do-it-yourselfer. Most

The low profile of this pickup topper makes it a good bet for getting through tight spots with overhanging tree limbs that would damage an over-the-cab camper. *(Photo courtesy Chevrolet Motor Div.)*

commercial models are dependably rainproof—something the less handy individual might not be able to attain with a homemade job.

The basic construction for a homemade pickup topper is shown in the illustration and applies to any conventional light truck, ½- or ¾-ton, regardless of box size. The topper should be built a little higher than the truck cab to provide headroom when you're seated inside. The roof construction, like the side panels, should be 2×2-inch framing and overlap the box. Cut two plywood panels to fit the roof. Make sure they butt together over a crossmember. Use epoxy on the faces of the butt joint, and seal the joint with a strip of fiberglass cloth epoxied in place or with a 1-inch-wide batten strip nailed and glued over the joint of the two roof panels.

Exterior plywood ¼-inch thick can be used for the side panels. Use ½-inch plywood for the back end and door. A saber saw can be used to cut the apertures for the windows. Position the front window to align with the rear window of the cab. For windows use ⅛-inch or ¼-inch clear plastic, cutting oversize pieces to install on the inside, covering both front and rear apertures. Mount the plastic windows with a combination of glue and short screws on the ½-inch plywood hinged back door and use small

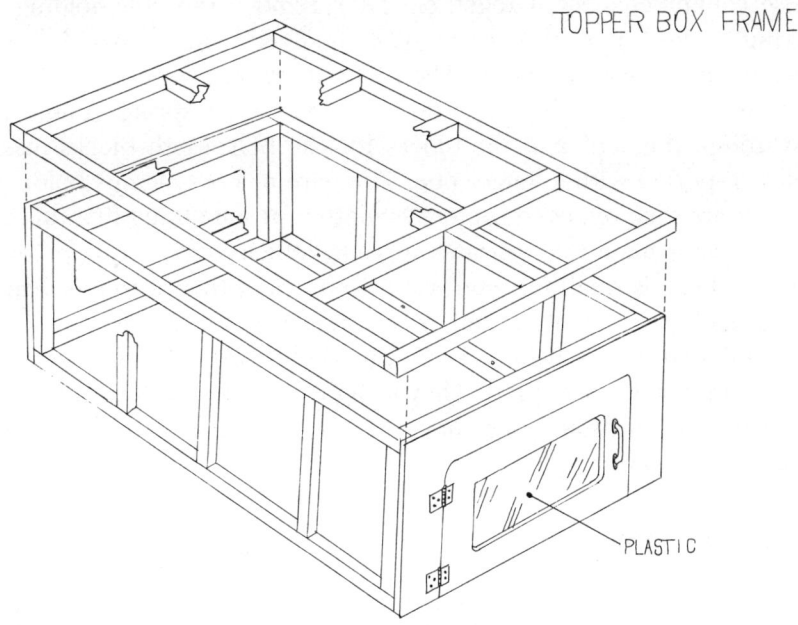

TOPPER BOX FRAME

PLASTIC

stove bolts for the front panel. Apply a silicone tub sealer or windshield sealer around the aperture edges to keep out rain seepage.

Small vents can be mounted on the sides for summer comfort. These are available at building stores.

ADVANTAGES OF SMALLER PICKUPS

Does a true hunting vehicle have to be four-wheel-drive? Not really. You can get through plenty of rough country with a six-cylinder, two-wheel-drive, half-ton pickup, provided it has enough road clearance. If you do get stuck, the vehicle is light enough to be jacked up so that limbs, rocks, or other materials can be put under the wheels. And with the smaller engine you get fair gas mileage; in fact, some hunters are going to the really compact foreign models that offer little camping space in back but great gas mileage.

Here's how some hunters gain extra wheel clearance on a pickup truck with coil springs. They add weight to the truck box until the coil springs are compressed. Then they tie the coil springs together with wire, or use two hose clamps connected together. They remove the bolt holding each coil spring to the frame. When weight is removed from the truck box, the coil springs rise above the frame. Then they insert one, or even two, blocks of wood cut from 2×6-inch lumber under each rear coil spring. A hole is first bored through the center of the blocks for the bolt. With blocks inserted, the bolt is replaced with a longer one. The wire or hose clamps holding the coil springs are then removed. Before you attempt something like this check a good service manual that pertains to your vehicle.

If your vehicle is small but you want more room than a topper can provide, you could use a tent trailer. A tent trailer is not a bad idea for the economy-minded hunter if he lives in a mild climate, but it's a poor choice for most cold-weather camping. They're light and can be towed by almost any kind of car, and since they have low resale value, good buys can be found in second-hand models.

LARGER CAMPERS

A popular hunting/camping vehicle is the bigger, slide-in truck camper, usually with a cab overhang for bed or storage space. They're heavy,

ADDING WHEEL CLEARANCE

BEFORE

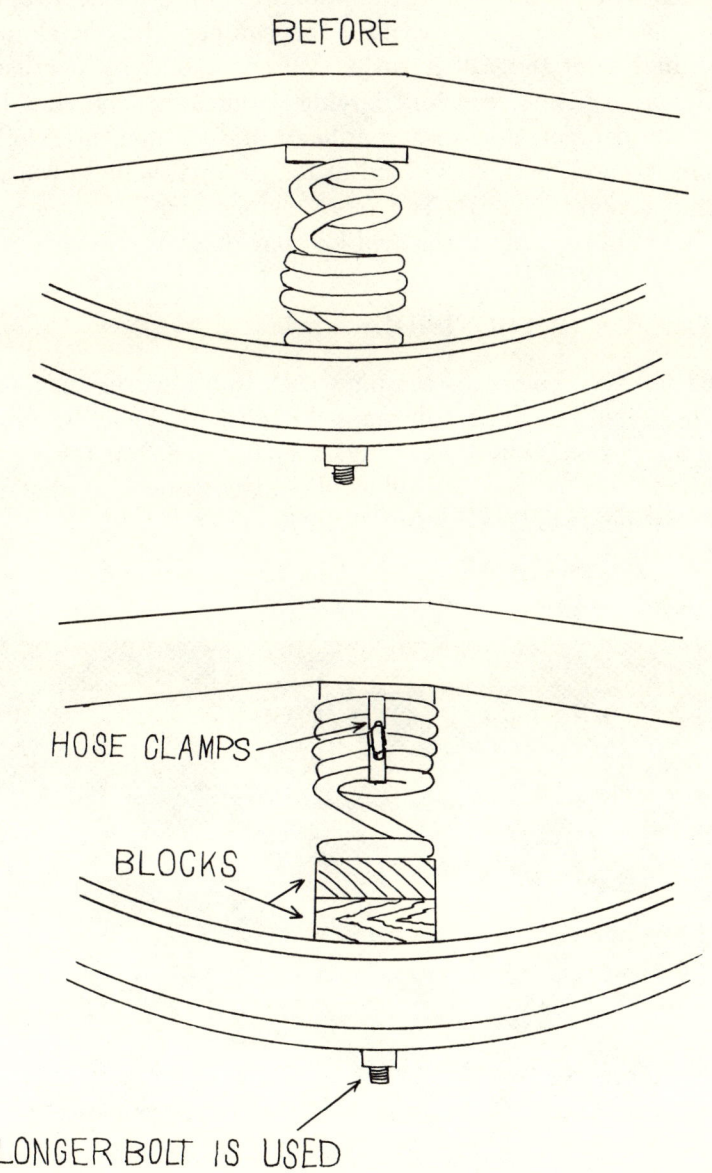

HOSE CLAMPS

BLOCKS

LONGER BOLT IS USED

though, and not usually very satisfactory with half-ton trucks. They reduce tire life and gas mileage, and if your truck camper is bogged down in mud or snow it's difficult to extract. It does, however, offer comfortable camping and is excellent for highway trips. Do not attempt to tackle a rough logging trail with one of these rigs because the camper's fragile aluminum skin towering high over the cab is easily dented or torn by overhanging tree limbs. If you're handy, consider buying a damaged one. But before you invest in any camper, new or secondhand, have a good idea of what you want from it—and be sure the kind of recreational vehicle you are buying is the kind you really need. The more chance you get to experience the various camping rigs, the easier will be your decision.

CAMP GEAR AND PROVISIONS

The person who combines camping with hunting trips generally camps to save money, although he still reaps the aesthetic benefits. He wants the least amount of fuss with his camping, since hunting time takes top priority. The methods and means that follow should cut down on that fuss, using practical but generally modestly priced items.

Big campers such as this one are ideal for long hunting trips, but are limited to good roads. *(Photo courtesy General Motors Corporation)*

For cooking and light, it's hard to beat propane. The Coleman Company offers excellent propane stoves and lanterns that will last for years. The fuel lights quickly and cooks efficiently. But avoid using small, disposable bottles of propane since the cost is prohibitive. Purchase an 11-pound or larger refillable tank. Adapters and extension hoses are available.

You can get every cooking utensil you'll need for camping by haunting garage sales. Avoid thin pots and pans; they burn easily. A cast-iron frypan is nothing you'll want to carry on a backpacking trip, but for most camping situations it's hard to beat. An old pressure cooker makes a great pot for conventional cooking. And unless you enjoy washing dishes, paper plates are worth the money.

To save time when you get the urge, a lot of your camping gear can be kept permanently in your camping vehicle. Even if you plan to use a tent, it's a real convenience to have the tent and most of your gear already packed in your car or truck and ready to go—at least during the hunting season.

Unless you enjoy cooking, keep the grocery list confined to easy-to-prepare foods. Hamburger and minute steaks are good. Potatoes, particularly American fries and hash-browns, are a camping staple. You can shorten the cooking time on fries and hash-browns by putting a cover on the frypan. When buying food for a trip, plan on two hot meals per day—breakfast and supper. You can get by with sandwiches and snacks during the day. Don't overlook a vegetable with the evening meal. A head of lettuce is an easy solution. Bring your favorite salad dressing.

For a simple overnight camp, try roasting wieners or Polish sausages over an open fire. Coffee, rolls, and fruit juice will do for breakfast. Sandwiches, apples, and oranges will fortify you during the day. Backcountry stores are not economical places to shop. The more you bring from home or purchase at big discount stores, the more you'll save. This holds true for gas for your vehicle, ammunition for weapons, and just about everything else. Camp near a water supply if possible, especially if you plan a long campout.

PLANNING AN ECONOMICAL TRIP

The pickup toppers we have already discussed at length are one route to inexpensive hunting. Manufacturers continue to bring out new styles and innovations in camping vehicles, tent trailers, trailers, and motor homes.

Some are designed for real economy, particularly if a camping vehicle can substitute for the family car, or you do a lot of traveling. If you're able to avoid motels and do your own cooking, you'll save a bundle.

You can save on long cross-country hunting trips by enlisting a couple of partners to share the expenses. This is especially advisable if you plan to travel in one of the self-propelled RVs, motor homes, vans, or campers. The quickest route to improving gas mileage with these rigs is to improve your driving habits.

Some camping rigs are large enough, and comfortable enough, that you might consider a family vacation/hunting trip. Much has been said about the advantages of a fall vacation, and most of it is true. If you plan to take your children out of school, give their teacher ample notice so advance homework can be assigned. A nonresident hunting license and other extras needed for hunting will raise the cost of your trip, but one trip is cheaper than two. Planning is half the fun, and while your wife plots out routes on the map that will be of interest to her and the rest of the family, you can plan your end of the trip, unless, of course, you all plan to hunt.

Whether you plan a family trip or simply a hunting trip with buddies, it is important to plan well in advance. Some nonresident licenses must be purchased almost a year ahead, some states offer considerably lower non-resident license fees than others, some do not allow nonresident hunting at all. Be sure you are clear on all points.

Florida, for example, offers a nonresident deer license for $26.50 (subject to change), and an extra $10 will open the gates for any hunter to one of the 44 wildlife management areas operated by the Game and Fresh Water Fish Commission for public hunting purposes. There are over 4 million acres of land included in the wildlife management area program. Public hunting areas such as these are a boon to the nonresident hunter. But be sure to write for complete details.

It's hard to imagine crowded California offering much in the way of public land, yet almost half of the state is county, state, BLM (Bureau of Land Management), and national forest land. This is public land and it gets hunted hard, but you can escape the crowds by climbing a little higher or walking a little farther.

Ask about the availability of public lands when writing the department of natural resources in the state you plan to hunt. And ask for any free maps. State tourism agencies are a good source for free maps and literature.

If deer is your quarry, ask for the past deer-kill records. This will pinpoint exactly what area of the state produces the most deer. High deer-kill areas generally mean high hunting pressure too. This *can* be an advantage, because it keeps the deer moving. It can also be something to avoid, particularly for a stranger to the area. In central and southern Wisconsin, for example, deer are thriving. This is agricultural deer range, and the increased demand for a place to hunt sometimes causes hunter-landowner conflicts. The quality of the hunting is far superior in the uncrowded northern forested areas of the state on land open to public hunting.

States such as Wyoming and Montana have large areas of public land and few people. This makes it relatively easy to find areas that contain heavy deer concentrations and few hunters. In many other states, however, there isn't much public land and what there is is surrounded by agricultural, privately owned land. The few public hunting lands teem with hunters, and the savvy deer rapidly disperse to adjacent private lands or wetlands with difficult access.

The best way to get permission to hunt privately owned land is to hunt alone or with not more than one companion. Most landowners quickly reject hunting groups.

Maps are useful in determining good hunting areas because they usually list public land, camping areas, and major access roads. Topographic maps show features such as narrow wooded areas between two open marshes and islands in swamps, both of which may harbor deer seeking refuge from hunters. Timber-type maps can reveal good feeding areas such as oak stands. Remember, however, that many maps are old and features such as trails may have long been abandoned and grown over.

Comprehensive map catalogs are now available that allow hunters, campers, and others to get specific maps or charts they want from one source, at one time, on one order form. The catalog is divided into two volumes, Eastern North America and Western North America. Each sells for $4.95, plus 90 cents for postage. Write to: U.S. Canadian Map Service Bureau, Ltd., Midwest Distribution Center, Box 249, 1066 American Drive, Neenah, Wis. 54956.

Most libraries have copying machines for public use. For one thin dime you can make a copy of any important area on a map. Make enough for every member of your hunting party. This is a must when hunting in wilderness country.

8
SUMMER HUNTING

Summer hunting is cheapest. Gun and ammo are often all the equipment you'll need. Crows, woodchucks, rockchucks, prairie dogs, and jackrabbits all provide interesting and challenging shooting, especially for the varmint-rifle enthusiast. And there are a lot of small fry: gophers, nutria, rock squirrels, Columbian ground squirrels, and even armadillos. Armadillos are good eating, as are young woodchucks and rockchucks. Rats, the kind found in dumps and around farms, are hyperactive and fast-moving, if somewhat loathsome, targets. Most of these small animals make sporting targets for .22 rimfires, pellet guns, blowguns, boomerangs, slings, and slingshots, and they provide excellent practice for the bowman.

Always check local regulations. The jackrabbit, for example, is a protected game animal in Minnesota with regulated hunting seasons, but is unprotected and fair game at any time in South Dakota. You may shoot woodchucks at any time in most of the eastern states and provinces, but Wisconsin allows you to kill them only if they're doing damage. Crow-shooting regulations are in flux nationwide. This is not to say that just because something moves you should kill it. But many of these creatures become pests around farms and ranches, and in the back-yard garden.

One example is the Columbian ground squirrel. An experiment was conducted some years ago to ascertain just how much grain a single ground squirrel might destroy. Two squirrelproof enclosures were built in a wheat field. A single adult Columbian was placed inside one. The harvest from the enclosed area with no squirrel was 40 pounds, plus nine straw bundles of equal size. From the squirrel enclosure only 4 pounds of wheat and one comparable bundle of straw were obtained. Equally staggering figures are available on jackrabbit depredation of wheat, alfalfa, watermelons, fruit trees, even haystacks. Woodchuck and prairie-dog holes are the bane of farmer and rancher.

Crows do serious damage to farm crops and wreak havoc with the eggs and young of song and game birds. Rats are carriers of many diseases and spoil foodstuffs with their droppings and urine. The list goes on and on. Overcrowding of any of these creatures invariably spells trouble. And hunting is a far better control measure than poison, although one often hears complaints that hunters do not kill enough! Poisoning had the prairie dog on the ropes throughout most of its range, but since that practice has largely been stopped the dogs are coming back swiftly and need control. Check with ranchers for trouble spots. Even porcupines can provide shooting opportunities. They are slow-witted creatures and the shooting is not particularly sporting, but porcupines do tremendous damage to desirable trees.

Summer is good for more than just hunting. It's the time to get out and try new handloads on paper targets; to pattern that new shotgun or to see how the old one handles your handloaded shotshells; to develop shooting skills plinking at tin cans and bottles; to scout new hunting spots.

The outdoorsman who is "up a creek" is probably having the time of his life, at least if he's in a canoe. Small creeks can lead to hidden hunting spots even within the shadow of city and town. You may discover pockets of wildlife rarely reached by others. Such knowledge, gained during the summer, will aid the savvy hunter later.

It may not be easy canoeing. A creek may be so narrow that you can barely make it around a bend with a 17-foot canoe. The water may be only inches deep, and you may have to haul your canoe over log jams and beaver dams.

Dry weather during the fall hunting seasons can lower the creek's water level so much that you'll have to give up any thought of a canoe. But if you've already discovered hunting hotspots, now you should be able to reach them on foot.

You may get in some great summer hunting by floating larger rivers and streams. In many areas of the United States and Canada you can expect to see woodchucks along the stream banks, since these are often the only places they can dig permanent dens in heavily farmed country. Crows are invariably found along rivers and streams, favoring them as nesting sites, and ground squirrels are common in the fields and pastures bordering streams. Some hunters in east Texas make quite a sport out of hunting nutria from a skiff at night. The nutria looks somewhat like an outsize muskrat, except that the face is blunt or squared and the long tail is round. These South American animals were first introduced in Louisiana and have now spread their range across the South. Although Louisiana trappers still take them, the market never has found a suitable use for the fur that would make it especially valuable. They are usually taken with .22 rimfires.

Sportsmen can get good crow shooting with scatterguns almost any morning in much of rural North America. You'll only need to rise before daylight and to know the whereabouts of backcountry dumps. Almost all of these dumps attract crows. By scouting early and late in the day, you can learn which get the most attention from crows. The most successful hunters arrive before daylight and quietly make their way to predetermined shooting sites selected on scouting trips. Blinds can be made from pieces of scrap wood or metal. Old car bodies make good blinds. Crows will arrive shortly after daybreak. Then the fun begins. But don't pick up the dead crows! Crows will circle after the initial shooting and the sight of their fallen comrades frequently sends them screaming in for a closer look. Hunters who are handy with a crow call can sometimes lure stragglers in a third time.

Camouflage and darkened faces help in fooling crows. It pays to stagger hunting spots so crows don't quit a dump entirely. Ammo can be almost any load, but field loads of No. 6 and No. 7½ are favorites.

Decoys are always a help in luring in crows. See the illustration for easy-to-make silhouette decoys shaped from coathangers and then wrapped in black electrician's tape.

While it is usually not listed as such, the woodchuck of the Eastern states and Canada is thought of by dedicated woodchuck hunters as a game

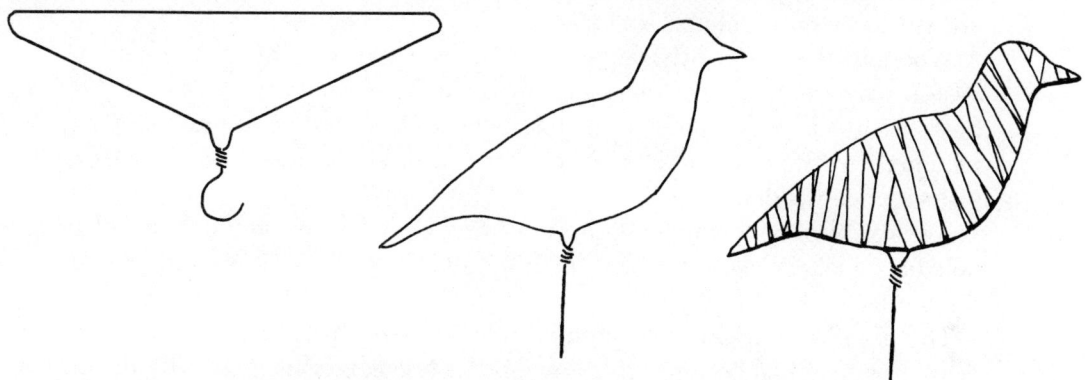

CLOTHES HANGER CROW DECOY

animal. The Eastern woodchuck has greatly increased its range during the past twenty years. The so-called permanent-pasture trend accounts for this. Thousands of acres have been sodded in permanent-pasture mixtures of various clovers and grass, and that's fine with woodchucks, who thrive on the green stuff. During the winter they do a lot of sleeping in underground dens.

Woodchuck hunters delight in telling of 500- to 600-yard shots made on chucks with high-priced custom rifles. The fact is that most woodchucks are killed at ranges under 200 yards, including those bagged with custom rifles. Most factory varmint rifles with scope sights properly zeroed in are capable of more accuracy than the shooter who handles them. With cool, accurate shooting, such rifles can kill chucks out to 300 yards.

Woodchucks can be hunted with .22 rimfire rifles if you use high-speed hollowpoints, but it is not recommended. It takes a shot in the brain to kill a woodchuck cleanly with these light loads. With a 5mm Remington or a .22 Winchester Magnum Rimfire you can have a try at chucks if you limit your range to within 50 yards. The .22 centerfires or larger rifles are best used on these astonishingly tough animals.

93

Chucks are most frequently found in fields of alfalfa and clover. The best times of the day are from about an hour after sunup until midmorning, and then from midafternoon until about a half-hour before sundown. During mild but cloudy days when a very light intermittent rain is falling, chucks are apt to be out at almost any time.

Woodchucks frequently have their dens right out in the fields and pastures where they feed, but more often they seek sheltered spots for their burrows. Rock piles, stone fence lines, woodpiles, and rocky areas of any kind are favorite denning sites. A hunter can often get a shot at a chuck as it sits up near its den.

A sharp blast on a whistle will often bring a curious woodchuck out of its hole for a look, or cause a chuck feeding in high cover to sit up and provide the hunter with a target.

The .243 Winchester is a popular rifle for use on both woodchuck and deer. For chuck shooting only, any of the hot centerfire .22s will do the trick, and the .222 is a favorite.

Hunters in the Western states have an equally intriguing summer target: the rockchuck, which is more properly known as the marmot. There are five

WHISTLE FOR CHUCKS

related varieties, but the yellow-bellied marmot (also called golden marmot) is the most common and ranges throughout the roughest and most mountainous portions of the West. Its usual natural habitat is around rock outcrops, rimrock, and rock slides, all of which must be adjacent to green ground vegetation.

An added attraction of hunting rockchucks, aside from the pleasant fact they're often hunted in scenic spots in company with such exotic big game as bighorn sheep and mountain goats (they thrive in elevations up to 10,000 feet), is that civilization is only a minor hindrance in the Western mountains. The Eastern woodchuck hunter, on the other hand, must always be vitally concerned with what is beyond his target. Dense population has made the hunting of Eastern woodchucks impossible in many sections of the country. About the only other person you're likely to meet while hunting rockchucks in the high mountains is another rockchuck hunter.

The same rifles suitable for Eastern woodchuck hunting are suitable for rockchucks. You can also bang away with heavier calibers such as the .270, .30-06, or 7mm magnum. Binoculars are handy. If you have one, a spotting scope is useful.

Rockchucks tend to live in groups. Find one and you've likely found a concentration of them. Rockchucks grow wary with heavy hunting pressure just as do Eastern woodchucks. They like to loiter in the afternoon sun on rock outcrops, but at the sight of a hunter, an alert rockchuck will give a loud piercing whistle and dive for cover.

Conservation should be practiced in hunting rockchucks or any creature. Whole communities of rockchucks have been wiped out in recent years. There is no justification for such a practice.

There is only one creature whose total extermination would be to the good of all, since they have no known place in the natural balance of nature. That is the Norway or brown rat. Norway rats are pale, grayish-brown in color, and 13 to 18 inches long. A 16-inch rat will normally have a body about 9 inches long and a sparsely furred tail about 7 inches long. They can provide some tricky summer shooting for the summer hunter in secluded dumps where shooting is not prohibited.

It's easy to tell if a dump has a rat population by standing quietly in the back edges of the dump during the last half-hour before dark. If rats are present, they will be seen and heard, scuttling about. They're hyperactive and rarely remain motionless for more than a second or two. It is fun shooting whether you are armed with a .22 rimfire, pellet gun, slingshot, or whatever. Because the light is usually poor during the best shooting time, the shooter with a slingshot will often have the best of it because he can shoot instinctively without having to rely on iron sights or scope crosshairs. Because rats are disease carriers, it's wise not to touch the quarry.

The prairie dog's slim build provides a good target for the rifleman. The targets are often myriad and fleeting. Prairie dogs quickly become wise to shooters and seem to delight in crouching within their cone-shaped doorways, exposing only a portion of the head to keep track of the hunter. Because their mounds are packed and sun-baked to the consistency of concrete, any bullet which hits the mound disintegrates or deflects. Pinpoint accuracy is required to take prairie dogs with any consistency.

An interesting way to cut down on the waste of ammunition and to put a premium on accurate shooting is to introduce competition into prairie-dog shooting. Two or three shooters can use an elimination process based on their performance. The shooters flip a coin for first shot and the winner gets to continue firing as long as he maintains a 100 percent string of kills. When he misses, the shooting goes to the next in order on the same basis.

While a lot of prairie-dog shooting is done on private lands, there are many shooting opportunities on public lands such as the federally owned grasslands near the Black Hills.

Few hunters get the amount of practice they need to hit running game with a rifle. An excellent moving practice target can be made simply and cheaply using a discarded automobile tire. Simply wedge a sheet of cardboard in the doughnut-like center of the tire. The cardboard should be large enough that it fits inside the rim of the tire and won't fall out. The target is then sent rolling down a hill by one person while another stands off to one side and cuts loose at the target with a rifle. Any hits will be recorded by bullet holes in the cardboard. The rougher and steeper the hill, the faster and more difficult the shooting.

9
BACKPACK HUNTING

Economy, escape from heavy hunting pressure, and the spirit of adventure and independence are probably all reasons for the trend toward backpack big-game hunting. More important, however, it allows you to penetrate terrain that would otherwise require the services of a guide and packstring. And good guides and horses don't come cheap. There is wonderful freedom in this kind of hunting. Your plans can be changed at any time because camp is on your back.

If you're hunting elk in Montana or Idaho and come upon a high-country park laced with a fresh elk sign, you can camp at the edge of the timber commanding a view of the park. Camp can simply be a foam pad laid on the ground with your sleeping bag on top. Daylight may show a bull elk standing in the park. If nothing shows, you can spend the day still-hunting. If you cook supper during midafternoon, you can then take another likely stand near fresh elk sign and take an evening stand in your sleeping bag. This can be very effective hunting, because you're on stand before daylight and remain on stand past dark.

The scene can easily be changed to northern Ontario, where you can camp for the night beside a beaver pond being visited by a giant bull moose. Or to the tundra of northern Quebec and along the route of traveling caribou. Or to northern Minnesota for the nerve-tingling experience of camping by a blueberry patch being visited by a hungry black bear. Or it could even be a camp near carrion being fed upon by coyotes. This is a good way to take these sly predators. Always camp downwind and a good distance from the hunting site. The locations and the quarry for this kind of hunting are almost limitless. About the only prerequisite is reasonably mild weather.

Ontario has mid-September moose hunting in the extreme northern portion of the province. Montana has early elk hunting in the primitive area just north of Yellowstone Park. Colorado offers high-country trophy mule-deer hunts in August. October deer hunting and mild weather are synonymous in most of the Western states. Backpackers who hunt with bow and arrow have early openings for a variety of big-game animals in almost every state and province. In some jurisdictions, bear hunters get extra hunting time and mild weather with spring hunting seasons.

Backpack hunting is often mountain hunting, and it's not to be approached lightly. It can be brutal, exhausting, and dangerous. A specialized method of hunting, it requires appropriate equipment and knowledge. Experience at backpacking is the first step. You should also study basic mountain-climbing skills. Technical rockclimbing techniques aren't needed, but the ability to walk surely under heavy load is. It's not uncommon to pack out 100 pounds of game meat in a load. An animal the size of a moose or elk means many such loads.

Every backpacker hunter should carry a first-aid kit and emergency gear. Obviously this, and everything else, must be kept to a minimum because of weight. Because you always have your pack (and therefore your camp) with you, you needn't take emergency rations or implements for shelter. A basic kit should include a first-aid kit, fire starters (a couple of plastic bags of kitchen matches and a candle stub will usually do), a police whistle and mirror for signaling, and, of course, a compass and knife. Some brands of compass also have mirrors, and some knives have a compass built into the handle. Weight-saving economy becomes all-important to the backpacking hunter, but you'll have learned many of the tricks if you've done some backpacking first.

Complete kitchen utensils for a backpacking hunt include a butane stove, pot, cup, spoon, and white-gas stove with windscreen. An overnight hunt can best be done with ready-to-eat food and no cooking gear. If you've

Discarded 35mm film container makes a waterproof match holder. Cut ⅛-inch from match ends for a better fit.

extra money you may want to experiment with freeze-dried and dehydrated foods. These are a good choice where water is plentiful. Some are very tasty but you may be disappointed with others. Most freeze-dried and dehydrated foods carry a high price tag. You can cut costs by buying packaged soups, cocoa, and other lightweight items that are sold as regular grocery fare.

Your clothing must adapt to everything from vigorous movement during warm days to sitting still during chilly mornings and evenings. Wool shirts and trousers are good. The trousers should be of fairly light, tightly woven wool like that in military dress trousers. Because long-underwear bottoms can be a nuisance to take off if the weather gets warm, it's best to forego these and wear a second pair of trousers if the weather turns cold. Multiple layers of clothing prepare you for a wide range of conditions. A lightweight windbreaker, gaiters for snow, and wool gloves may be useful.

Footwear is all-important. You *can* get by with regular hunting boots with Vibram soles, such as those manufactured by Herman, Browning, Redwing, and others, but your feet won't be as well protected should they come down hard on sharp rocks while you're carrying an extra-heavy load. Nor will the uppers likely give enough support should you twist your ankle with that load. Remember that we're talking here of mountainous, rocky terrain.

A medium-weight European-style climbing boot is acceptable for mountain backpack hunting. Although often overly stiff, they are readily available, and usually of good quality. The sole should be between ¼ and 7/16 inch thick, and the soles stitched and screwed or nailed on. Many hunters have found the Danner boot ideal. You can make overly stiff boots more comfortable by adding closed-cell foam insoles. Be prepared to pay a lot for quality boots; there's no escaping it. Also be sure to break them in before attempting a backpacking hunt.

Sleeping bags ran be had with down or Dacron 88 or Fiberfill. Down packs into less space and is a little lighter. Mummy-style is warmest if you don't suffer from claustrophobia. As for filling, 2½ pounds of down or the equivalent amount of synthetic is about right. You will need a foam pad that should reach mid-thigh. Your pad should be of closed-cell foam or it will soak up moisture.

You must have a poncho, not only as rain garb, but for a ground cloth and/or rain shelter. The light tarp mentioned in Chapter 7 can provide adequate shelter for the lone backpack hunter. A tent is usually too heavy and bulky for a lone hunter to carry, but for two or three men hunting together, an alpine tent is worthwhile. Uncoated nylon tents with coated rain flies will keep you dry. Segmented tent poles held together by elastic cord are handy. They assemble themselves when you pull them out of the bag. You want a well-designed tent that can be quickly erected.

Choice of rifle for backpack hunting is a personal thing, but avoid heavy magnums. You want a rifle that you are familiar with and that's not too heavy. Fixed-power scopes are lighter than variable scopes. To save weight, a rifle barrel over 22 inches can be cut back and recrowned. The butt stock can be drilled and wood routed from the barrel channel. Iron sights can be removed. You can do this yourself or hire a competent gunsmith.

Once you have a big-game animal down, the work begins. A 4-inch sheath knife and a foldup-style bone saw are all you'll need. Some hunters simply carry a hacksaw blade for deer-size animals. You may want to carry the whole hacksaw for animals the size of moose and elk. Small hoists are available, but about the only time they come in handy is to hang a carcass at base camp or at home.

To reduce weight, the meat should be boned out. Boning is similar to skinning except you are separating muscle groups from bone instead of skin from meat. It's relatively easy to do an acceptable job. A hacked-up hide isn't worth much, but hacked-up meat is just as edible.

Put the meat in heavy, reusable polyethylene bags, and if your pack has a single large top compartment, stow it there. Meat carried in your pack compartment is a less awkward load, since no lashing is needed.

Plans for homemade backpacks are available but are not recommended for heavy loads. A strong pack frame is needed then, too, and should be of welded aluminum or magnesium. Screwed or clamped frame construction is fine for normal backpacking but is not satisfactory for really heavy loads. The best pack bag is nylon duck and should be attached by grommets and pins. The pack must have a padded hip band. It should be adjusted to ride above your hip bones and below your waist.

You must be in good physical condition if you're going to try backpack hunting. Some men can carry 150 pounds. But don't attempt a load that's too much for *you*. This is not a practice to be taken lightly. You have to be dedicated and possibly a little crazy. Read *Aerobics* or *New Aerobics* by Kenneth Cooper. Using this, *and your doctor's advice*, work up to a 30-point week. That is your year-round minimum. From there you work up to hunting condition.

When you are in good shape, at 30 to 50 points, see your doctor again. Be sure to tell him what you plan. Then start additional running and hiking, not avoiding hills or rough spots but tackling them head on. And start backpacking. Once your legs can handle 50 pounds without tiring, experiment with heavier loads to see how they feel. If you can't handle this weight, backpack hunting isn't for you. But if you can, and want to enjoy good hunting without a guide and packstring, this is the way to do it.

If you can get a copy, read Clarence Ellis' double-length magazine article, *Hunting via Backpack*, which appeared in the July 1976 issue of *The American Hunter*. The magazine is published by the National Rifle Association of America. Write: *The American Hunter*, 1600 Rhode Island Ave. N.W., Washington, D.C.

10
HUNTING AND TRAPPING

The hunter who can combine trapping with weekend or extended hunting trips is fortunate. One or two mink, raccoon, fox, or coyote pelts can help defray the cost of a week in deer camp or a weekend stint of chasing after pheasant. At today's high fur prices, the hunter/trapper may even come out ahead. Some sample fur prices paid by a fur buyer in one northern Minnesota community during the 1976-77 season: muskrat $4.50, mink $30, raccoon $30, fox $60, coyote $60. These are modest figures. Trappers who sell their goods directly to auctions get more. The same fur buyer was paying up to $125 for bobcat. Trappers selling direct to a West Coast auction received over $300 per bobcat skin during one sale. Contact your local trapper's association for information on selling direct to auctions.

Some preparations are necessary to make this approach to trapping work. It does little good to stumble onto a surefire set location for coyote while, for example, you're hunting sharptail grouse if you left at home your bottle of coyote scent or the small spade needed for making the "dirt-hole" set. (This set and others will be explained in detail later in this chapter.) Well before the hunting and trapping seasons, build a box in which to store all your trapping gear. Then make it a permanent fixture in car trunk or truck box. A good way to keep gas and oil odors from permeating your gear is to keep the box outside your vehicle, as on a cartop carrier.

The trapping you squeeze in on hunting trips will not require many traps, but you never know the kind of furbearer you are going to encounter. Store traps of several sizes in the box.

Trappers like to dye their traps first with a solution of wood bark. This is a job best done outside. A fireplace can be improvised by placing rocks in a U-shape and putting several iron bars across the rocks to support the tub used for boiling the traps.

The first step in treating traps is to boil them in water. This will remove oil from new traps and excessive rust from older ones. After the traps have boiled for an hour, pour off the oil, dirt, and old trap wax that have risen to the surface. If the traps are new, remove them from the tub and leave them out in the weather for a couple of weeks to rust. It's important that traps have a coating of rust, because smooth shiny steel will not take on a good color. To ensure that the inside of the trap jaws get a coating of color, put a nail or chain link between the jaws. If the traps are already rusty, bring clean water to a boil and add bark from hardwoods such as soft maple, white oak, or green butternut, or sumac bulbs, or walnut hulls, or other material or trees common to the area. Evergreen bark should not be used, however, since it produces an overly concentrated odor.

A short cut is to use 1 pound of commercial wood dye to each 5 gallons of water. Wood dye is available at trapper's supply houses and sporting-goods stores. It is not expensive.

If time permits, allow the traps to sit for several days in the water and wood-dye or bark solution. This will give the tannic acid in the dye or bark time to etch itself into the metal and will give a more lasting color. This treatment frees traps of the odors of steel and rust and imparts a natural woodsy smell. It also makes them easier to conceal.

In the same box used for storing traps, keep such accessories as a small spade, hand trowel, rubber gloves, dirt sifter (a 10-inch framework of wood with ¼-inch-mesh screen across the bottom), stakes, lashing wire, and hatchet. Build a separate compartment for bait and lure bottles.

Recommended traps for muskrat are the No. 1 or 1½ Victor or Blake & Lamb stoploss trap, as well as the No. 110 Victor Conibear and No. 1 Blake & Lamb sure-grip traps. The muskrat, more than any other furbearer, is capable of escaping from the steel trap. The stop-loss trap prevents the

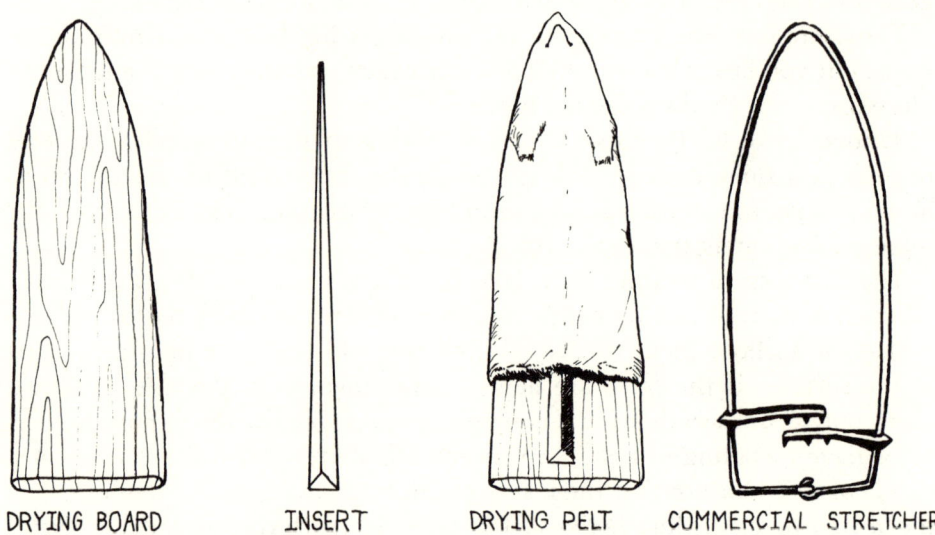

DRYING BOARD   INSERT   DRYING PELT   COMMERCIAL STRETCHER

muskrat from twisting free. The sure-grip, or body-grip, trap is designed to catch the animal around the neck or chest, killing it instantly. It doesn't always happen exactly that way, but they rarely escape from this trap.

For mink and raccoon trapping the No. 1½ Victor coilspring is good. The No. 1½ longspring or underspring (jump) trap will do the job, too. The No. 1½ trap will hold a number of furbearers including marten, skunk, oppossum, and weasel.

Fox trappers invariably choose the Victor or Blake & Lamb No. 2 coilspring. These traps are easy to conceal and work well with the popular "dirt-hole" set.

The No. 3 Oneida and Blake & Lamb in either underspring (jump) or double longspring are recommended for coyote and bobcat.

For beaver, use the Oneida and Blake & Lamb No. 4 in underspring or double longspring. An excellent choice, where it can be used, is the Victor Conibear No. 330 body-grip trap. This is a killer-type trap that is very powerful and must be handled with care.

You can make your own wooden fur stretchers. You can get the idea of how wooden fur stretchers should be shaped by examining commercial steel

104

stretchers, or go to the nearest fur buyer and ask to borrow some of his wooden fur stretchers to use as models. It pays to become acquainted with the fur buyer. He will answer your questions on the preparation and handling of animal furs. It is to his advantage that you bring in well-handled furs.

If you are not experienced in skinning, fleshing, and drying pelts, don't let this deter you. For buyers will buy animals that have not been skinned, generally deducting a small amount from the pelt value. Skinning, fleshing, and drying of pelts are skills you will want to acquire. They all add to the overall enjoyment of trapping.

MAKING A DIRT-HOLE SET

The dirt-hole set is useful for the hunter/trapper because it will take a variety of furbearers including fox, coyote, bobcat, raccoon, skunk, opossum, even mink. The basis of the dirt-hole set is the habit of foxes and other wild canines of digging holes to bury food they want to eat later. The trapper attempts to imitate such a food cache. The set is even more effective because animals delight in robbing food caches. The dirt-hole set should be made out in the open, away from high grass, trees, large rocks, and stumps. This is because an animal, in approaching what it thinks is the food cache of another, does not want to be ambushed.

When making this set for fox, wear clean rubber gloves and rubber footwear. With a small shovel or gardener's hand trowel, cut a triangular clump of sod about one foot from corner to corner. The corner where the hole is to be dug should be against a low rock or other backing the fox can see over. Shake some of the excess dirt from the sod into the excavated area. Toss the sod as far as you can into nearby high grass or carry it away with you after completing the set. Next dig a hole with your trowel about 3 inches in diameter and 6 inches deep, and at a 45-degree angle under the backing. Scatter this dirt as far as you can throw it. Now dig a trap bed directly in front of the hole so one jaw of the trap is 1 inch from the edge of the hole. Put this dirt in your sifter. The trap bed should be deep enough so the trap will sit slightly below the level of the surrounding dirt.

Before setting the trap, drive a stake into the trap bed. The trap chain is wired to the trap stake by the fourth link from the trap. Pound the stake completely into the ground and slightly below the level of the trap bed.

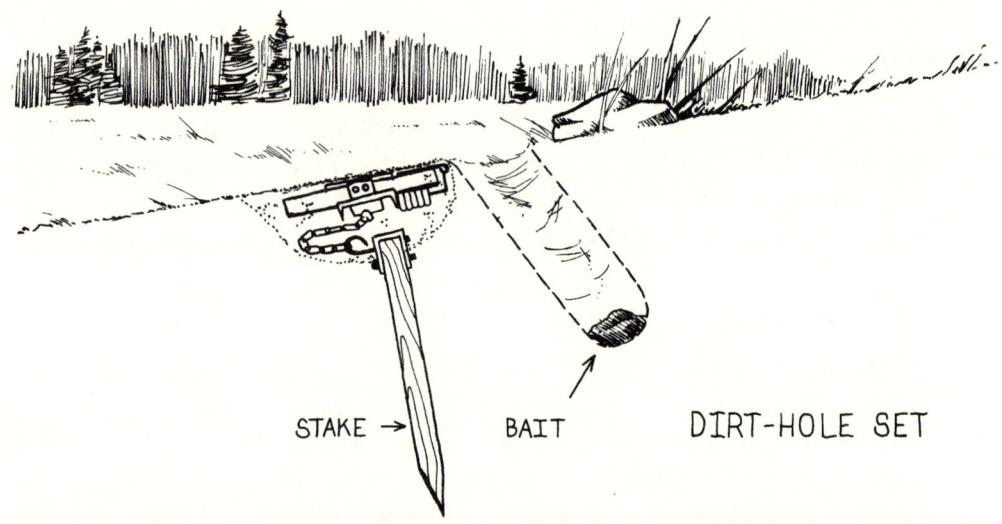

STAKE →   BAIT   DIRT-HOLE SET

Now take a 4½ × 7-inch sheet of wax paper, tear a slit for the trap dog, and then place it over the trap pan with the ends under the trap jaws. See the illustration. Set the trap firmly in the trap bed with the trap dog, or trigger mechanism, toward the hole. Now take your dirt sifter and sift the dirt in it over the trap to a depth of about ¼ inch.

A stiff piece of wire works well for spearing bait from the bait jar. Drop the bait into the hole, being careful to not spill juice on the buried trap. This could cause the fox to dig where the trap is, and this usually results in a sprung trap rather than a trapped fox. Pour a few drops of good gland lure on the edge of the hole, letting it run down inside. Spray the spot where you have crouched, and the trap bed, with red-fox urine.

MAKING BLIND SETS

Blind sets are popular for taking minks, muskrats, and raccoons. This is simply setting traps where you believe the animals will step. Minks have the habit of investigating every narrow passageway, hole, brushpile, or space under overhanging tree roots along creek, river, or lake shore. A trap placed in a narrow passageway and under 2 inches of water will catch mink. If a passageway is too wide, narrow it with weathered sticks or rocks. Wedge them into the creek bottom to narrow a passageway and force the mink to step into the trap. Muskrats and raccoons will tumble to the same set.

There are many possible blind sets for muskrats. Look for their droppings (similar to rabbit droppings) on rocks and logs. Muskrats will climb onto these to enjoy a snack at leisure. A trap set where the muskrat crawls out of the water is sure to connect.

Many blind sets will take raccoons. Traps can be set where the animals enter and leave the water. Tracks, trails, and droppings are easy to find along waterways. Raccoons also spend a lot of time on land. A tempting bait is fish. Try the dirt-hole set for raccoons, using fish for bait.

MAKING SNARE SETS

During winter hunts in snow, you can make very productive fur catches using steel snares. The self-locking steel snare is ideally suited for catching foxes, coyotes, bobcats, and lynxes when the snow lies deep. One of the best things about using snares is their lightness. They weigh only ounces and you can carry a half-dozen in the pocket of your hunting coat.

Before you even consider using snares, check the local regulations and

BLIND SET

SNARE SET

then get in-depth information from the local conservation officer. Restrictions on the use of steel snares will vary with the state or province. Generally, snaring is legal only in areas of very wild terrain where there is little chance of catching dogs. At that you may be advised of restrictions as to snare length and size of the snare noose. Snaring in deer trails is usually illegal.

Snaring is most effective when soft, deep snow induces foxes, coyotes, and wild cats to stick to established trails. A trail may appear as a single track because each time the animal returns it places its feet in the same tracks. Even the winding, helter-skelter tracks made by a fox hunting rabbits in a thicket of willows will be followed step by step by the fox when it returns.

In making a snare set for foxes, lean a sapling 3 to 4 inches in diameter across and a foot or so above the trail—unless you have found a natural opening where the trail passes under a limb or vine. Hang the noose directly below the sapling. Wire the other end of the snare to a tree or the sapling. The sapling across the trail forces the fox to lower its head and guides it into the snare. The noose for fox snaring should be about 8 inches in diameter. The bottom of the noose should be about 5 inches above the trail. When snares are set in rabbit trails, often the case when foxes are hunting rabbits, the rabbit can run under the noose but the longer-legged fox gets caught.

You can use weed stalks or small twigs thrust into the snow to help hold the snare in place. This helps to break up the outline of the snare. Snares need not be treated in any way as long as they are kept free of foreign odors and gloves are worn when making sets. Very shiny snares, however, should either be darkened or whitewashed.

MAKING DEADFALLS

The common deadfall with a figure-four trigger arrangement as shown in the illustration seems awfully primitive by today's standards. Yet it is not unusual for professional trappers to use this old method occasionally for capturing a particularly trap-wise furbearer. Its advantage is its freedom from the odor of steel. One trapper told of a trap-wise wolverine that cost him an estimated $1,000 in furbearers stolen from his traps. He finally killed the wolverine in a deadfall set.

By studying the illustration you can see how the trigger sticks are notched and assembled. There are many variations.

DEADFALL SET

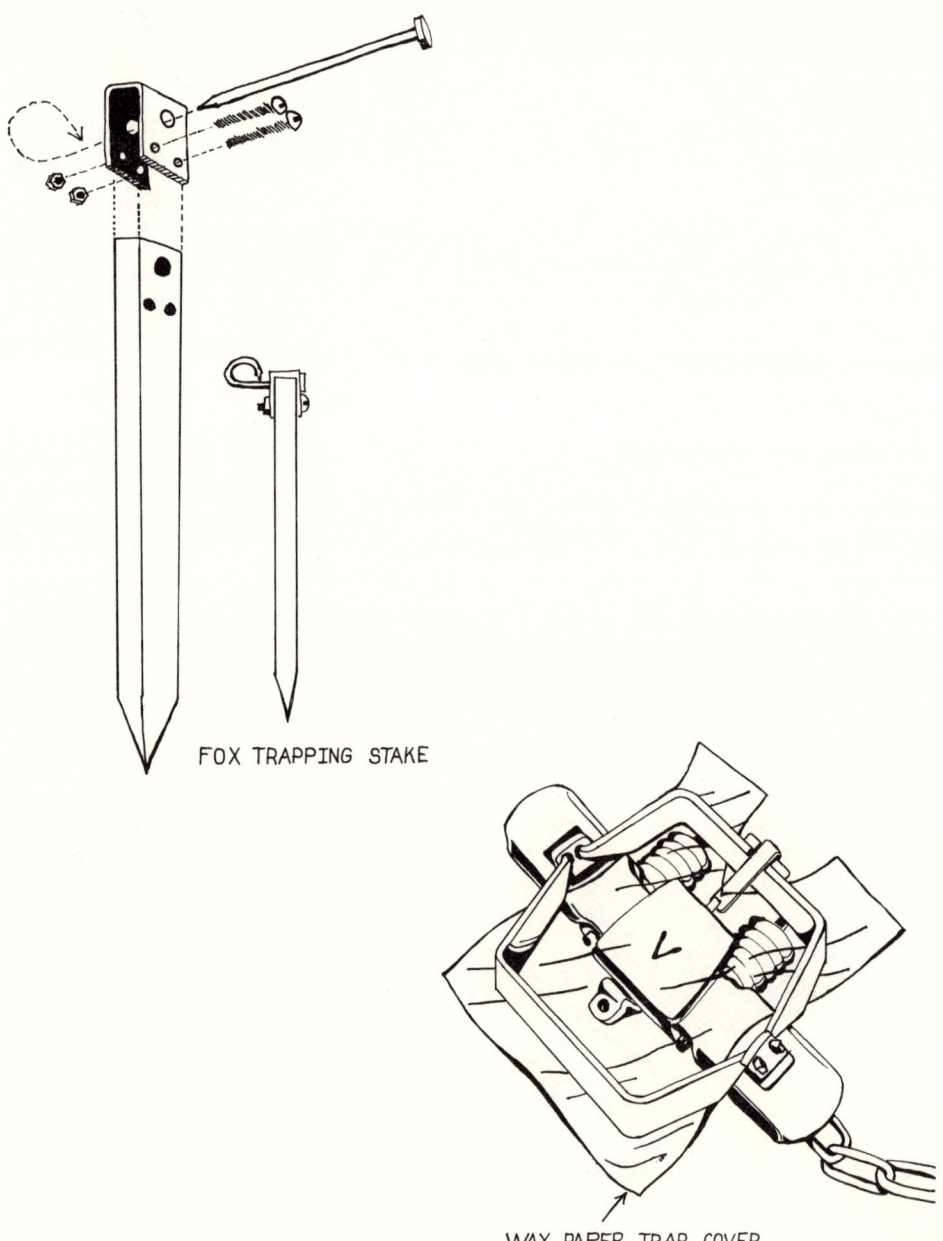

FOX TRAPPING STAKE

WAX PAPER TRAP COVER

MAKING TRAPPING STAKES

An excellent stake for fox trapping is made from old hardwood flooring, usually about 12 inches long for clay soil, longer for sand. A piece of sheet metal is fitted over the top of the stake and held in place with two nuts and bolts to prevent splitting when pounding on the stake. As the final touch, drive a nail through the stake and sheet metal and then form a loop in the pointed end of the nail. The trap chain can then be wired to this loop.

WAX-PAPER TRAP COVER

Wax paper is popular for covering traps before further concealing the traps with dirt, leaves, or whatever is the natural material at the set locations. The wax paper prevents dirt or other covering getting under the trap pan and preventing the trap from operating. Wax paper has the added advantage that it is not affected by dampness and freezing temperatures. Such conditions could render a trap inoperable.

11
WATERFOWL

Jump-shooting and pass-shooting are two low-cost methods of hunting ducks. Jump-shooting is a technique for marsh-feeding ducks, such as mallards, black ducks, gadwalls, shovelers, and teal. The only accessories needed are hip boots. These are preferable to waders because they are lighter and more comfortable for walking. Because jump-shooting usually involves fairly close-range shooting, the hunter can get by with a 12-gauge upland gun such as a double-barrel bored improved cylinder and modified. The modified choice setting is a good choice for a single-barrel or pump with a variable-choke device. Magnum loads are not required. Express or high-base loads in No. 6 shot will furnish enough zap for most of your shots.

Jump-shooting involves sneaking close to a farm pond, lakeshore, creek, marsh, or water-filled ditch where there are ducks and flaring or "jumping" them so they fly, and then shooting them on the wing.

Anyone can enjoy this kind of hunting. Membership in an exclusive club is not required. There are nearly 750,000 farm ponds across America. Access is simply a matter of obtaining landowner permission. This is usually not difficult for one or two shooters, the right number for this kind of hunting.

The best approach to a farm pond or other low-lying water is by the lowest available ground. Start the approach from a crouch and then get down and crawl in the final stage of the stalk. To crawl, get in a prone position and lay your gun across the crook in your elbows. Then, keeping your head and buttocks down, move forward by advancing the right elbow and right knee, then the left elbow and left knee. If you reach water and are still not within range of your targets, keep as low as possible and wade into the water. There's usually enough high vegetation along the water's edge to conceal you.

Sometimes you can see ducks landing in a pond or swimming. Other times you'll just have to assume that ducks are present and make your stalk on speculation. Newcomers to the method often lose patience under these conditions and stand erect too soon, thinking that no ducks are around. Then a flock of fat mallards flushes out of range from a far corner of the pond. The hunter soon learns to keep low until every possibility has been checked out.

When walking a creek or ditch it's best to walk against any flow of water. The majority of birds will be facing upstream, into the current, and this will give you a slight edge. You can also walk shallow marshy areas with high vegetation. In this case, walk slightly stooped over and watch for openings in the vegetation; they can signal pools of open water. Crouch even lower when approaching these possible hotspots.

Marshes that are too deep to wade can be hunted by canoe. One man handles the paddle while the other sits in the bow with shotgun at the ready and watches for flushing ducks. This also works on small rivers and streams. Some camouflage over the canoe's bow will help. You can make simple camouflage by poking tree limbs butt first under the front seat of the canoe with the smaller branches and leaves extending over the bow. Burlap bags draped over the sides will help to subdue the shininess of an aluminum canoe. The more winding the waterway the easier it will be to get within shooting range of ducks. Watch for puddles of backwater off to the side of the main stream. These are often hotspots. These backwaters are usually hunted best by leaving your craft and stalking.

When birds are flushed they may not know where you are and may swing by you, offering a pass shot. Whenever birds are in the air, try to get into some sort of cover.

Pass-shooting is equally low-priced. Equipment for pass-shooting includes camouflage clothes, some sort of blind, and a hard-hitting gun. Full-choke barrels and magnum loads in No. 4 shot are the usual choice. Blinds for pass-shooting are usually portable, because passes shift locations as new migrants arrive, and because constant and concentrated shooting along one pass will make birds wary and they will shift routes.

A good share of your time should be spent watching the flight route of ducks. A pair of binoculars is useful. The borders of preserves and refuges are always good spots to watch. Ducks, and sometimes geese, will rest in these sanctuaries by day and move out from them morning and evening to feed. Once you locate the routes they're using, you're on your way to good shooting. Generally the hunter locates himself near where the birds first leave their resting site and are still within gun range. Sometimes a knoll affords this kind of shooting, or a point extending into the lake or marsh. Often these "passes" are on dry land and the hunter can wear comfortable insulated field boots.

These routes do change, and a pass that's hot one day may not necessarily be so the next.

Always take care in setting up a blind. Waterfowl suspect anything new. Keep your blind no higher than the surrounding vegetation. If you have to set up in the middle of a stubble field, you're better off digging a slit trench or lying flat under a trap. You can often take advantage of some natural cover.

For many, hunting over decoys is what waterfowl hunting is all about. It needn't be terribly expensive for those hunters who have access to public hunting grounds or private property. You'll want to use a boat, motor, push-pole, decoys, and a portable blind. If you own a johnboat, you can convert it each fall into a remarkably efficient duck boat.

DUCK BOATS

You can transform a johnboat into a duck boat by adding plywood decking fore, aft, and along gunwales. To make an area in the center of the boat for lying down, remove the center seat and install a sheet of plywood on the bottom of the boat. For comfort, cover this plywood with outdoor carpeting or use a closed-cell foam pad. A keel added to the bottom will make sculling easier. To increase flotation, add foam fore and aft. By thinking ahead, this modification can be done in such a way that the boat is easily converted back to a fishing craft for the summer months.

MODIFIED JOHNBOAT

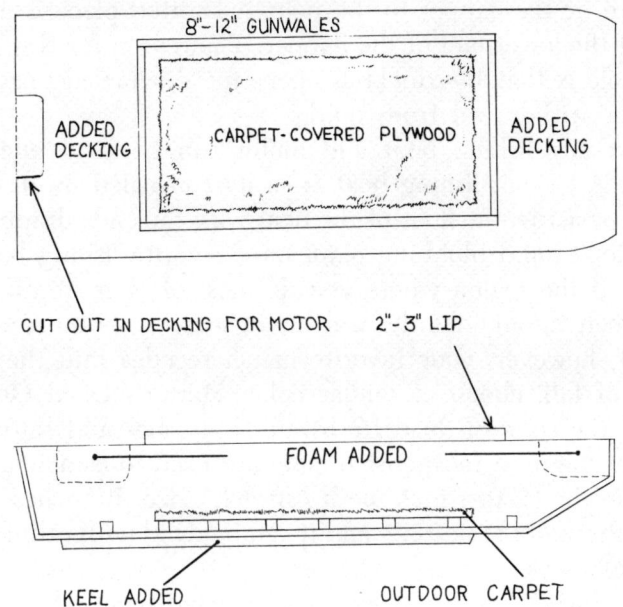

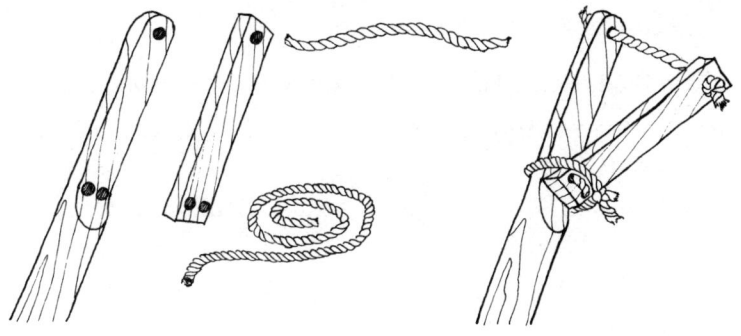

PUSHPOLE

You can make your own pushpole by cutting a long, straight pole and carving flat the last 10 inches or so of the small end. Drill three ½-inch holes through the flat surface to match three holes in a flapper made from scrap ¾-inch lumber. This is shown clearly in the illustration. Clothesline rope is used to tie the flapper to the pole. A knotted piece is used to check the swing of the lower end of the flapper. The reason for this kind of design in a pushpole is that the duckbill opens for shoving against the bottom and closes for withdrawal from mud.

Almost any fishing boat and motor can be used effectively for duck hunting. A 14-foot fishing boat is easily concealed by draping one or two large tarps across the floor of the boat with the ends draping over the sides. If you don't mind blobbing paint on a favorite fishing boat, by all means paint it. If the region where you do most of your hunting remains essentially green throughout the waterfowl season, lay on a coat of olive-drab paint. If, however, your favorite marsh recedes into the golds, tans, and browns of fall, choose a similar color. Herter's Dead Grass paint closely matches the color of dead freshwater bulrushes and saltwater marsh hay.

One of the most inexpensive materials used to camouflage a boat is fish-netting in the ½-to-1-inch mesh (stretch) size. Branches and grass can be pushed through the netting, and it can be dyed with ordinary garment dyes available in supermarkets.

If your boat is made of wood, an easy way to conceal it is by stapling grass to it with a staple gun. This ploy is used by famous waterfowler Norman Strung. Simply take a hank of grass and twist it twice. Set a staple at the top of the twist and another at the bottom.

PLANS AND KITS FOR DUCK BOATS

Plans will cost $5-$10, kits $60 and up.

Baldwin Boat, Hoxie Hill Road, Orrington, Maine 04474. Kits.

Clark Craft, 16-0 Aqua Lane, Tonawanda, N.Y. 14150. Plans and Kits. Catalog, $1.

Glen-L Marine Designs, 9152 Rosecrans, Bellflower, Calif. 90706. Plans and kits. Catalog. $1.

Glenwood Marine Equipment, 1627 West El Segundo Boulevard, Gardens, Calif. 90249. Kits.

PORTABLE BLIND

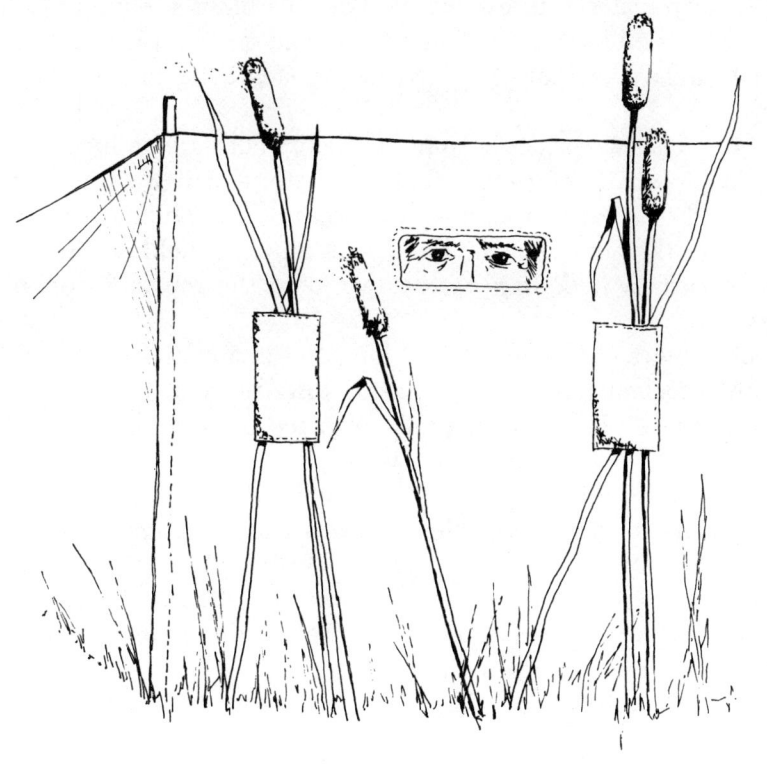

117

Mystic Seaport Historical Association (Attn: Curatorial Dept.), Mystic, Conn. 06355. Plans only, including such old-timers as a 15-foot scull boat, 12-foot Barnegat Bay sneakbox, 12-foot Connecticut River duck boat, and 10-foot brant duck boat.

Riverside Canoes, Box 5595, Riverside, Calif. 92507. Kits.

Sportscraft, Box 636-0, Allentown, N.J. 08501. Plans and kits.

Trailcraft, 2020 N.E. Place, Concordia, Kans. 66901. Kits.

MAKING A PORTABLE BLIND

The portable blind shown in the illustration is designed primarily for shore use but can be utilized even in wet marshy areas. Anchor it to long extension poles set in the water.

Good cheap material to use for the portable blind is burlap. Camouflage it with blobs of oil-base stain. Three stains that go well together are walnut, beechnut, and yellow oak. Blob streaks of each color in a confused linear pattern.

The blind has two pieces, a front and back; both are 40 inches in height. The front piece is a total of 12 feet in length, and it is supported by five 5-foot lengths of ½-inch thin-wall conduit. The conduit legs extend 20 inches below the bottom of the blind. The burlap is held on the conduit by a sewn-in curtain fold. It is further wired to the top and bottom of the conduit.

The back piece of burlap is 8 feet long and is supported by three lengths of conduit attached in the same manner as those in front.

The two-piece blind is held firmly in place by driving the conduit legs into the ground.

You'll find it useful to sew two slots about 1½ inches wide and 6 inches long in the front blind. This allows you to watch incoming birds without exposing yourself.

It also pays to sew on burlap tabs. All manner of natural material such as cattails or marsh grass can be inserted through these tabs and will help to break up the outline of the blind.

Because it is lightweight, the blind can be rolled up and easily carried.

HOMEMADE DECOYS

It's not hard to make your own decoys. Discarded telephone poles are free for the asking in many areas, and the wood makes ideal decoy bodies. Medium-size poles are best because there's less wood to remove. Cut the pole into 15-inch lengths. That's about the size of an average drake mallard. Split the wood lengthwise. A little shaping using a half-round wood rasp turns each half-block into one decoy body. Taper slightly to the front, round off the block front and rear, and you have a very suitable decoy shape. See the illustration. Do not remove the cuts made by the rasp; they simulate feathers and enhance the decoy's appearance.

You can purchase heads and eyes at sporting-goods stores or you can make your own from 2×6-inch blocks of wood as shown. Drill a hole ¼ inch deep for the neck to fit into the body of the decoy. Using the wood rasp, blend the bottom of the neck contour to merge with the body. Set the heads on the bodies at different angles for more realism.

Because telephone poles are treated against post powder beetles, the surface is not very absorbent. That should eliminate the need for more than one heavy coat of paint.

119

PHONE POLE DECOY

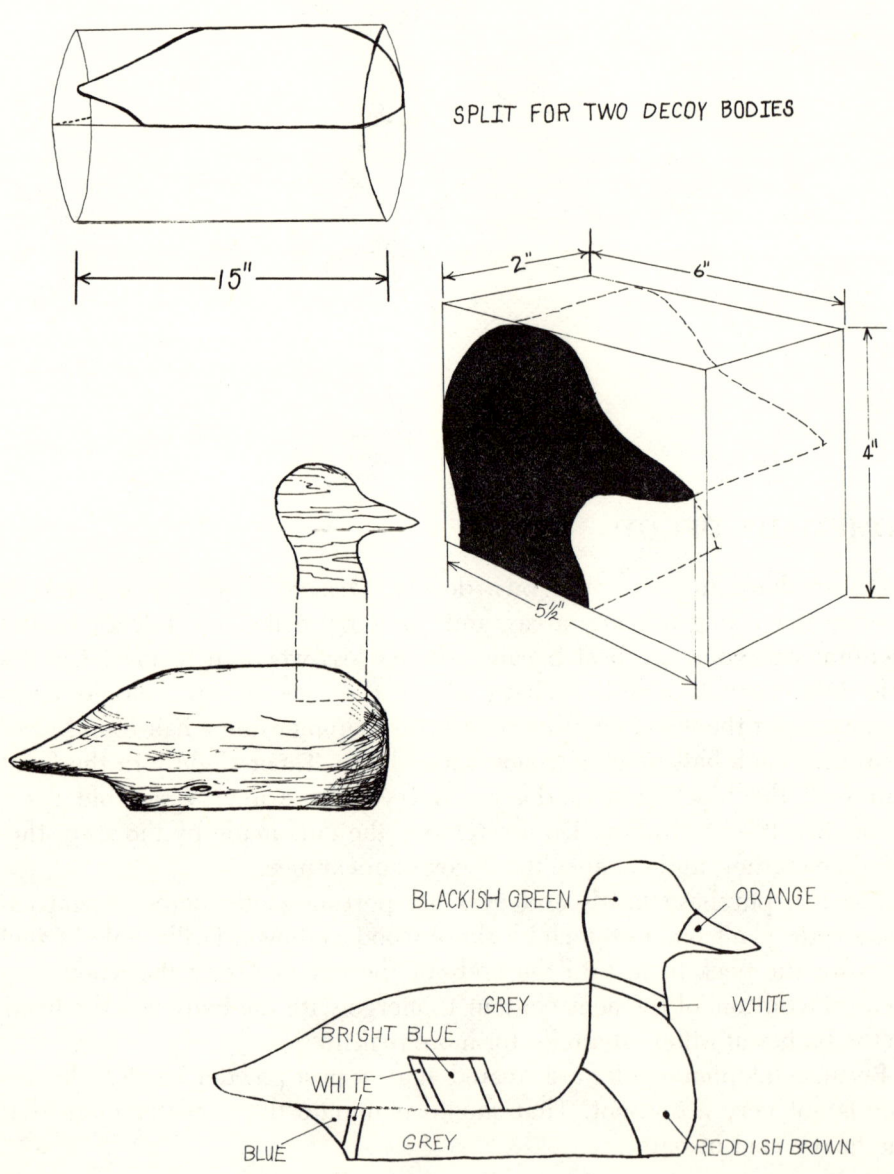

SPLIT FOR TWO DECOY BODIES

15"

2"   6"   4"

5½"

BLACKISH GREEN   ORANGE

GREY   WHITE

BRIGHT BLUE

WHITE

BLUE   GREY   REDDISH BROWN

Paint all decoys over the entire body and head with gray paint. After the paint has dried, paint on the colors shown in the illustration. Use flat paint to prevent glare.

Insert a screw eye in the bottom of the decoy near the front of the body; that's where you'll tie the decoy weight. The flat bottom makes these decoys ride upright even in rough water.

SETTING OUT DECOYS

Waterfowl are inclined to decoy more readily to their own kind. The divers prefer generous space for landing, while the puddle ducks are content to sit down in a tight space among the decoys. The savvy hunter will anticipate the driver's needs and leave an open space in the decoys within easy gun range of his blind. During pleasant weather, decoys should be spread out. Bunch them up in bad weather. A lot of decoys are needed to lure in bluebills, redheads, and canvasbacks; 100 decoys make a nice spread. Marsh-feeding birds such as mallards and teal can be lured in with anywhere from a pair to a dozen decoys.

However, sometimes a larger spread is in order. If, for example, you know another hunter is rigged in an adjoining creek with eight or 10 decoys, it is worthwhile to use a larger setting so as to attract attention a little farther away and thus get the birds coming toward your decoys first.

Sizable decoy spreads are particularly effective during a blow. In bad storms ducks gather in large bunches for shelter.

A useful ploy is to have several oversize decoys just outside the main setting. Incoming birds see these fine specimens first and are encouraged to join the flock. Geese are commonly used as "confidence" decoys. Because they're wise birds, they clearly indicate that all is okay. These oversize decoys have another function. They are easily seen and can be used to mark distance from your blind or boat, providing an accurate gauge of range.

Experts agree that you will get more birds to decoy if the wind is blowing across the blind, slightly quartering your back.

Divers in particular will come in more readily to a crossing wind. A wind blowing parallel to land gives the impression of plenty of water ahead of the spread, as ducks always fly into the wind to land. A rig that draws birds directly to shore is likely to be associated with danger. Waterfowl coming directly in are also more likely to spot you and may flare out of range as you rise to shoot.

OTHER WILDFOWLING TIPS

More than anything else, ducks notice movement. When you're hunting from a blind over decoys, stay hidden to avoid scaring ducks or geese before they are in range. The most common mistake is to stand around in full view until a flight of ducks is spotted. When you dive for the blind it may be too late. When ducks see movement they rarely come any closer.

In the North, during the late hunting season, a makeshift blind can be made by piling ice cakes on the shore high enough to conceal you. A blind can be made of stone the same way. Because ducks notice movement, you may be better off positioning yourself in front of the rocks rather than behind them where it will be necessary to poke your head up and down while watching for incoming ducks. When there's snow, you can put up a white sheet as a blind. You can also drape yourself in a white sheet. Cut a hole for your head and slits for your arms.

Use a forked twig to remove the gut from waterfowl without opening the stomach cavity.

The bad taste often attributed to ducks and geese often stems from poor handling in the field. The duck hunter has a problem. If he opens the stomach cavity of the ducks he bags, it makes the later task of waxing and removing pinfeathers difficult. He has to avoid getting wax into the open stomach cavity.

Fortunately, it is possible to remove a duck's entrails without cutting into the bird, making the waxing job easier and preventing dust and foreign matter from entering the stomach cavity. It is not possible to remove all of the stomach and organs of a duck without opening the stomach cavity, but you can remove the portion that is the first to spoil. This is the intestinal tract, the gut.

Simply cut a thinner-than-pencil-thin forked stick. The fork should be cut to ¼ inch in length and angle back from the end of the stick, like a fish hook. Insert this forked stick into the duck's anal passage, give a slight twist, and draw the stick out slowly. The gut will follow. Once you have it started it can be pulled out by hand .

When you clean ducks and geese, *save the down*! It can be used in making a sleeping bag, vest, jacket, or any number of cold-weather clothes and accessories.

12
UPLAND GAME BIRDS

PHEASANT

A mature cock pheasant will average 2¾ pounds and have a 30-inch wingspan and 35-inch length, including the long tail feathers. The bright, gaudy good looks, succulent eating qualities, inherent cunning, and availability of the ringneck pheasant make it a favorite with hunters. There are open seasons on pheasant in 36 states and four Canadian provinces. Those hunters who live within the pheasant's range can, at times, find these birds living within the shadow of city skyscraper and in suburban vacant lots. This ability to survive in spite of civilization makes the pheasant a good bet for economical close-to-home hunting.

The 12-gauge in pump or automatic is a favorite choice of shotgun for pheasant. A modified choke setting is satisfactory for all-round use. Loads in high-base No. 5 and No. 6 shot are about right for pheasant. As you get into the late season and the birds are flushing wild, a full choke is better.

The pheasant's normal feeding schedule is a couple of hours after sunrise and another couple of hours beginning in midafternoon. Generally this feeding schedule is upset early in the season by considerable hunting pressure, and the early-morning feeding may last into the early afternoon. This works to the advantage of large groups who have permission to hunt fields of corn and soybeans.

When hunting a cornfield, members of the hunting party should space themselves from one corner to a point half the width of the field, if it is a large one, and then walk the full length of the field. Then they return by walking the other half of the field. Driving works best when hunters follow the furrows. If you make a drive across a field the birds are likely to run to the left or right, but if you follow the furrows the pheasants will continue to the end of the field. Driving is one of the most effective methods of pheasant hunting.

Woodlots are generally overlooked by pheasant hunters, yet are often midday hotspots. It is considerably easier to gain permission to hunt a woodlot than a field of corn or soybeans. Oddly, one rarely flushes a hen pheasant. Woodlots are the domain of the rooster. A woodlot with acorn-bearing oak trees and scattered openings amid tangled thickets is a good prospect. If the woodlot is situated amid fields of corn and soybeans it's the kind of location one or two hunters should never pass up. It could be a loafing and casual feeding spot for every rooster in the neighborhood. Two hunters spaced 20 yards apart and walking along the outer edge of the woodlot will almost always have good shooting.

Other midday loafing spots used by pheasant are thickets of high grass and weeds. Such locations are easier for you to handle alone than are large cultivated fields. The birds are more inclined to hold tight and flush within range in heavy cover.

Very large areas of swamp and grassland are good late-afternoon prospects. Pheasants can be spotted flying in to roost in such locations during the last hour of daylight. You can pinpoint a rooster's landing site and then walk out and flush it. If the cover is thick grassy swale, the bird will be inclined to hold tight rather than run. If the cover is heavy but no bird flushes, don't give up too easily. A smart old rooster will sometimes hold remarkably tight.

Look for pheasants seeking shelter from the wind on cold blustery days. Hedgerows, fences, stone walls, gullies, creek bottoms, and swampy spots all provide cover. Large areas of grass and cattails can be tackled by concentrating your efforts where islands of trees or clumps of bushes and high willows grow. These islands of trees are often surprisingly open near the ground. Rooster pheasants like to browse and scratch not unlike farmyard chickens. They can't do that in swamp grass or cattails. Walk slowly, zigzagging, or you may walk past wily cock birds. Stop occasionally and just stand still for several minutes. That will cause a rooster pheasant to think it has been spotted and send it cackling into the air.

RUFFED GROUSE AND WOODCOCK

In some states where habitat loss has severely reduced pheasant numbers, the ruffed grouse now ranks as the number one favorite game bird. In other states it's always had that spot. The grouse is a plump bird 15 to 19 inches long, with rather short, rounded wings that spread 22 to 25 inches. The tail, 4½ to 7½ inches long, spreads into a broad fan.

The ruffed grouse is found throughout most of Canada, from the New England states to the Appalachian Mountains, throughout the upper Midwest, and sprinkled, sometimes abundantly, in the Northwestern states. You should know that it's actually called a pheasant in the South, a partridge in some parts of the U.S., and a birch partridge in Canada.

Because the ruffed grouse is a woods bird, hunters have problems locating and hitting them early in the season when the foliage is still lush. One solution is to concentrate your early-season efforts in fenced-off woodlots and cow pastures where the walking is easy.

While the ruffed grouse is normally associated with heavy cover, it is surprising how open a woods can be and still produce an occasional bird. Sometimes a patch of cover in one corner of an otherwise comparatively open woodlot will produce two or three birds season after season. If the hunter has a half-dozen or so such spots in mind his success is almost assured.

The ideal woods offers not only the occasional open shot but a lot of birds as well. Such an area is only lightly pastured during the summer months, promoting open lanes of grass and closely cropped beds of clover, a food much favored by the ruffed grouse. These open lanes let in sunshine that encourages the growth of heavy patches of bushes and briars. The perfect spot has hardwoods and thickets of aspen and birch, a stand of spruce or cedar for roosting, and a tinkling brook with clear spring water.

Ruffed grouse are normally flushed in heavy cover, but experienced grouse hunters know they favor openings. Grouse scratch for tidbits the same as barnyard chickens and rooster pheasants, and for this they need a little leg room. When hunters approach the birds head for heavy cover.

A northwoods hunters will often find that trails constitute many of the openings in heavy cover. An old trail carpeted with clover and wild strawberry and edged by thickets of aspen and birch, sumac, or hazel is the most common ruffed-grouse environment in the northern coniferous zones.

During the late season, evergreen thickets are worth investigating. Grouse like to roost in evergreens and, as the season progresses, spend many more hours in their roost. During late-season hunts you'll have to leave the easily walked trails, as the birds are now widely scattered; but in deep snow, watch for their snow holes in those same trails and in clearings. By roosting under snow, the ruffed grouse avoids bitterly cold surface temperatures.

Ruffed grouse make short flights of 75 to 100 yards. This gives the hunter a second, third, and sometimes a half-dozen chances. Often the grouse will fly in a straight line, and the persistent hunter can easily raise the bird again. But more often a grouse will stop short in the dense crown of a pine or balsam, or veer sharply to one side and run after landing, or occasionally a bird will swing sharply upward from gliding flight to perch in the branches of a tall pine.

Use your ears when hunting ruffed grouse. Listen for their fall drumming—a warning to other male grouse to stay out of the area. The male bird makes the sound by rapidly beating his wings while perched on a favorite log. It sounds like a tractor being started up miles distant, but the grouse may be only 50 yards away. Listen for the faint rustling of the grouse walking in dry leaves, or the nervous *prrrrt, prrrrt* emitted by grouse when a hunter draws near. In the fall and winter the ruffed grouse feeds noisily on buds atop aspen trees.

Hitting ruffed grouse on the wing is very difficult for the novice and very trying at times for the experienced hunter. Don't wait for the perfect shot. They come only rarely. Ignore the leaves, trees, and branches; get on the bird and shoot! It's a fragile bird; it doesn't take much to knock a ruffed grouse down. Fortunately, it doesn't take much to find the downed bird either. Ruffed grouse are not nearly as tenacious of life as are pheasant.

Light shotguns with open bores are favorite grouse guns. Improved cylinder is a good choice of choke. A side-by-side double-barrel bored improved cylinder and modified is just right. Use low-base loads of No. 7½ or No. 8 shot.

Woodcock are often found right along with ruffed grouse. Guns and loads recommended for ruffed grouse will handle woodcock, too, but even lighter shot sizes such as No. 9 are recommended for strictly woodcock shooting.

Woodcock are virtually ignored in Minnesota, Wisconsin, and Michigan, but eagerly sought in New England. In Virginia, only one out of every 53 hunters pursues woodcock. Yet some of the heaviest concentrations of the birds are found south of the Mason-Dixon line.

Although not much larger than a robin, woodcock provide wonderful shooting opportunities. In some coverts hunters can hunt resident woodcock the whole season long. More often the bulk of the hunter's bag will be migratory birds which come into a region at almost any time during the fall. Major migrations depend on the locale. In Virginia, for example, the flights are the heaviest around the first of November. Farther north, the flights are much earlier.

Both ruffed grouse and woodcock prefer moist places. This is especially true of the grouse early in the season. It likes succulent plant life; the woodcock needs soft ground to probe for worms with its long bill.

Dense cover along streams is favorite woodcock cover. Some covers will be very narrow, with a few shoreline birches and alders being the only likely holding lines. The lone hunter can quickly check the likely spots in only a couple of hours of hunting, walking first on one side of the stream and then coming back on the other. Such light cover rarely holds many birds, but the shots you do get are often easy ones.

Abundant woodcock will be found where damp boggy soil rich in earthworms and sufficient cover stretches for 40 yards or more on either side of the stream. These large areas are best hunted in a zigzag pattern working up each side of the creek.

As with ruffed grouse, woodcock can be flushed a second and even a third time. If it appears that the woodcock has flown a considerable distance it's best to ignore it and try for another—unless the birds are very scarce.

Woodcock are unnerved by long pauses; in fact, about 90 percent of the woodcock flush while you are standing still. This is to your advantage. When you're stopped and ready, anticipating the flush, your chances of putting shot in the path of the bird are greatly increased. Get into the habit of stopping every 30 to 50 feet and simply waiting silently with your gun at the ready position. Pause for at least 20 or 30 seconds.

Woodcock are sometimes difficult to retrieve because they're small. When you see a woodcock fall, immediately rivet your eyes to that spot. Then, with your peripheral vision, note any shrubs or trees next to the spot that have some identifiable characteristic about them. It's a good idea to drop your spent shell or hang your cap before going to make the retrieve, in case you need to come back for realigning where you shot from. Then walk straight to the bird. Quite often the bird will have fallen a little beyond where you thought, because of its momentum.

Hunters may be put off by the gamy flavor of woodcock. If you don't care for wild duck you almost certainly won't rave about woodcock. If you don't like woodcock straight, cut the meat from the bone and cut it into small pieces to add to casseroles and baked dishes. It will add delicious tang, flavor, and body. You can do this with any game bird. It's also a handy way of dealing with game when there really isn't enough for a good meal.

SHARPTAIL GROUSE

Sharptails are big-country birds. Some of the best sharptail hunting is in the Western states and Canadian prairies. Fewer are found in the northern counties of the Great Lakes states. A wide-ranging pointing dog is often considered a must to locate sharptails, but the dogless hunter can also locate and flush sharptails. The 12-gauge shotgun bored modified or full with high-base No. 6 shells is a good combination for the longer-range shots you'll take at sharptails.

During the early morning and late afternoon, watch for sharptails feeding in stubble fields and other low-vegetation areas. Then look for clumps of willows or aspen thickets nearby. This is where the birds will spend the remainder of the day. It's in such thickets that you should concentrate your efforts.

It isn't always easy. Sharptails run and skulk, sit tight, flush wild, or slip between hunters. One of the best ways to combat the last problem is to have hunters walk close, say within 10 yards of each other. This will discourage birds that would normally slip through or hold tight. Obviously a party of hunters can't cover as much ground using this method, but their chances of flushing birds in their path will be greater than if they were strung out with large gaps between shooters.

If you're alone you can better handle a heavy clump of cover found on the edge of farmland or prairie by first walking around the entire outer edge of the cover. Then, back at your starting point, walk through the willow clump, aspen stand, or alder grove in a zigzag pattern.

The theory behind first circling the cover is that it confuses the birds. They know somebody has been on all sides of the cover; can they run out safely? This tactic alone can help hold birds inside a cover so the hunter can put additional pressure on them when he enters. Convince yourself that every cover holds birds. Without this confidence, you may neglect your careful plan, and simply blunder along.

In some areas of the Great Lakes states, sharptails live out their lives in rather damp, boggy terrain. Hunters can sometimes penetrate this terrain by following railroad tracks. Sharptails are frequently flushed from the high grass bordering the tracks. You should also explore any dry knolls in the otherwise wet terrain. Sometimes you can sight sharptails far ahead feeding near the rails. Generally they'll flush before you're within range. If the country is open enough, however, you may see where they land. Knee-high rubber boots are handy for slopping through wet swamps to follow these birds.

TURKEY

More than 20 states all over the country have turkey seasons in the spring, and almost 40 have fall seasons. Turkey hunting is now available to thousands who never dreamed they'd have the opportunity. Even Minnesota, which never had native wild turkey even in the earliest of times, is now considering a limited hunt in the southeastern corner of the state, where turkeys have been successfully planted.

Wild turkeys look like domestic turkeys except that they're built along slimmer and racier lines. The wild turkey has to hustle to stay alive. The distinguishing marks of a wild turkey are its black-and-brown tail feathers; those of the domesticated turkey are white-and-black. The average adult wild turkey cock weighs 14-17 pounds, while the female weighs 8-10 pounds.

High-base loads of No. 6 shot in 12-gauge shotguns are standard fare. Some hunters like to have a couple of No. 2 shells in their guns for backup shots. Generally a full or modified barrel is best.

In some states, rifles are legal for turkey hunting. They are most popular in the Western states, where longer-range shots are common. A good choice is the .22 Rimfire Magnum. The hollowpoint loads tear up some meat but are deadly. Shots can be effective to 100 yards.

In the fall, the hunter attempts to still-hunt within shotgun range of a flock, or drove, of turkeys, make his shot, and either hit or miss. A miss is not the letdown it might normally be. A flock of fall or winter turkeys is made up of mostly young turkeys, and they will regroup at, or very close to, the spot from which they were scattered. This is an excellent opportunity for the hunter, and perhaps others in his party, to call the birds back together and pick them off.

For tyros, calling can be frustrating. Turkey hunting is very new to many hunters, and most do not know how to call. Until you learn, there are other methods you can use. One is detecting by their sign where turkeys are entering an opening early or late in the day. Look for tracks, feathers, and droppings. Turkeys visit waterholes. The birds love to follow old trails and paths in their wanderings, and it is sometimes possible to take a stand near one of them and shoot a bird. Watch for tracks and feathers along old roads and trails. By scouting thoroughly, you may locate several waylaying spots. In the Western states, game trails snaking along mountain slopes may show turkey tracks and dropped feathers. If you can find a place where two well-used trails or paths cross, or a side draw that comes out to a small stream, it is probably a good bet, particularly if tracks show that birds habitually pass the place when going to and from roosting, feeding, or resting places.

But the real drama in turkey hunting lies in using a call. In the fall or winter when a flock of young birds have been scattered, the whistling *key-key* of the young turkey is by far the most reliable. The young birds will come to lost calls produced on any type of caller. Hunters usually have their favorites. Regardless of the caller, it's important that you locate the precise spot from which the turkeys are flushed when scattered. The speed with which they return to the scatter point will depend on a number of factors, including the time of the day, the nature of the threat that scattered them, and the ages of the birds in the flock. Turkeys scattered early in the day will usually regroup quickly, often beginning to call shortly after the hunter has concealed himself. Birds scattered later in the day will wait until late in the evening before regrouping. A flock that is split up right before sunset will make an effort to regroup just after dawn the next morning.

The one major threat to this strategy is a failure to effectively scatter the birds. Poor dispersion of the birds will mean they will reunite soon after landing in close proximity to one another with no need to return to the spot where they flushed.

You needn't worry about calling too much when working with scattered young turkeys in the fall and winter; in fact, the turkeys will often become suspicious if you call sparingly. In the spring, frequent calls may arouse the turkey's suspicion, but in the fall and winter the lost turkey expects other members of the flock to respond readily, and it will be to your advantage to answer every call a bird makes.

Spring gobbler hunting, killing just the male of the species, is the newest sport in many states. This bird only recently became legal game in the spring after being protected for several generations.

The purist gets most of his thrill out of calling the bird, seeing him strut and hearing him gobble. The kill is anticlimactic, although the hunter now has the makings of a legendary meal. The wild turkey is usually not as fat as a domestic one nor as tender, but it is just as flavorful.

You should try to locate several turkeys before the spring season opens. You can do this simply enough by driving along back roads and stopping every half-mile or so and giving a call. Do it at sunrise, because gobblers are most likely to respond then. When a gobbler responds, you can mark the spot as a place to try during the season. Some hunters like to get out and call the gobbler in. This gives you a better idea of the terrain and the gobbler's territory. But don't do this too often. A good rule is to call them once and then leave them alone until the season.

The call is that of a lonesome hen. With a box or slate caller, even the uninitiated can master the skill in a few minutes by following the instructions with the caller. The call may sound scratchy or strange to your ears, but try it in the woods. Once you have the chance to hear wild hen turkeys, you will soon realize that there is a different-pitched voice for every hen. Many a turkey hunter has been surprised by a hen making a sound that had him cursing an amateur turkey caller for messing up his hunt.

When a gobbler answers your call, move up to within 100 yards of the bird as quickly, and as quietly, as you can. Foliage is so thick that you can do this without being seen by the turkey. If you are in the mountains, you must always get on the same ridge as the gobbler. They will not cross a hollow to get to the most romantic-sounding caller.

Crouch near some natural camouflage; a fallen tree or stump will do. And you'd better be camouflaged from head to foot. That includes a face mask and gloves. Then resume calling. Chances are the gobbler will answer immediately, if he hasn't seen or heard you. The most widely accepted rule is not to call too often. Do not call as long as the tom is gobbling. When he quits sounding off, wait a couple of minutes and revive his interest with another call.

If the bird stops gobbling, don't relax. Many an old tom quits gobbling when he's close and comes running right in without a sound.

133

MAKING A TURKEY BOX CALL

Make your turkey box call from dry cedar of the type used in lining clothes closets. This yelper features double handles. See the illustration. The bottom handle provides a grip so that the fingers do not touch the 1/16-inch sounding-board sides. The other handle is attached loosely with a screw, and is slid or rocked across the edges of the sounding box to produce the yelp of the wild turkey. The directions in the illustration are self-explanatory. The important part is to practice. Then use the call sparingly. Sound a series of yelps every 15 to 20 minutes.

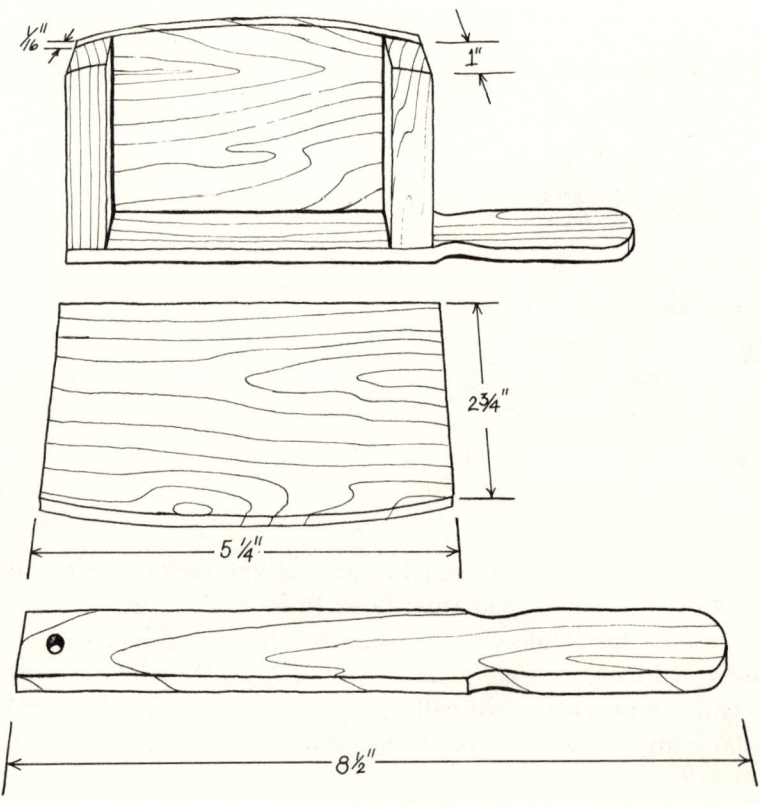

13
SQUIRRELS

Gray and fox squirrels are hunters' favorites. Both are a delight for the economy-minded shooter. You can hunt them with the low-priced .22 rimfire rifle, although in areas of the South, where glimpses of squirrels are fleeting, hunters prefer shotguns. Squirrels can also be killed with the more powerful of the pellet rifles if you stick to head shots only. If you use a pellet rifle, or any of the silent limited-range weapons, you can hunt squirrels in the vicinity of buildings and urban development. Add to this the fact that squirrels are no pushovers and you have the makings of good cheap hunting from fall through the winter. In a number of states, squirrel hunting is open in summer.

The eastern gray squirrel is found all across the eastern United States. The western gray inhabits a narrow strip along the Pacific Coast. Fox squirrels are found across most of the same range as the eastern gray squirrel, but not as far north, and farther west of the Mississippi. The gray is 15 to 20 inches long, 7 to 10 inches of that length being a bushy tail. Fox squirrels are considerably larger, although the smaller gray is considered the better eating.

Early-fall hunting is productive. Hickory trees are laden with fruit. These

Eyeglass pouch makes convenient case for .22 rimfire ammo.

trees turn yellow before most of the other forest species. The hunter can pick out those yellow crowns at a distance and look each one over. Squirrels sometimes work on hickory trees until each has been totally stripped of nuts. In the early fall, squirrels are more numerous than at any other time of the year. Natural mortality has not made serious inroads in populations, and hunters have not yet placed pressure on the bushytails to wise them up. Because squirrels are not hibernators, they must be in good condition to survive the winter months. This means plenty of activity when the fall mast crops are ripe. They must not only eat enormous quantities, they must store nuts and acorns as well. All of which adds up to much frantic activity by squirrels in the early fall, and many targets for early-season hunters.

Hunter success is proportional to the number of squirrels in any given woods. Look for woods with large, mature oaks and hickories that produce abundant quantities of nuts. You can estimate the squirrel population by the amount of hulls and husks in evidence on the forest floor. When possible, do this kind of scouting just before the season.

Another clue is the presence of nests and dens. Dens are usually located in old trees that have succumbed to disease and insect attack. Branches fall off and the scars are enlarged by woodpeckers searching for larvae or a nest site. These become enlarged over the years and sooner or later squirrels discover them and move in. Nests in the tree branches are invariably made of leaves. An abundance of leaf nests can indicate many squirrels are in the area, although leaf nests are quite often only temporarily used by squirrels to raise their young and then abandoned in favor of den trees that offer secure winter shelter. River banks are choice locations to find mature trees, both those that are still producing fruit and those that are now providing den sites.

Early-fall woods are still in full leaf, and you can readily ambush squirrels as they travel between den and feeding areas. You can wear camouflage, but it is more important to remain motionless. Squirrel activity is often so feverish that the busy animals never notice motionless hunters. In the East, a good ambush point is the intersection of two stone walls. Large trees often grow along these walls and the walls act as perfect runways.

Near a well-laden hickory or oak, you should approach slowly. When you sight a squirrel, freeze. Wait for the bushytail to feed. Then close in quietly and pick your shot.

Patience is often the key to success. Squirrels don't hole up for long when fall food is available. Squirrels that have been put to flight can still be taken by the hunter who assumes a comfortable position and waits them out. This is particularly effective in a stand of mature hardwoods. Here you are in position to greet squirrels as they emerge from their dens or travel toward them.

Don't pick up a downed squirrel immediately. Moving from a stand to recover downed game will end the hunting temporarily.

Stand-hunting is a deliberate kind of endeavor. There is seldom reason to hurry a shot; you can wait for a good one, take your time, and squeeze off a shot, or carefully release an arrow or slung projectile.

Still-hunting, moving quietly through the woods with frequent pauses, is another method that works. When a squirrel is sighted, it often is running for cover. Left to its own resources, the squirrel will almost invariably head for the nearest den tree. You can sometimes panic the squirrel into scampering up the nearest tree—one, you hope, without a den—by running full tilt after the animal.

Once the squirrel has been treed, you should position yourself where you have a good view of many branches. Pick up a heavy branch and then sit quietly for a few minutes. Then hurl the branch to the opposite side of the tree. The squirrel, thinking you've moved, will scramble to your side of the tree and offer a shot.

If you're hunting alone, try taking along a long length of stout twine. When a squirrel is treed, tie one end of the twine to a bush on one side of the tree and then move to the opposite side of the tree. After waiting for things to settle down, jerk on the end of the twine, causing the bush to shake. This startles the squirrel, which then moves to your side and presents a good target.

Two or more hunters together should take turns shooting. The one whose turn it is to shoot assumes a comfortable position allowing a view of many branches, while his partner moves to the opposite side of the tree in an attempt to move the squirrel to the shooter's side. Another two-hunter system is for both hunters to move quietly around the tree opposite each other until one of them sees the squirrel. He then takes the shot, or waits while his partner creates a disturbance in an effort to get the squirrel to shows its head and provide the best target for a clean, killing shot.

Windy days are notoriously poor for squirrel hunting. Because the wind muffles sound, squirrels are reluctant to venture to the ground for fear of being ambushed by predators or hunters. If the option is to hunt on a windy day or not at all, two hunters can still make a go of it. Two hunters can watch the tree limbs between them by walking abreast and about 20 yards apart. A squirrel that is startled by one hunter will scramble to the opposite side of the tree limb and expose itself to the other hunter. This requires considerable alertness on the part of the hunters. Watch for movement.

Floating a river or small stream in a canoe or light boat is an interesting and often productive way to hunt squirrels. The trip can be more fun if combined with an overnight campout. And the gear is easy to transport in the craft.

Some favor shotguns for float hunting, since the shots are often at squirrels scampering up a tree as the boat rounds a bend in the stream. The rifle purist, however, will stick with his .22 rimfire for ultimate sport, usually taking head shots only.

Quiet is essential in drifting a woodland stream. Your boat as well as your clothing should be camouflaged or of subdued tones, although this is not essential. The real secret lies in using your eyes and ears. Frequently you can beach the boat while moving away from the stream to hunt out a choice wooded location.

Squirrels dropped in the water will float long enough for you to retrieve them.

By late season, wind, rain, and snow have stripped the hardwoods of their foliage, and spotting a treed squirrel is easier. Getting one treed is not, however. Getting close enough to shoot one on the ground is even more difficult. Squirrels can spot you from a distance. Stalking close enough for a shot is a real test of woodsmanship.

An unpicked field of ripe corn is a tempting meal for hungry squirrels. The fox squirrel is especially daring, and ventures long distances from the nearest tree. Even after the corn has been picked there will be corn on the ground that was missed by the mechanical picker, and squirrels will continue to feed on this. If the field is not plowed, squirrels will dig through deep snow to reach the cobs. It is easy to see when squirrels are feeding in a cornfield. Sometimes they carry the cobs into the woods and leave the husks at the base of trees and stumps.

The hunter with sharp ears has a decided advantage in squirrel hunting. Squirrels will variously grunt, purr, chatter, and even growl. The sound of nutshells falling to the ground and the rustling of a squirrel moving in dry leaves are also giveaways.

A good squirrel dog can double your success. Hunting with a dog is a fast-paced kind of hunting, with the dog running ahead, following the scent, then the sounds, and finally sight-chasing squirrels.

A dog will force the squirrel to run up the first tree it comes to, preventing it from choosing a den tree. That is something the less agile hunter cannot copy. If you own a dog that simply hasn't made the grade as a bird dog, you can salvage your investment by using it on squirrels. If the dog likes to hunt, it won't take much to encourage it on squirrels; in fact, many a dog that has never done any hunting, aside from chasing the neighborhood cat, will immediately take to sight-chasing squirrels.

Even if a dog is a bit overweight or getting older, there's no real problem. Discovering that you have a helpmate in your family pet will add a new dimension to your hunting.

Don't overlook the use of binoculars in squirrel hunting. A lightweight pair are very useful for spotting a treed squirrel and for scanning small clumps of trees that are located in otherwise open terrain. Fox squirrels feel right at home in such isolated hangouts, while the gray prefers larger woods. Distant squirrels are particularly easy to spot against a snowy background.

While squirrels are almost always active in the fall, that's not the case in winter. Winter hunting can vary from fantastic one day to nothing the next. Barometric pressures and other forces probably have an effect on squirrel activity. You can learn a lot just by observing squirrels in your own yard or in a city park. If squirrels are active and much in evidence, it can pay to head for your favorite squirrel woods.

Squirrels are late risers during the cold months, and will feed into the late-morning hours. Cold temperatures alone will not keep them holed up, and a crisp sunny day will see them out and about at high noon absorbing some sunshine. Really raw, windy days are poor.

Camouflage should be white for snowtime hunting. You must be extra-cautious, too. Take a few steps, stop, listen and look for five minutes, then take a few more steps. If you have chosen a winter's day when the bushy-tails simply are not active, you can still make use of your time observing their tracks and trails in the snow. The next time you hunt you can approach these activity centers with special alertness.

There are several kinds of squirrel calls on the market. Some are mouth-operated like crow and varmint calls, but others are of the hand-operated bellows type. You do not attempt to lure the squirrel in but rather simply to make it give away its location. You imitate the familiar bark of a squirrel, prompting your quarry to sound off and give away its location. Two coins struck edge to edge produce a reasonable facsimile of a squirrel chuckling or barking.

You can sell gray, black, red, or fox squirrel tails to Sheldon's, Inc., P.O. Box 526, Antigo, Wis. 54409. This firm makes the well-known Mepps lures, and they use the tails for hook dressing on spinners. Good-quality gray squirrel tails bring 8 cents each, and good-quality fox or black squirrel tails 10 cents each. Common red squirrel tails bring 4 cents each. Premium-quality tails are worth 3 cents more. Postage is refunded on 50 or more tails.

Over 30 million squirrels are bagged each year, and by selling the tails, squirrel hunters are simply utilizing a by-product of the game they harvest for the table. Besides, a few tails will help pay for ammo on the next outing.

Tails can be dried or green and sent by parcel post or UPS. Treat them as follows:

1. Do not put tails in a plastic bag for shipment.
2. Keep away from flies; do not send tails on which flies have laid eggs. Best storage is in a deep freeze.
3. Salt butt end of tail generously; use either dry salt or dip in a strong saltwater solution.
4. Be sure tail is straight before shipping. Tails that dry in a curled position cannot be used.
5. Do not remove the bone from the tail. The people at Sheldon's prefer to have the bone left in the tail, although they'll buy them without it.
6. The best time to ship is during the cold months, although dried tails may be shipped anytime.

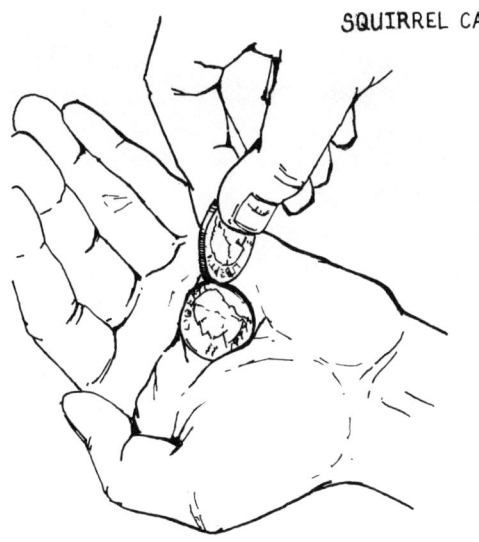

SQUIRREL CALL

14
DOVES

The mourning dove is a sleek, beautiful bird weighing only 4 to 5 ounces. It is the most widespread of any of our native game birds, nesting in all the 48 contiguous states, Mexico, and all of southern Canada. The wintering range of the mourning dove includes most of the United States and extends as far south as Panama. It is a hardy bird, but cold weather forces it out of the northern states.

There's been a lot of research on the mourning dove. For the most part it's been over the status of the bird. The argument as to whether the mourning dove should be classified as a game bird or song bird continues. The result of research, the hunter is quick to point out, shows that the dove's natural mortality runs between 50 and 70 percent regardless of hunting. Even with this mortality rate, its numbers remain fairly constant. It's classified as a game bird in 31 states.

The opportunity for good cheap hunting is within easy driving distance if you live in a state that is open to dove hunting. The annual harvest of about 40 million birds seems to support the dove's gastronomic reputation as well.

Shotguns and fine shot, usually No. 9, 8, or 7½ in field or high-base loads, are the basic equipment required. Dove hunters are particularly wise to handload, because when the shooting gets fast and furious it's easy to use a lot of shells. A dove with wind on its tail is a difficult target. Estimates place the number of shells emptied annually at doves at 200 million —for 40 million birds, that's five shells per bird.

Dove season generally opens the first week in September and offers the first shooting opportunity of the season. In Tennessee, there has been a split dove season for many years. During the first part of the season, the month of September, hunters gun for what are referred to as native doves, doves which have nested in the state. The second season, usually mid-October to mid-November, finds them gunning for "Yankee doves," birds that have migrated down from states farther north. Usually by this time cold snaps and food scarcities have sent the native doves winging southward. Other states experience similar migrations.

Finding where the doves are concentrated is the secret to consistently good dove shooting. Generally this takes place where the birds are feeding.

Some of the best dove territory is around livestock farms. The reason is that silage is used for feed by dairy and beef farmers. Silage is made from the harvested cornstalk. The entire cornstalk and ear is chopped and blown into a wagon. With the entire stalk removed from the field, only a clean, low stubble remains. Doves relish such openness with much waste grain on the ground.

Another favorite feeding ground, often found on the same farm, is a harvested wheat field where the wheat stubble has been baled to use for winter livestock bedding. Again, a clean field with low stubble is created. The waste grain is out in the open where the birds can find it.

When you can find them, fields of commercially grown sunflowers will provide excellent shooting opportunities. Intensive shooting will drive doves from most feeding areas, but it is almost impossible to drive them away from sunflowers.

The best feeding spots late in the season are picked cornfields. Other domestic crops that make up a dove's diet are millet, milo, peanuts, maize, and various field peas.

Wild foods also attract doves. In some areas, such as the Texas "brush country," there is not much farming. Two outstanding wild foods are croton, often called "dove weed," and wild sunflower. Ragweed, foxtail, and pigweed are also eagerly sought. While tough for the hunter to walk through,

143

these weeds are generally quite open near the ground. This is a requisite for doves, which do not like to feed in dense ground cover.

Doves do not feed from a stalk or head, but only on the ground, on fallen grain or seeds. They do not scratch for food. Unripened or unharvested crops may not offer enough fallen forage to bring birds in. The same field, however, may be a sizzler a week or so later.

To ensure good shooting, you should scout back roads, looking for the mentioned kinds of field conditions and noting which fields have dove activity. By scouting just before the season opening you can start the season off with good shooting.

Around midafternoon is a good time to scout prospective fields. The birds will be very active then. Binoculars are handy for viewing more distant fields. You should continue this kind of observation into the season, because after two or three weeks the doves will be shuttling about from one area to another because of weather, hunting pressure, and farming activities. Also, as the season progresses, migrating birds will be moving in. Most good dove shooting during the late season in October in the Midwest takes place in harvested cornfields. Often late-season doves will be seen loafing in the trees, on telephone wires, and on the ground near these fields during midday. When loafing on the ground they can be very easy to overlook because they don't move much. Careful observation is needed to locate late-season birds.

For the actual shooting, hunters choose shooting sites around the edge of a field in early afternoon and wait for the arrival of the birds. (More than half the dove-hunting states limit dove shooting to the afternoon hours.) Flocks will come into a field from several different directions. Hunters generally conceal themselves in fenceline cover. Camouflage clothing helps, and it pays to remain motionless when birds are approaching. The sun glinting off a wristwatch or gun barrel can cause birds to fly wide of the shooter. Once you get set on a good stand in or around the edge of a feeding field, you should stay put until you get your limit. Fidgety dove shooters who keep moving around rarely get their limit.

Waterhole shooting is another method of dove hunting. Waterholes used by doves can be found only through observation. A general rule is that when water is everywhere, waterhole shooting is not likely to be as good as when water is fairly scarce.

In selecting a shooting site, watch where most birds go to drink at a waterhole. Usually they will come in where there is a bare, muddy flat along one edge of a waterhole. Such a location is easy to land on, and the birds can walk to water. Doves do not hop and cannot walk well in heavy grass. Also watch for dead snags near a waterhole. Doves love to perch on these between drinks of water. Sometimes a hunter will place a few dove decoys in such a snag and a few on the ground by the waterhole where he has actually observed birds landing.

The routine of a dove's day is roughly as follows. About dawn they fly from roost to feed, then make a flight to water, and thence to a midday resting area. By midafternoon the birds are again heading out to feed, followed by a flight to water. At sunset they return to the resting area, or roost. Thus feed-field shoots are best during the first half of the morning (where legal) and the middle to late afternoon. Waterhole shoots are best in late morning and late afternoon.

When shooting over a waterhole, a good gimmick is to bring along a casting rod and a surface plug. Birds dropped onto the water won't sink, and you can retrieve them by pinpoint casting and pulling them in.

Doves sometimes fly several miles from or to food, water, and roost. This can allow you to get good pass-shooting. Getting under such flights offers shots at swiftly flying birds. It is a good idea after bagging a few birds on a pass to remove and open the crops. This may tell you what they're feeding on and where. By tracing back the direction from which the birds came, you may find an abundance of the forage the birds' crops contained— and thereby set up an excellent feeding-field shoot.

When you drop a dove, keep your eye on that spot and pick it up immediately. Doves are small and blend so well with grass or brush that they are difficult to find. A good retriever can help, although some dogs are not happy retrieving doves because the feathers come off in bunches in their mouths.

Because doves are migratory birds, they come under federal regulations and may not be covered in your state's regular hunting-laws pamphlet. A supplementary sheet for migratory birds is usually available where licenses are sold. Ask for it.

Another source of information is the U.S. Fish and Wildlife Service, Department of the Interior, Washington, D.C. 20240. Ask for the publication that contains the federal regulations governing the hunting seasons, limits, and shooting-hour schedules for doves.

15
DEER

Deer are the most popular big-game animals in the United States and the cheapest to hunt. Whitetails are the most widely distributed and receive the most hunting pressure. States with the highest concentrations are Michigan, Minnesota, Pennsylvania, Wisconsin, and Texas. Only five states have whitetail numbers so low as to be negligible: California, Colorado, Kansas, Nevada, and Utah.

Whitetails can thrive practically in your back yard. The brush-loving whitetail can subsist in almost any kind of foliage, croplands or natural forest cover. Edge country, where farmland and forest meet, is favorite habitat. So is the second growth that follows fire or logging operations.

The antler tines of the whitetail are unbranched and extend upward from the main beam. The tail is brown on top and white underneath.

Mule deer are confined to the Western states, Mexico, northwestern Canada, and Alaska. Their antlers are usually higher than the whitetail antlers, and they are branched. The main beam is evenly divided at the first fork. Each branch then divides again. Its tail is black-tipped. The blacktail deer of the Pacific Coast is considered one of the mules. The tail of the blacktail is black on top from tip to base.

The mule deer is considerably more tolerant of open country than is the whitetail, although increased hunting pressure is causing the mule deer to seek shelter more and more in heavy timber.

The choice of rifle for deer hunting depends on whether it is to be used strictly for deer hunting or if it is also expected to handle the super-accuracy required for varmint shooting. If the rifle is to be used for larger game such as moose and elk, this must be considered. The choices are covered in Chapter 1.

Where rifles are not allowed by law and shotguns must be used, the best choice is a 12-gauge, of magazine type, with a single sighting plane (double-barrel guns are notoriously poor at handling slugs). Slugs are fairly accurate out to 100 yards if conventional sights are installed. Buckshot is used in some states but is not as effective as rifled slugs. Range with buckshot is limited to under 40 yards.

Accurate bullet placement is very important. The range at which most whitetails are killed, less than 60 yards, should require only one well-placed shot. The best point-of-aim is the lung area, located in the center of the chest cavity. This is almost pie-plate in size. If your shot is a little high, this will result in a spine shot, which is also lethal; if it is a little low, it will hit the heart. A deer hit in the lungs will rarely travel more than 50 feet.

Deer hunting is often as cheap, or as expensive, as you care to make it. You can hunt from home for a few dollars, but a week in deer camp is a different story, since nickel-dime poker is a misnomer.

Generally deer habitat is of two major types—the forested range and the agricultural range. Often the agricultural range carries the highest deer densities. The best agricultural habitat can be described as a mixture of woodlands consisting of large tracts. In many areas, large marshes, river bottomlands, or swamps can substitute for the woodlands. In the agricultural habitat, the fields can serve as the primary food source and the woodlands as escape cover and merely a secondary food source, so the type of woods is not as important as it is in the forested range.

Many hunters prefer the traditional forested range for their hunting, and here also there are things to look for. The best deer habitat is an area dominated by sun-loving trees, particularly aspen and/or jack pine. Of course, this rule breaks down as we go north because of severe winters. Large areas of Canada are in aspen or jack pine, but hold few if any deer.

Can you estimate deer numbers by their sign? The systematic reading of deer sign is used in formal deer surveys, of which the deer-pellet (droppings) survey is a prime example. It is not practical for you to run the number of survey courses required to produce a statistically reliable result, but in a general sense we can say that the greater the amount of sign that is present, the greater the number of deer that are present.

If you're trying to determine the extent of a local population of deer in states such as Florida, the best method may be to drive the dirt roads on a morning following a rain and observe the deer tracks that cross the roads. This is no real survey; nevertheless, trying to determine population by walking through the woods is almost impossible because of the tropical vegetation which obscures tracks, trails, and droppings.

Conservation officers (game wardens) are a good source of information on deer numbers. In patrolling their districts and checking deer kills, they find the areas of plentiful deer numbers and will have some idea of the hunting pressure in these areas. Talk with farmers, foresters, store owners, and other hunters. Sometimes a casual reference to a good area proves profitable. But don't plan a hunt on hearsay; get out and explore the area on foot. Camp in it. Hunt small game in it. Drive its back roads early and late in the day. Ideally, a hunter who really wants to learn about deer hunting should be out at all times of the year scouting for sign.

Once you have chosen an area for deer hunting, you should narrow the field even more by locating good spots for standing or still-hunting, or where you and your partners can make drives. You should do this scouting as close to the hunting season as possible. Deer can change their location quite suddenly because of a killing frost, snow cover, leaf fall, or many other reasons, mostly related to availability of food and cover. If you are a two-season hunter, your early-season hunting with bow and arrow will prepare you for the rifle season and settle, as well, the question of whether or not you have made a wise choice of hunting areas.

Drives are used most frequently in the Eastern states, where the quarry is the whitetail. This is the deployment of a group of hunters, some to stands on known deer runs, and others to drive the cover in a still-hunting manner, pushing the game out to the standers. Drives are most productive during midday when the game is bedded down. Deer will follow known trails and escape routes. One or two drives in an area will give the hunters all the knowledge they need to conduct efficient drives in future hunts. Areas should not be driven too often, as this will eventually push the game out of one location. Once a week is about right to drive a specific area. If you establish several adjoining areas for drives, this method can be used effectively for a day's hunt.

Standers need not necessarily form a straight line along the edge of the woods being driven. A rough U-shape is better, because pushed deer will often sneak out to the sides, especially toward the end of a drive. The standers are stationed downwind, so as not to be winded by escaping deer. The drivers have the wind at their backs, because they *want* the deer to scent them. That will move the deer toward the standers.

The most effective drives employ "backstops," a few hunters who follow the drivers, straggling a good distance behind to intercept game that attempts to slip through the drivers. This is especially important when hunting whitetails, and it is also a good idea when driving mule deer through a thicket or canyon.

Still-hunting is the most commonly used method of hunting deer and perhaps the most exciting. It calls for the most skill as a woodsman. Still-hunting is no less than stalking before the actual sighting of game takes place. The still-hunter moves cautiously until game is sighted, then takes his shot or moves into position for a shot. It is best done early and late in the day when game is up and about feeding. It is a stop-and-go routine with a great deal of looking and minimum of movement.

Only on occasion will you see the entire animal. More often it is a small patch of white that draws your attention, or sometimes the barely seen flicker of an ear caught out of the corner of the eye, or a slight nonconforming shade of color, or a stick that is an antler.

All the while you must guide your feet through loose rocks, over crunching twigs, around stumps, listening, watching. Some even claim they can smell deer.

You must be convinced that you are going to see a buck any second, every second. Only this kind of positive thinking will keep your senses attuned to the right frequency all the time. If you hear something, don't swing your head toward the sound. Such a movement could panic a buck. Search with your eyes first, then very, very slowly move your head in the direction of the sound until you can see. Fine-tune your eyes, nose, and ears to the highest possible degree. Slow stalking isn't a new method of hunting; it's really the oldest. You'll get a great deal of satisfaction from hunting deer this way.

Successful hunting from a blind or stand requires the right choice of a vantage point over a game trail, escape route, or cover of any kind utilized by deer when moving between bedding and feeding ground. The prevailing wind direction should be noted in planning these locations. Always try to locate your stand downwind of where you think deer will appear. The blind or stand should, if possible, be located above the line of vision of game. The experienced build their stands to *stand on*, and they make them solid, so they won't squeak at the slightest shifting of weight. The hunter can stand *against* the tree without the slightest giveaway of noise or movement.

A common error in selecting a stand is to choose a location overlooking an open field or logged-over area near a roadside. When hunters and their cars descend upon the deer woods complete with campers, trailers, and tents, deer abandon these open feeding areas or feed only after dark. The best location for a stand is where deer can travel and feed without feeling exposed. Whitetails are even more shy of openings when snow blankets the ground.

It is best to choose a semi-opening among trees and underbrush. One rewarding thing about trail watching is that the deer are moving slowly; standing shots are common. It is not difficult to pick an opening in the underbrush for a shot. A scope sight makes it easier. A favorite stand location is a narrow neck of woodland that winds between open swampland or abandoned fields. Whitetails will use these sheltered routes to reach feeding or bedding areas. These are real hotspots if buck scrapes and rubs are found.

Generally the area where deer are feeding will show the most tracks, since deer come from different parts of the woods to eat where food is plentiful, but it's wise to select a stand location closer to the deer's bedding site. You won't find many tracks near bedding sites, but the bucks often give away their routes by rubbing saplings and leaving scrapes if the rut is near.

Scrapes are small patches of earth cleared of leaves and sod by the buck's hooves. The buck urinates in the cleared patch. The scrape is an invitation to does to hang around for the buck to return with romance on its mind.

The closer you can position yourself to a possible bedding site the better your chances of intercepting the buck in the daylight. His bed is the last place he reaches in the morning and the first place he leaves in the afternoon. With hunters in the woods, you can expect deer to appear almost anytime, but it pays to be prepared for their normal movements, unpredictable as they may be.

When hunting pressure is heavy, look for possible escape routes. These are usually discovered only after many years of hunting in an area. A deer hunter in Minnesota had a stand halfway between two roads, where two points of trees crossed open grass bordering a creek. Normally there were few tracks or other sign at this location. However, once the season was underway, deer that were pressed by hunters from either road used the points of trees for cover as they crossed the open grass along the creek. Deer often abandon well-established trails once there is hunting pressure. A good escape route is a hotspot.

FIELD-DRESSING YOUR DEER

Once you've downed a buck it pays to open the stomach cavity as soon as possible. Follow the initial cut shown in figure 1 in the illustration of field dressing, leaving a patch of hide around the sex organs of the animal. Cut through the outer hide only. Then, as shown in figure 2, cut through the abdominal flesh, using your finger as a guide to avoid cutting into the intestines.

Before making the circular cut around the anus, pinch the anus opening closed with one hand. This keeps the skin taut and makes it easier to sink the knife in to one side of the anus and, following the circular bone formation, cut completely around the anus. This is a deep cut. Use the entire length of the blade. With the colon thus freed, you can usually pull the sex organs and colon free in one piece.

Remove the innards by vigorous pulling toward the rear of the carcass. Usually this will have to be helped by judicious cutting of the tissues holding these organs against the back.

Now cut away the diaphragm membrane that separates the stomach from the chest cavity. As this point a torrent of blood may pour out into the stomach cavity of a lung-shot animal. Tip the animal over to remove this blood. At this point it's possible to reach into the chest cavity, past the lungs, and grasp the animal's gullet and windpipe. Pull these backward, gaining as much of their length as possible; then with the other hand cut

1. INITIAL CUT

2. GUIDING BLADE

FIELD DRESSING

the windpipe and gullet off as far forward as possible. The lungs and heart are pulled free with a little cutting.

Now turn the animal over and dump out any accumulated blood. At this point it's a good idea to prop the carcass stomach-down on a log. Spread the hind legs to open the stomach cavity and permit drainage. If the animal's chest is resting on the log the carcass will be sufficiently off the ground and can properly cool (see figure 3). If you have to leave the carcass overnight, it will keep very well in this position. Foxes, coyotes, and other predators will rarely bother such a carcass because your human scent will still be very strong.

When dragging the deer out of the woods, first loop the drag rope around its neck and then bring it forward and loop it around the deer's nose as shown in figure 4. Back at camp, hang the deer in a shed or in a shaded spot from a tree limb. Prop the stomach cavity open with a stick as in figure 5.

TROPHY PREPARATION

If you plan to have your deer mounted, *do not* cut open the chest cavity. If the head is to be mounted it is necessary to bring in plenty of hide with the head, and this should be cut *behind* the neck only. If you want a shoulder mount it is absolutely necessary to start skinning well behind the front leg. Even with a neck mount it's well to start skinning behind the front leg, because taxidermists can do a neater job if they have surplus hide to work with.

Start skinning just behind the front leg straight up to the backbone and completely down the other side behind the front leg on that side. Then cut across and around the front of the legs and across the chest just above the opening made in field-dressing the deer. Then make a cut up the back of the neck, but instead of going all the way as shown in the illustration of trophy preparation, stop about halfway up the back of the neck. Skin the hide out to this point and then sever the neck. Your taxidermist can complete the skinning. You will want to do the whole job as shown in the illustration only if you expect to be in the field for an extended period.

The cheapest of all solutions is to save only the rack. Saw through the skull as shown in the illustration for a skull mount.

153

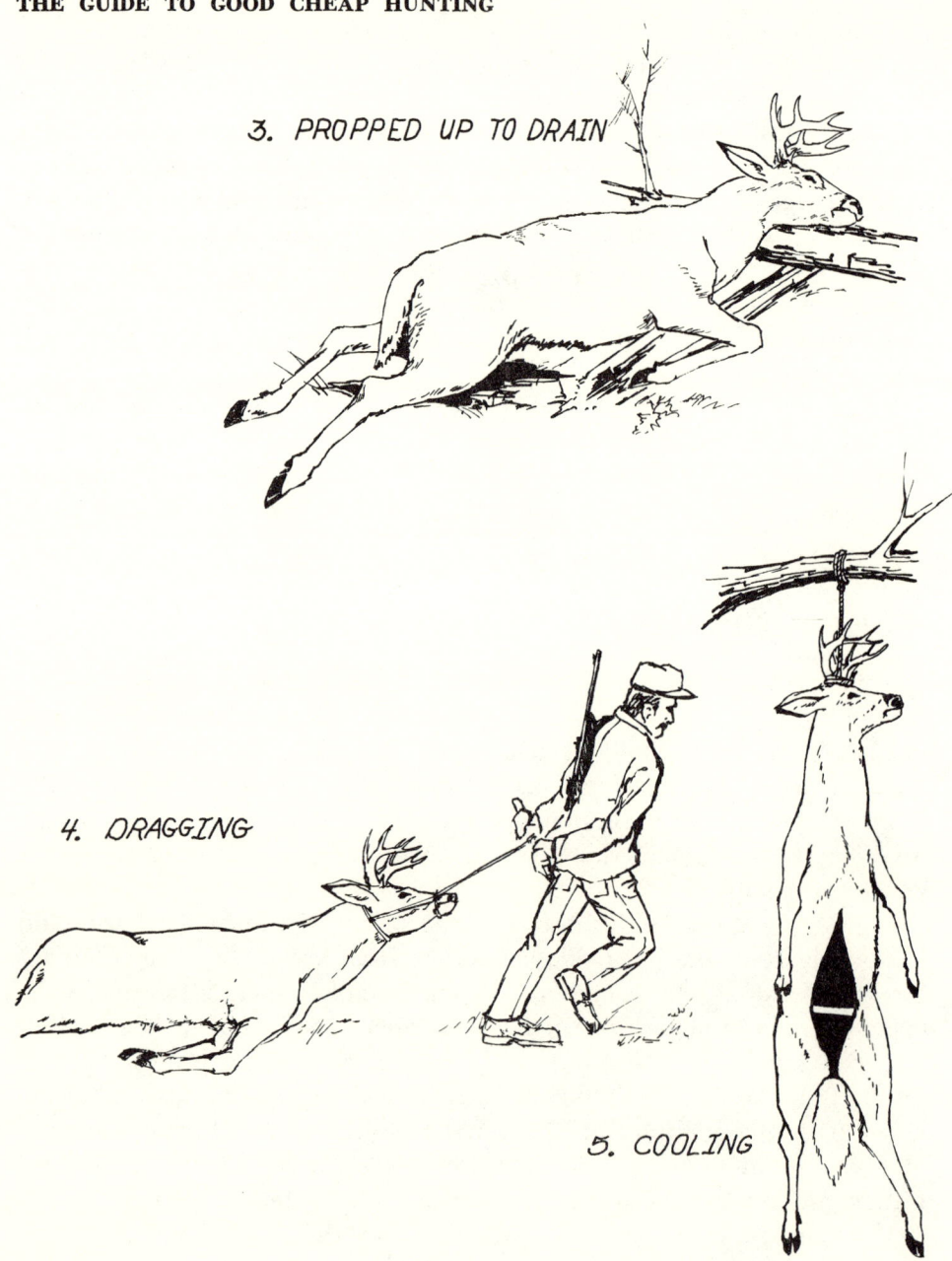

3. PROPPED UP TO DRAIN

4. DRAGGING

5. COOLING

TROPHY PREPARATION

MAKING HOISTS AND STANDS

A block and tackle is handy for hanging a deer, but it is cheaper to use a rope as shown in the illustration. A rope hoist is formed by tying one end of a rope to the head of the deer and then forming two loops in the rope above that point. You can use either of the two knots shown, the blood bight or the perfection knot. It's not necessary to start from the end of the rope for either of these knots. Once the loops have been tied, the other end of the rope is thrown over a tree limb or rafter and then brought through the lower loop and then the upper loop. Now the deer can be hoisted by pulling on this end of the rope.

In areas where tree stands are legal, you can make a portable stand like that shown in the drawing. Here are details the drawing does not provide. The belt that fastens the rear of the stand to the trunk of the tree can be fastened to the tarp hooks by simply looping the belt around the hooks and then around the tree or by cutting the belt into two separate parts, the

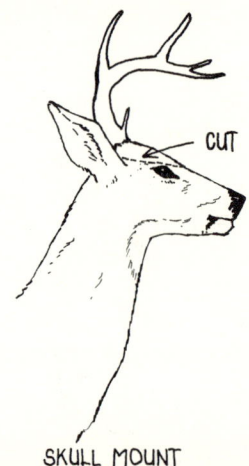

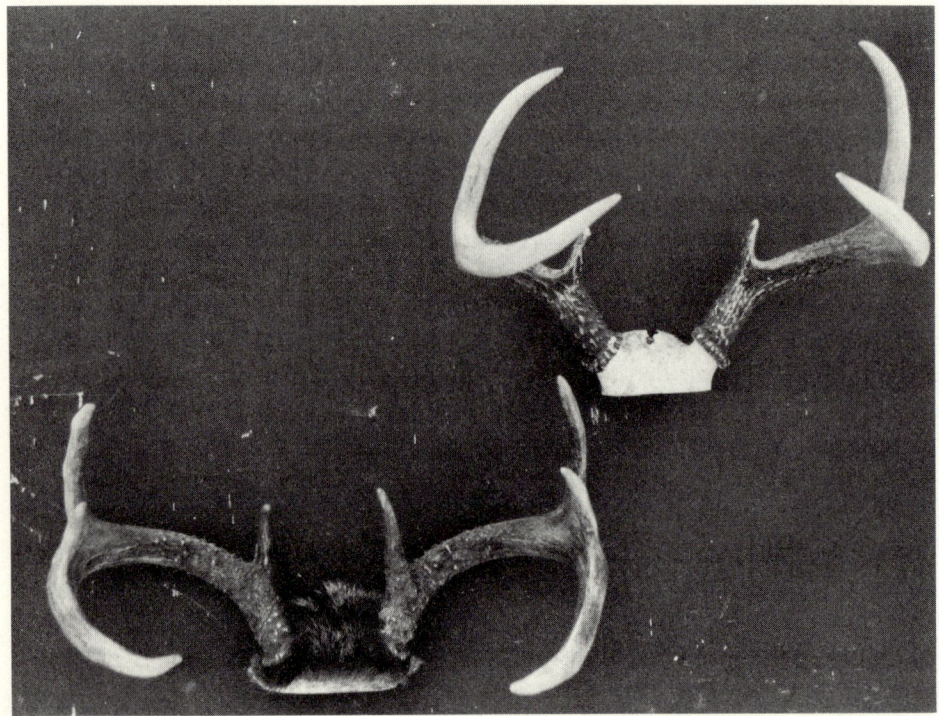

Skull mounts are lasting mementos of the hunt yet cost nothing.

156

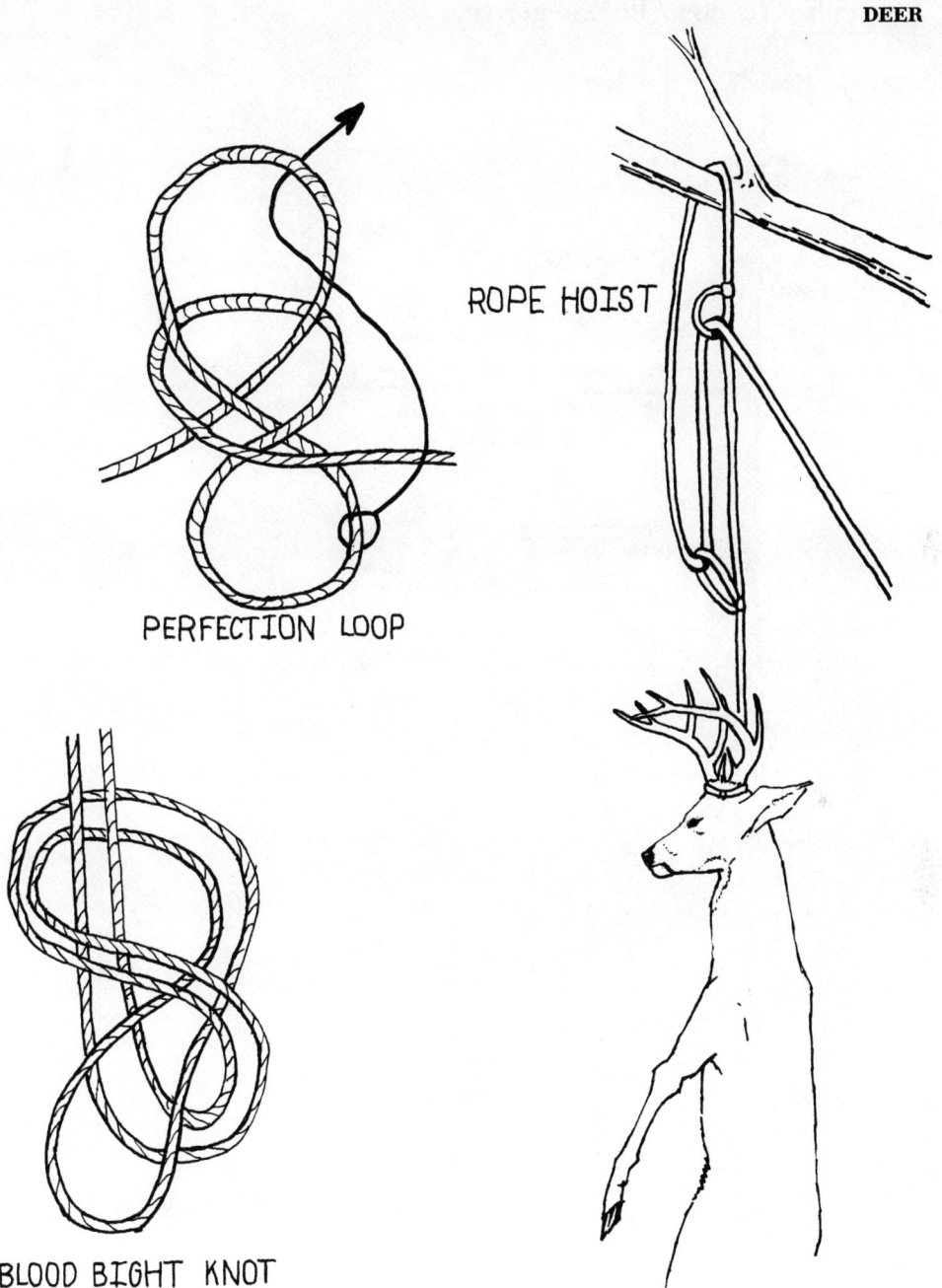

ROPE HOIST

PERFECTION LOOP

BLOOD BIGHT KNOT

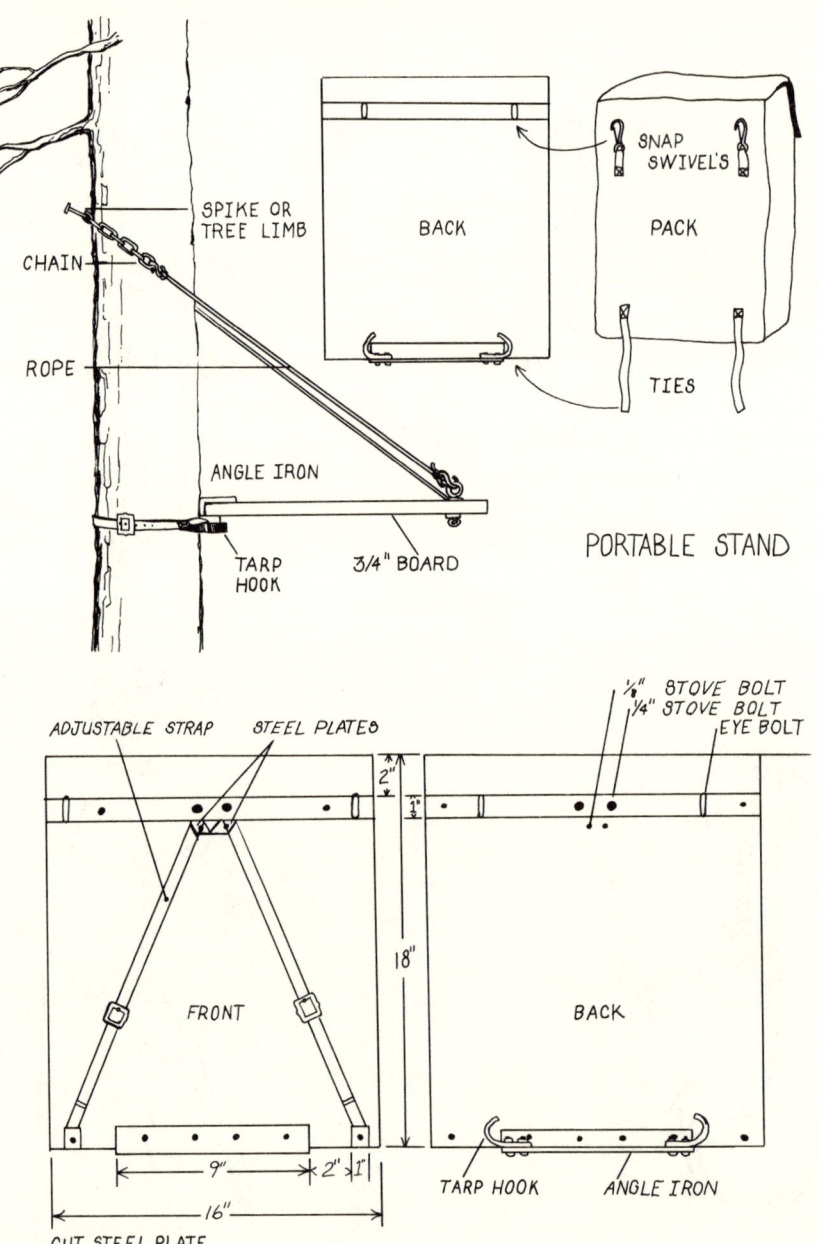

SPIKE OR
TREE LIMB

CHAIN

ROPE

ANGLE IRON

TARP
HOOK

3/4" BOARD

BACK

SNAP
SWIVEL'S

PACK

TIES

PORTABLE STAND

ADJUSTABLE STRAP   STEEL PLATES

⅛" STOVE BOLT
¼" STOVE BOLT
EYE BOLT

2"

1"

FRONT

18"

BACK

9"   2" 1"

16"

CUT STEEL PLATE
FOR WASHER

TARP HOOK   ANGLE IRON

buckle end being the shortest length. This is to allow flexibility if a smaller tree is chosen. The ends of the two pieces can be folded into loops and sewn or riveted.

A rope and chain are used to support the stand. Use ¼-inch 1,200-pound anchor rope with S hooks attached at both ends of the two ropes used. The ropes should be 3 feet long with slack for adjustment.

The chain rather than the rope is used to grip the upper portion of the trunk. Chains that work well for gripping bark are 3/o lock-link and 2/o twist-link machine chain.

Because of the shoulder straps, the tree stand resembles a packboard, and can function as one. You can even attach a commercial pack sack. If you want to make such a pack, buy at least a yard of orange canvas. Use heavy-duty polyester thread to sew the seams, swivel hooks, and ties for attaching pack to board. The pack can be used to carry the gear needed to erect the stand as well as any other equipment.

While the Pennsylvania Game Commission owns over a million acres, many hunters are welcome on private land such as paper-company holdings. Hunting is permitted on more than 90 percent of the 70 million acres of woodlands managed by timber companies. *(Photo courtesy Jim Bashline)*

16
BEAR

Black bears are widely distributed throughout the northern forested states, the mountain states in the East and in the West, and most of Canada and Alaska.

In a day of soaring nonresident license fees, the tab for black-bear hunting remains within reason in most states and provinces. A spring bear license in Ontario costs the nonresident only $15. A $10 export fee is required if the hunter is successful.

The black bear is an overlooked trophy throughout most of its range. It is only in recent years that hunters have come to realize the superb hunting experience these animals can provide. A black-bear pelt with head mount is an impressive trophy. The meat is palatable and considered by many to be excellent.

The average adult bear weighs 125 to 250 pounds, but you could run into one weighing 350 to 550 pounds. Although I've killed many bears with the .243 cartridge, something like the .270, 30-06, or .308 is more suitable.

Many black bears are killed ahead of dogs. The sport is limited, however, to those who own dogs or are friends or clients of someone who does. Fortunately, there are equally exciting means of hunting black bears for the individual or small party of hunters on their own. These include hunting in the early fall when bears are stuffing themselves in preparation for winter hibernation, and spring hunts that coincide with the annual spring sucker spawning run in Ontario and other provinces and states that have spring seasons. Another method is to use bait. Baiting is sometimes the only way to hunt black bears in heavily forested terrain. Check your local regulations for the legality of baiting and spring hunting.

If there was a great deal to fear from black bears, Lynn Rogers of the Department of Ecology at the University of Minnesota probably wouldn't be around. Rogers, working toward his Ph.D in ecology with a wildlife minor, is possibly the best-known black-bear expert in the United States. During a recent six-year study, he gained a wide variety of data from 756 captures of 252 individual black bears in northern Minnesota.

"I crawled into the den, put my head on the mother bear's chest, and tried to time her heartbeat," Rogers related. "All of a sudden, she raised her head and looked at me eyeball to eyeball. Her heart had been going at about eight beats a minute, but it was doing 250 by the time I got out of there—and so was mine!"

Contrary to old myths, the bear doesn't snarl fiercely and display an awesome array of teeth, Rogers says. When it's mad, it slaps its front feet down hard while running and "huffs and puffs." But Rogers maintains that it will usually stop 15 to 20 feet away, turn around, and run in the opposite direction. He admits there are exceptions.

In the spring the black bear's primary food is grass, first brown and then green, the buds of aspen and birch trees, wild sarsaparilla, and other common greens, And they will catch spawning fish. Suckers are especially easy prey. Suckers spawn in shallow riffles, water only inches deep; this makes it easy for bears to catch them.

Water temperature of 55 degrees will start the sucker spawning run. In northern Ontario, suckers normally spawn around May 10 to May 15. Suckers will leave a lake via an inlet and travel upstream in the creek to spawn. Usually the run stops at the first natural barrier, such as a waterfall, and the suckers will spawn in the riffles below the falls. When no barriers are encountered the spawning may take place wherever there are shallow riffles. A natural barrier with shallow riffles below is ideal. This crowds the fish into one central location, and getting a shot at a black bear

Creeks that are hosts to spawning suckers are good bets for spring hunting.

is only a matter of positioning yourself downwind of the location during the early morning and late afternoon. If the location is fairly secluded, black bears may show up at any time.

Hunters can add to the attractiveness of the situation by scattering sucker carcasses on shore. The smell will lure bears from a distance.

Look for bear tracks and droppings along and near a creek to determine if bears are in the area. Sometimes a hotspot can be found where suckers are forced to swim through a narrow opening such as a break in a beaver dam. Look for bear tracks plastered in the mud along the top of the dam. A beaver dam may also be used as a regular crossing by bears traveling from one area to another. Also watch grassy clearings near streams, as bears will still feel the need to eat grass and other greens.

Black-bear hunting is probably most fascinating in the early fall. Often nocturnal, the black bear becomes very active during daylight hours in late August and early September in the northern coniferous zones of the United States and Canada. This splurge of eating may come a little later in more southerly climes. It is brought on by the need to fatten up for winter hibernation.

It is not uncommon for a bear to put in a full day of feeding in a blueberry patch, wild-plum thicket, or oak grove, pausing only for an occasional nap. This the bear will do right on the spot. Should you be stalking a bear that suddenly lies down for a nap, your best recourse is to wait until the bear wakes, is again on its feet, and in view for a shot rather than risk approaching closer or making a noise to alert the bear. A running bear makes a difficult target.

As the season progresses, wild fruit and nuts grow scarce and the bears less active. Snow and cold have nothing to do with a bear's hibernating except they are the factors climaxing the bear's food supply. Bear dens are not as cozy as legend would have it—a poor den can be 34 degrees below zero inside. A bear is so well protected against cold, however, that it could curl up outside and sleep under a heavy insulating blanket of snow.

Getting a fall black bear in your rifle sights depends largely on finding a concentration of fresh sign, selecting a vantage point downwind, and then waiting it out. Tracks and droppings are more meaningful when they accompany signs of feeding; broken limbs of oak, wild plum, and apple trees; bushes of blueberry, raspberry, cranberry, and currant that are flattened or interspersed with trails. Bears prefer berries that grow in clusters making for easy picking and quick mouthfuls. In bountiful years the blueberry crop will last into September, and the opening of bear season. Bears will travel long distances from their home range to feed on blueberries, and in some areas they are attracted by acorn-bearing oaks.

Tracks are often the most difficult sign to find. The broad, padded foot of the black bear leaves little indentation except in mud and sand. The front footprint shows most clearly. If you can find a clear hind footprint, here are some observations you can make based on the combined measurement of the widest and longest part of the pad: less than 6 inches a cub, over 10 inches an adult male. In a Washington State study, no female collected had a combined length-plus-width pad value equal to 10 inches, whereas 86 percent of the males four years old or older had values of at least 10 inches.

Using bait, where legal, is probably one of the easiest ways for the novice to kill a bear. It can also be time-consuming and frustrating.

Bait is generally set out in several locations a week or so before the season opens. Bait can simply be placed at random, but faster results are obtained when it's placed near fresh bear tracks, trails, and droppings. When bait is taken at a location, more bait is put out to keep the bear coming to this easy meal. What is frustrating is having the bear eat all of the bait at one feeding. When this occurs, the bear may not return.

If bait remains after the bear has fed, you can be assured that the bear will return the next night. More bait should be put out at this time to ensure that the supply does not run out. Once the bear is coming regularly, the hunter is almost sure of getting a shot.

Almost any kind of meat scrap, fat, and bone available at butcher shops will attract bear. It need not be spoiled as many seem to believe. The only advantage of spoiled bait is that it can be detected from a greater distance.

There are a couple of ways to ensure that a bear does not eat all of your bait and thereby lose interest. One way is to have the bait in a tightly covered oil drum. Cut a hole in the side of the drum just large enough for the bear to insert its paw. This will slow down its eating and make the bait last for quite a while. Another method is to drill several holes in a log and fill them with honey or similar sweet liquid. Bears have a sweet tooth and will work on the log for many nights. Honey and bacon are two items that are dessert to a bear.

Best location for bait is a *small* forest clearing. Place the bait near one edge of the clearing. Bears are shy and will approach the bait from the cover behind. Station yourself across the clearing from the bear and downwind. Best time to watch bait is during the last three hours of the day.

Bears killed in spring or fall taste equally good. Bear roast is especially savory. Cook in a covered pan, nestling the roast in a bed of celery leaves, fresh parsley, chopped onion, and carrot; season with salt, pepper, and marjoram. Cooked at 300 degrees for five hours, you can cut it with a fork. The flavor hovers between beef and rendered pork. Cold, it makes a great sandwich.

Some hunters worry unduly about trichinosis, the man-originated disease contracted by hogs or bears when they eat man's leftovers. It is preventable by thoroughly cooking, and if contracted is a treatable disease. Curiously, the danger of trichinosis is very low in heavily hunted areas, because there is a good chance a bear so afflicted will be killed by a hunter and the disease not spread. In a wilderness area the bear may die a natural death and as many as a dozen other bears will feed on the carcass and contract the disease.

Studies show that black-bear cubs may be self-sufficient when as young as 5½ months. Cubs of a sow bear killed in September will survive and go into hibernation that winter. *Do not* kill the cubs because of the mistaken notion that they will not survive.

Most hunters will consider having a bear pelt mounted if the animal is an outstanding trophy. A black bear with a summer coat or one only partially in the stage of developing or shedding a prime coat cannot be successfully tanned. The individual hairs will fall out during the tanning process. So timing is important in planning a fall or spring hunt.

In Minnesota, for example, a bear shot during the first week in September may not be suitable for tanning. The obvious solution is to hunt late in the season, but recent studies indicate that some bears hibernate as early as October 1 because of poor food supply. This is the exception, but lack of natural foods by that time of year curtails bear activity. Few bears are moving about by the October 21 closing. By the second week in September, most bears are sporting a fairly thick prime coat suitable for tanning. Most spring hunts, unless you hunt into the month of June, will produce bear with prime winter coats.

SKINNING A BEAR

When they get a bear hide for tanning, taxidermists prefer that the feet and head of the animal be attached to the hide. The skinning of the feet and head is a job they prefer to do themselves. They are good at it.

Here is how to handle the skinning job. First open the abdomen as you would a deer's and remove the sex organs, anus, intestines, and vital organs. That will ensure good eating.

(When hunting bears or other big game in comparatively mild weather, it also helps to sprinkle pepper inside the carcass after the animal has been field-dressed and hung in a shady spot. This helps to seal in the flavor and repel flies and other insects.)

Next make a cut in the hide from the top of the opened stomach cavity to the animal's throat. Then make a cut from each hind foot pad to the anus area. Make a cut also from the base of the front foot pads to the center cut, following the contours of the leg. Then start working the hide away from the carcass, using your knife to cut away tissue. Once the hide is worked loose on a leg, cut through the leg bone near the foot, being careful not to cut the hide. This leaves the foot attached to the hide. Once the hide is worked loose down to the bear's head, sever the head and leave it attached to hide.

If you cannot get to a taxidermist or freeze the hide, and the weather is warm, salt the flesh side of the hide liberally. Use two or three pounds of salt. Dump it into the ears as well. Then roll the hide into a ball with the fur side out, and keep it in a cool, shaded spot.

If you do not care to go to the expense of having the hide tanned and mounted, consider selling it to a taxidermist. It will help defray the cost of the hunting trip.

17
BUTCHERING

Butchering your own deer not only saves money, it ensures that you get the meat from the deer you shot. It is not uncommon for butchers to toss the scrap cuts from many deer into one pile and then make equal amounts of hamburger for each customer from the pile. Some of those deer may not have been as carefuly handled in the field as was yours. And once you can handle the butchering of a deer, you can as easily handle a moose, an elk, and even a bear.

Good butchering begins in the field. Chapter 15 gives the details of handling a deer or similar animal in the field.

Once you have the deer home, it should be hung in a shed, garage, or other sheltered and shaded enclosure. If the weather is unseasonably warm, it is wise to start butchering at the first opportunity. In colder weather the meat can hang for a week or more to "age." Farmers who butcher a steer in midwinter commonly hang the carcass for a week or so, keeping a small fire going in a stove to prevent the meat from freezing. It is merely necessary to keep the temperature above the freezing point. Others believe that alternate freezing and thawing actually help to age the meat.

It should be pointed out that many experienced deer hunters who do their own butchering find no difference between meat that has been butchered immediately and meat that has been allowed to age. I've often eaten fresh-killed deer in camp and enjoyed it thoroughly. So have many others.

The first step in butchering is to skin the deer, and, like every step of the butchering process, this is best done with a sharp knife. With the deer hanging by its head, make a cut from the opened stomach cavity to the throat. At the top of this cut, continue around the deer's neck until it is girdled. Make a girdling cut around each leg below the hock joint. Then make a cut across the chest from one girdled front leg to the other. Repeat with the hind legs, following the curve of the leg to the anus area. The hide can now be peeled off, starting at the neck and working downward. You will have to cut away clinging tissue with a knife.

Do not throw away the hide. You can sell it to a raw-fur buyer, have it tanned at a commercial tannery and then sell it for a profit to someone who works in leather, have it tanned and then make mittens, gloves, and other items yourself, or preserve the hide with the hair on as a wall ornament. The Home Tanning Kit put out by Lawrence of Portland, Ore., costs $6 and contains enough chemicals and tanning compound for two average-size hides. The kit includes four pages of instructions, which are easy to follow. Deer-hide rugs are only for show, as the hair is brittle and will break if walked on.

The gamy flavor associated with venison originates primarily in the muscle sheaths or membranes. The membranes and fat seem to deteriorate after a short time in the freezer, and that can spoil the meat. Experienced venison chasers also believe that the bone gives a gamy flavor to the meat. By deboning most of the venison and removing every bit of fat and membrane, you can eliminate gamy flavor and save on freezer space as well.

Start by having a large table or clean workbench. A 4 × 8-foot panel of clean plywood can be placed over an otherwise scruffy workbench and provide a clean working surface.

Start by separating the hindquarters by splitting the backbone lengthwise with a crosscut saw. Stop the cut at the forward end of the hips (between 3 and 4 in the diagram).

Remove one haunch (hind leg) by cutting with a knife along the forward curve of the haunch to the backbone (between 3 and 4 in the diagram). Saw through the backbone. This should be at the same point where you

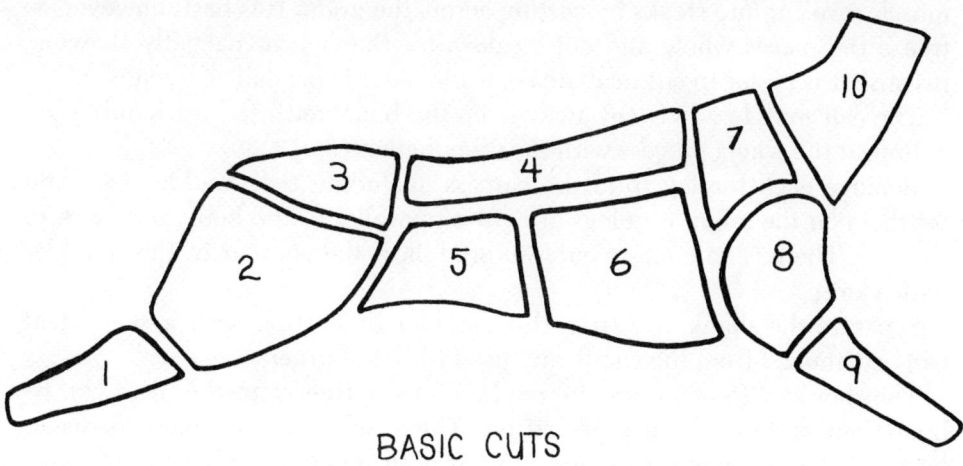

BASIC CUTS

stopped the lengthwise cut through the backbone. Remove the other haunch in the same manner.

Place one haunch on the table, with the inside of the leg down. Use a knife to cut rump (3) away from thigh. The cut should separate the ball-and-socket joint. Feel for this joint with your fingers. Turn the haunch over to complete this cut. Rump roast (3) is ready for the freezer after wrapping in freezer wrap.

The haunch (2) is deboned by separating the various layers of muscle. This is done by first stripping away outside membranes. With the inside of the leg up, use a knife to free the edge of the thinnest muscle. Then pull it off the rest of the way with your hands. Now separate major muscles of the haunch by pulling them apart with your hands. It is easier than cutting. Muscles will separate easily and expose interior membranes. Peel this away with a knife. Use a knife to cut away interior muscle that is firmly attached to the thighbone above the joint.

Go over all the cuts of meat and strip remaining membranes and fat. Some muscle sheaths can be pulled off with the fingers, while others must be peeled with a knife.

Major cuts from the haunch are ready for cooking or freezing. Thigh muscles are cut into steaks by cutting across the grain. It is best, however, to freeze the pieces whole and cut steaks after thawing or partially thawing, because it is easier to cut neat steaks if the meat is partially frozen.

The calf muscle (1) is cut away from the bone and used for hamburger. Repeat the whole process with the other haunch.

Remove each foreleg from the carcass, including the shoulder (8), and set them on the table. Forelegs are cut off parallel to the body and close to the ribs. There is no bone to cut. Simply follow the contour of the shoulder with a knife.

Separate the shank (9) from the shoulder by cutting with a saw. Meat can be trimmed from the shank and used for hamburger.

The shoulder (8) can now be readied for the freezer or the meat can be boned out and membranes peeled off. This results in a flat piece of meat, best utilized by rolling it up and tying it with butcher's twine as pot roast.

With the remainder of the carcass on the table, cut two long strips of meat from along the backstrap (4). Cut a strip from each side of the backbone. Try to cut to the bone on the first pass to avoid creating scraps. This is choice meat. Strip the membrane from the backstraps by pulling the membrane against a knife laid flat on the table. Backstraps are cut into small but tasty steaks. Try these little steaks for breakfast with eggs and hash-browns.

Flank meat (5) is cut away on both sides. It can be broiled if it's from a young and tender deer. Otherwise, add it to the hamburger meat.

Meat from the neck (10) can be cut free and used for hamburger.

Meat on the outside of the rib cage (6) is cut away with a shaving motion of knife. Also cut away meat from between the ribs. This is used for hamburger. Some prefer to omit this step and cut the ribs into short lengths for barbecue.

A butcher who deals with wild game will grind all the scraps into hamburger for a nominal fee. To ensure having good hamburger, remove every bit of fat (tallow) that you can. This is time-consuming but worthwhile.

Other big-game animals can be handled in the same way, although you may need a helping hand with elk or moose. Black bear is also handled the same. But a word of warning: first let a bear carcass hang for a couple of days after skinning. The fat on bear is slippery and messy right after skinning, but in a day or two will dry and be easier to handle. Some folks like to boil down the bear fat and make shortening.

18
WINTER RABBIT HUNTING

Hunters are missing half the hunting time allotted to them if they think the season is over with the close of deer hunting. Cottontails, snowshoes, and jackrabbits furnish several more months of action. In many states grouse, pheasants, and squirrels remain open into the winter months. For some, winter predator hunting, covered in the next chapter, is the high point of the season.

Lengthy, expensive trips are rarely undertaken when the quarry sought is one of the rabbits or hares. Rabbits are very adaptable, especially the common eastern cottontail. It can find shelter in an overgrown city dump almost as well as in brushy woods areas.

Jackrabbits survive in wide-open farm fields adjacent to suburban housing developments.

Snowshoe hares are ignored by hunters throughout most of their range, and the hunting goes begging.

Cottontails, and this includes the eastern cottontail, the mountain cottontail, the New England cottontail, the desert cottontail, the brush rabbit, the marsh rabbit, the swamp rabbit, and the pygmy rabbit, are America's number-one small-game animal. And it is not hard to understand why. They are

Warm winter boots are made even warmer with extra sole inserts cut from old carpeting.

available to hunters in every state. And they are probably the finest eating of small game.

Shotguns are good for taking cottontails on the run. Use low-base loads in No. 6 or 7½ shot. The .22 rimfire rifle is a good choice for stalking cottontails on the sit, using the Long Rifle cartridge.

You should take note whenever you see a woodlot that shows signs that a landowner has been cutting trees or brush. A common practice is to heap the excess branch tips into piles, usually for burning at a later date. Fresh brush piles are hotspots for cottontails. They feed on the tender branch tips and buds, and find refuge under the piles.

Cottontails can be routed from brush piles by getting on top and jumping up and down. You'll need a shotgun because the shots will be at fast-stepping bunnies. Often a cottontail will scoot under another pile before you have a chance to shoot. And if that pile contains heavy stumps or branches, the cottontail will live for another day. You can make your own brush piles if you own woodland.

Sometimes long rows of brush piles will be found where whole woodlots have been cut or bulldozed. Such piles will usually contain too many stumps and heavy branches to be considered for routing cottontails. But on warm, sunny winter days the bunnies will sit along the outer edges of the piles to soak in the winter sun. This makes them a target for the hunter armed with a .22 rimfire rifle. Sunny winter days are generally the best for hunting cottontails by any method. Windy, bitterly cold days are the worst.

Look for cottontails in weed-choked ditches, brushy fencerows, hedges, or otherwise heavy cover adjacent to openings. They love edges.

If you locate a cottontail's form (bed) in the snow, you have a good chance of locating the bunny. If there is no snow, look for an oval depression in the weeds and grass. Chances are the cottontail is sitting nearby in another form, usually within 40 yards. Mark the empty form with your cap or handkerchief by hanging it from a high branch, then start working in small circles from the marker. In a way the small circular routes you take will resemble the outline of petals on a flower, with the marker being the center. Forms are often found by walking a zigzag course along heavily used rabbit trails.

In some areas, raising beagle hounds and chasing cottontails is a way of life. Cottontails are ideal for chasing with hounds because they tend to circle. You should find an elevated view near where the cottontail was first flushed and wait for it to circle back. When they cannot find a stump or windfall to stand on, some hunters will improvise, using a stepladder kept handy in the car trunk. If there is snow, you can see where hound and quarry have passed through an opening and wait there. Over the years, certain escape routes used by the rabbits will become evident. Favorite crossings become fabled hotspots.

Jackrabbits are unsurpassed as targets for the hunter. Because of the odd shape, size, and location of the jackrabbit's eyes, it can see to the front, side, and behind at the same time. It has acute hearing and a keen sense of smell. When pushed, it can leap from 15 to 20 feet and hit 35 miles an hour.

There are three subspecies of jackrabbits—the whitetail, blacktail, and antelope. The whitetail variety is found throughout southern British Columbia, Alberta, Saskatchewan, and Manitoba into Wisconsin and west to Washington, and south to New Mexico. In the winter, in their northern range, they develop a white winter coat. The tail is always white. Farther south they replace their normal summer brown with pale gray. Ears are tipped with black.

The most abundant jackrabbit is the blacktail. It is common throughout the West and Southwest, but is absent across most of the northern states and Canada. The blacktail has a black streak on the top of its tail. Its ears are black-tipped and considerably larger than those of the whitetail jack rabbit. The blacktail is grayish-brown and weighs 3 to 7 pounds.

The third variety of jackrabbit is the antelope jackrabbit. It has huge ears, up to 9 inches from skull to tip, and a very small head. The ears lack the black tip found on those of the whitetail and blacktail. Its general coloration is gray with a whitish cast along the sides and hips. The antelope jackrabbit makes its home in Mexico but its range extends into Arizona.

If you're using a shotgun, high-base loads in No. 2 and No. 4 shot are good choices in 12 gauge with a full-choke barrel. Others prefer rifles chambered for the hot centerfire .22s—the .22-.250, .222, .223, etc. In the really wide-open spaces of the West, hunters can use the .243, 6mm, .25-06, and even the heavier .30-06 and .270. There is no better practice for the big-game hunter than to use his heavy artillery on jacks.

Still others prefer to use the .22 rimfire rifle when hunting jacks because it is cheap to shoot. In some areas it is not unusual to burn up 100 rounds a day.

All jacks are nocturnal. The only daylight feeding they do is in early morning and late afternoon. Usually you must jump them from their beds. Whitetails prefer large open-type farms with big stubble fields. Winter-wheat fields are good. Walk along the edges of cover next to stubble fields and hunt brushy benches or draws near the fields.

Winter is a favorite time for hunting jacks. Tracks in the snow quickly indicate if a section is worth hunting. If the snow is not deep, jacks will bed in the furrows of plowed fields. Hunters should space themselves 50 to 100 yards apart to work a plowed field. It appears the rougher the field and the deeper the furrows, the more attractive it is to jacks.

As the snow deepens, a jack will burrow a short tunnel into the snow for a bed. Sometimes you can get very close before it will run, but once a jack has been flushed a few times and shot at it is educated and may start running while you are still 150 yards away.

Jacks will seek more sheltered bedding sites after the plowed fields fill with snow. Look for them in old gravel pits and on the leeward side of snow fences, farm machinery that has been left in the field, bushes, and brushy fencelines. Small willow swamps are good bedding sites.

Blacktails are usually found in gently rolling sagebrush country, open enough to allow plenty of banging away. During the day the jacks usually sit in, or on, the edge of draws. Walk along and keep a sharp eye out 50 to 60 yards ahead, as they often try to sneak out.

A good time to find the antelope jackrabbit is after a good rain. The jacks leave their soaked brush or grass hideouts and seek open sunny spots.

Do not underestimate the eating qualities of a young jackrabbit. Fillet the meat from the bone, cut it into bite-size pieces, and simmer it before finally browning the meat.

Snowshoe hares are found throughout Canada and Alaska and all across the northern tier of states and extend southward into the Appalachian Mountains, Rocky Mountains, and California high country.

The snowshoe is white in winter, dark brown in summer. It is bigger than most cottontails and will weigh from 2 to 4 pounds. Its large hind feet enable it to move about in deep snow.

The snowshoe is not nearly as adaptable as the cottontail and will have nothing to do with such civilized fare as may be found in the typical garden. Twig ends and buds are the two main foodstuffs of snowshoes in winter. When these items grow scarce they will eat a great deal of bark from the trunks of aspen and alder saplings.

Snowshoes are undoubtedly the least clever of the rabbits and hares. What they lack in brainpower is made up for by the difficulty in seeing them. Look for them in thickets of second-growth aspen resulting from logging or fire. These are choice locations if there is a minimum of slashings. and windfalls. The snowshoe will run off under a protective screen of criss-crossing logs and slashings, and you won't see it if the cover is too heavy.

The .22 rimfire is ideal for stalking snowshoes in their beds. Snowshoes avoid the hunter by remaining motionless while he walks by or by running out ahead of him. You can spot the snowshoe that is sitting tight by zig-zagging through cover that shows a heavy concentration of tracks and drop-pings. Spotting a motionless snowshoe is often a matter of looking from the right angle.

The snowshoes that cause problems are those that run out ahead of you unseen. If the snow conditions are noisy, as when there is a crust on the sur-face, most of the snowshoes will be running out ahead of you.

When approaching a heavy concentration of sign such as may be found around a windfall, always look beyond this cover. It is very easy to flush snowshoes from heavy cover, but their flight is swift and silent. Always look as far ahead as you can. At the sight or sound of an approaching hunter, the snowshoe will leave its bed but often will run only a few feet and stop. That is your chance. If you fail to see this first short run, the snowshoe will probably escape.

Be selective in choosing hunting sites. Move as quietly as possible through cover and keep looking as far ahead as you can. Watch for movement and watch for the snowshoe's telltale black eye.

MAKING SNOWSHOES FOR WINTER HUNTING

The Ojibwa-style snowshoe in its beginning stages in the illustration is the best style for the do-it-yourselfer. The one great advantage of the Ojibwa style, which may also be constructed without an upturn at the front, is that its pointed front knifes through deep snow and does not pile up with snow. Because there is a great deal of detail involved in making snowshoes —that is, snowshoes of any quality—you'd be wise to read the detailed instructions in *The Snowshoe Book*, by William Osgood and Leslie J. Hurley.

OJIBWA SNOWSHOE JIG

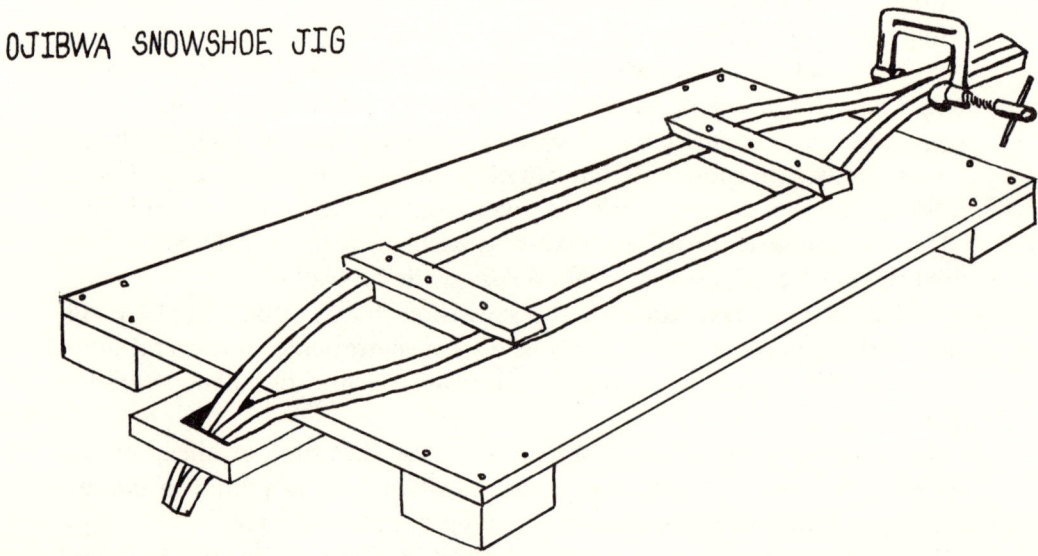

RUBBER SNOWSHOE HARNESS →
ATTACHED WITH LEATHER THONGS

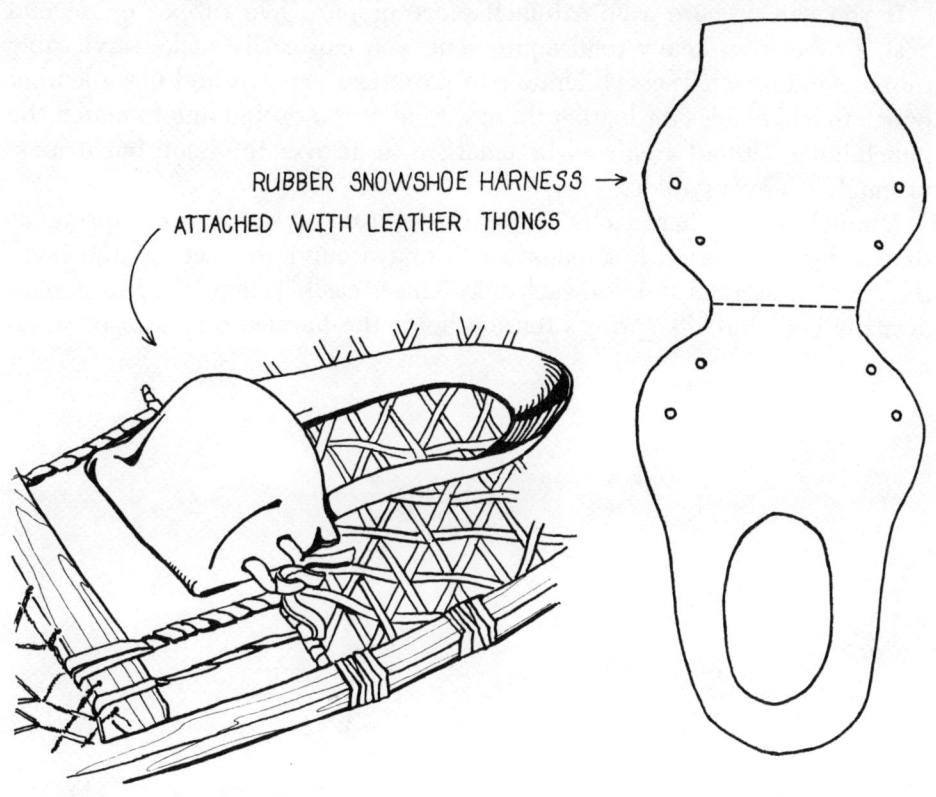

QUICK-RELEASE
SCREEN DOOR SPRING

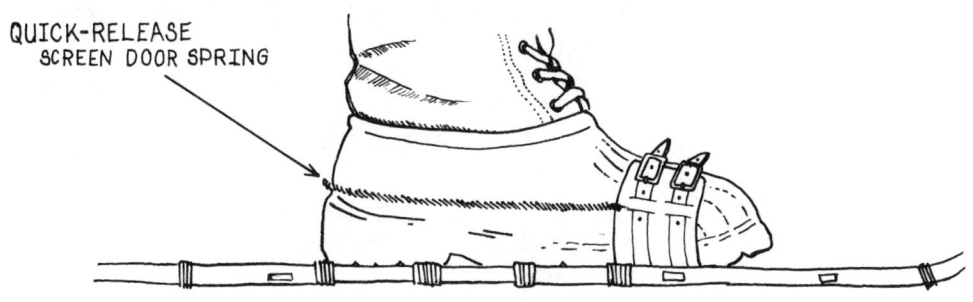

177

If you can procure a 20×10-inch piece of pure live rubber or, second best, a tube from heavy road equipment, you can easily make serviceable rubber snowshoe harnesses. Draw two patterns as shown and use a leather punch to make holes for leather thongs. Fold at the dotted line to match the punch holes. Cutout area may be enlarged to fit over the boot, but it must fit snugly over your ankle.

A quick-release harness is easily made from a screen-door spring as shown. Simply stretch a screen-door spring around the heel of the boot, then hook it into the strap on each side. This is easily removed by stretching over the heel, but the spring's tension holds the harness on the boot when in place.

19
WINTER PREDATOR HUNTING

With today's fur prices it is possible to come home from a winter predator hunt money ahead. Coyote, fox, and bobcat pelts are bringing top dollar. This is quite a bonus when you consider that winter predator hunting is fascinating anyhow. However, because of the value of pelts, many more hunters and trappers are pursuing these animals; the game has grown both scarce and wary. When predator numbers are low, only the most trapwise and hunter-wise of their numbers survive. Successfully stalking and killing such a predator calls for the utmost in hunting and shooting skill, and sometimes requires a great deal of stamina on the part of the hunter.

FOXES AND COYOTES

The red fox is about the size of a small dog. The fur is reddish above, white underneath, with blackish legs and feet. Ears are pointed and stand erect. The tail is full and tipped with white. The silver, cross, black, and others are color phases of the red coat and have the same characteristics.

The red fox is the most widespread of the foxes. It is found throughout most of North America with the exception of the extreme Southeast and Southwest and the Plains states.

The red fox can be hunted with the .22 rimfire, but generally something larger is recommended. Shots at foxes are often long, and one of the hot .22 centerfires is about right. Hunters take them with even larger calibers such as the .30-06 or .270 where they can be used safely. The .22 Winchester Magnum Rimfire (.22 WMR) or the Remington 5mm Rimfire Magnum can be used in settled areas. Using either of these would require accurate shooting, because the red fox is very tough; a poorly placed shot, even with one of the centerfires, will only wound. If you use a shotgun, high-base 12-gauge magnum loads in No. 2 shot with a full-choke barrel is about right.

Stalking red foxes as they nap on sheltered hillsides is one of the most interesting and challenging ways to hunt them. This is best suited to fairly open country with gently rolling hills. Typically, such terrain is farming country with scattered woodlots and swamps that edge upon cultivated fields. By midwinter the fields and pastures are shrouded in snow and the napping red fox becomes visible to the experienced hunter who uses binoculars to spot them on the leeward side of hills, log piles, fenceline snowdrifts, haystacks, and den entrances.

Some believe that foxes always lie sheltered from the winter wind because it is warmer; others believe the wind interferes with the animals acute hearing. Whatever the reason, or reasons, always expect the red fox to lie out of the wind.

Large, roadless sections of farm country are always prime places to look for foxes—say, a mile wide by 3 miles long. You should first drive completely around the section looking for fox tracks entering and exiting the area if it is new to you. You should also watch for foxes. It is not uncommon to sight a fox napping from the roadside. Some hunters mount powerful spotting scopes on the edge of the car window to aid in spotting foxes. But the real sport lies in walking in on foot or on snowshoes and meeting the fox on more equal terms.

You should walk into the wind when possible. As you near the crest of one hill your attention should be riveted on the next. You'll need to stop frequently and use your binoculars or rifle scope. The red fox will lie curled up, as will other members of the canine family, with the tip of its tail warming the tip of its nose. This furry ball will appear about a foot in diameter and have a soft outline. Rocks and clods of frozen dirt have hard, clearly defined outlines. Watch for the fox's pointed ears.

If you are alert you will see the fox before the fox sees you. It is then a matter of ducking out of sight and moving forward in a crouch, then crawling on hands and knees, and finally squirming ahead on your stomach until you can see the fox and shoot at it from the steady prone position. If the fox is lying at great range, you will have to plan a longer stalk, one that will bring you within range of the fox without alerting it.

Foxes are light sleepers. You'll rarely need to wait more than 10 minutes before one raises its head for a look at the surrounding terrain. You're home free once you're lying within range of the fox, because even though the fox looks your way it will see so little of you it won't become alarmed. Lie quietly for a minute or two to catch your breath. Then place the scope cross hairs where they will do the most good and squeeze off a shot. Remember that the fox gives off body heat and will sink a little way into snow. The most common reason for missing is shooting too high; the bullet whistles through the thick and fluffed fur on the fox's back.

With the advent of the snowmobile on the winter scene, foxes are less inclined to lie in the open. Often they prefer the thick cattails of a swamp, or they will lie in high grass and swale. In such cases your first sight of the fox will be a running view as the fox seeks escape. If you miss the running shot, you can take up the fox's track in the snow. This time the fox may bed down where you can see it.

The most important thing in open-country fox hunting is to be constantly looking ahead. Foxes are normally nocturnal, but it is not unusual to see one up and about during midday. A snowfall during midday will cause a fox to leave its bed and begin hunting, possibly because the conditions are favorable for catching mice and rabbits. Mating urges during January and February will cause foxes to move about during midday. They seem especially prone to daylight activity on warm and sunny days.

Another method that will take foxes, and coyotes and bobcats as well, is the judicious use of a predator call. Most are designed to imitate the cry of a rabbit in distress. Others are designed to imitate a bird in distress. Frank Martin of Lewistown, Mont., is able to call foxes and coyotes by squeaking through the fingers of his hand. Hunters have employed rubber mice, dolls, and other toys that emit squeals or squeaks when squeezed. These may sound like mice, birds, or rabbits to a hungry predator.

The dying-rabbit call is still the winter standby, and imitating it on a predator call is not that difficult, especially if a tape or record is purchased with the call. A little practice is all that is necessary, since the distress cry of a rabbit or hare will vary with the animal.

The difficult part is getting into position where your quarry will not see or hear you. Camouflage clothing is a must. A pair of coveralls dyed white is a good start for hunting in snow. Top off with white cap and mittens. White masking tape can be wrapped around a rifle and scope. You can fashion a temporary arrangement with an old white sheet. Simply cut a hole for your head in the center of the sheet and wear it as you would a poncho.

Tracks in the snow give graphic evidence of the presence of foxes, coyotes, or bobcats. Once you have in mind a potential calling site you should approach it with the utmost caution. Do not slam your car door. Ease it closed gently. Use gullies, heavy cover, anything possible to reach the calling site undetected.

In the case of red foxes, you'll get best results by calling from a vantage point where you can see in all directions. Foxes will come more readily to a call if the country is open and they too can see in all directions. Because you must call from out in the open, you should lie prone. A ground sheet of heavy plastic will keep you dry. A white sheet spread over a prone hunter makes him almost invisible. Other good calling sites are the light cover found along fencelines in otherwise open fields and pastures. Calling foxes from such vantage points is far more effective than calling from a woods' edge. It is easier to conceal yourself in a woods, but such a backdrop poses a threat to the quarry.

The best calling times are early and late in the day, when the animals are most likely to be up and hunting and there is little to no wind. Night is also a good time, especially between dusk and midnight. Norman Johnson of Bloomington, Minn., often calls foxes on moonlit nights. Sometimes he will first stalk close to a fox that he hears barking. Foxes bark often at night, especially in moonlight, to claim their territory or locate their mate, which may have strayed away a mile or so. Such barking helps the hunter to pinpoint a fox's location. But it is not easy. The moonlight hunter leaves a dark shadow projected against the snow that's often visible to foxes. Sounds also carry better in the cold night, making it more difficult to stalk a fox, especially over noisy, crusty snow.

Night hunting with a light is legal in some states. A red-lens light is superior to conventional white. Tests have proved that animals are oblivious to the red beam; they cannot see red light. However, for actual shooting, it pays to switch to a more brilliant white light.

Foxes and coyotes that are within hearing of a call will come in within 10 minutes, and sometimes a lot sooner. It is not unusual to have a fox or coyote gallop straight in within a matter of three minutes. Bobcats approach more cautiously and take advantage of every bit of cover. Figure close to 30 minutes for bobcat.

Not every predator will respond to a call. An animal that is resting with a full stomach will not be inclined to leave its bed. That is why early, late, and after-dark calling are best. An animal that is up and prowling about is more likely to be lured in by the chance for an easy meal. In many places, predators are wise to calling. A fox, coyote, or bobcat that has been lured in and then seen the hunter or been shot at and missed is not likely to make the same mistake again. Foxes and coyotes have been known to turn and run in the other direction at the first blast of a predator call.

Coyotes range from the shores of the Arctic Ocean to southern Mexico, covering the continent eastward to the Mississippi. In recent years this range has spread to include all the Great Lakes region, almost all of the Midwest, and on into New York, New Hampshire, and Vermont.

In an area where coyote numbers are high and where no calling has been done within a year or so, an experienced caller may expect to call up at least one coyote every stop. Some have lured in as many as eight coyotes to one stand. That's enough to make your hair stand on end. That kind of action takes a lot of know-how and considerable respect for the animal. It means the hunter must do everything right. And even then it helps to be lucky.

The coyote's senses are superb. His nose is excellent, his hearing is razor-keen, and he is one of the few animals that can recognize the motionless shape of a man as a *man*. Camouflage is a must. And because coyotes will circle to seek your wind, a little olfactory camouflage helps. Some of the scents sold to conceal the deer hunter's odor will help, especially coyote urine, available at sporting-goods stores and trapper's supply houses. You must approach the calling site with the utmost caution. Experienced callers actually stalk their intended calling site as if they expected to find the coyote bedded down in the exact spot they plan to call.

Your first few calls should be subdued. Too loud calling at first may startle nearby coyotes. If none shows within a couple of minutes, step up the volume of your call. Even then, increase gradually to full volume for a few bleats, but don't keep it up. On a still day, a coyote can hear a normal long-range predator call for a mile.

BOBCATS

The bobcat is found throughout the entire United States, although only rarely in the Plains states, and southward into Mexico. His range overlaps that of the lynx in southern Canada and the northern United States.

The upper parts of the bobcat's body range from gray to reddish brown, becoming lighter along the lower sides. The undersides are white with dark spots and streaks, especially on the legs, chin, and throat. A full-grown tom bobcat taken in one of the northern states may weigh 30 pounds, although larger ones have been reported.

Hunting with one or two hounds is the usual way of taking bobcats. A bobcat will circle from a dog, but snap a twig or rattle a snowshoe on a windfall and you will alert the bobcat to your presence and he will stay one jump ahead of you for mile after torturous mile.

Stalk quietly when approaching a bobcat at bay. The presence of humans panics a bobcat. Even with a bobcat in a tree, it pays to move in quietly and shoot at the first good opportunity.

Probably the most important element in killing a bobcat ahead of hounds is to start the dogs on the freshest track you can find. In deep, soft snow it's possible to make a kill in under 20 minutes when the hounds have been set on a fresh track.

If you get the chance to join a winter bobcat hunt with hounds, be prepared for tough hiking or snowshoeing and bring enough warm clothing to keep you comfortable should you be posted on a stand. Snowmobiles are sometimes used to locate bobcat tracks. An old 12-gauge, single-shot is a good choice for riding a machine or snowshoeing over windfalls. High-base loads in No. 2 shot are a favorite choice in factory ammo. Rifles, except .22 rimfires, are rarely used, because they damage a bobcat's fur.

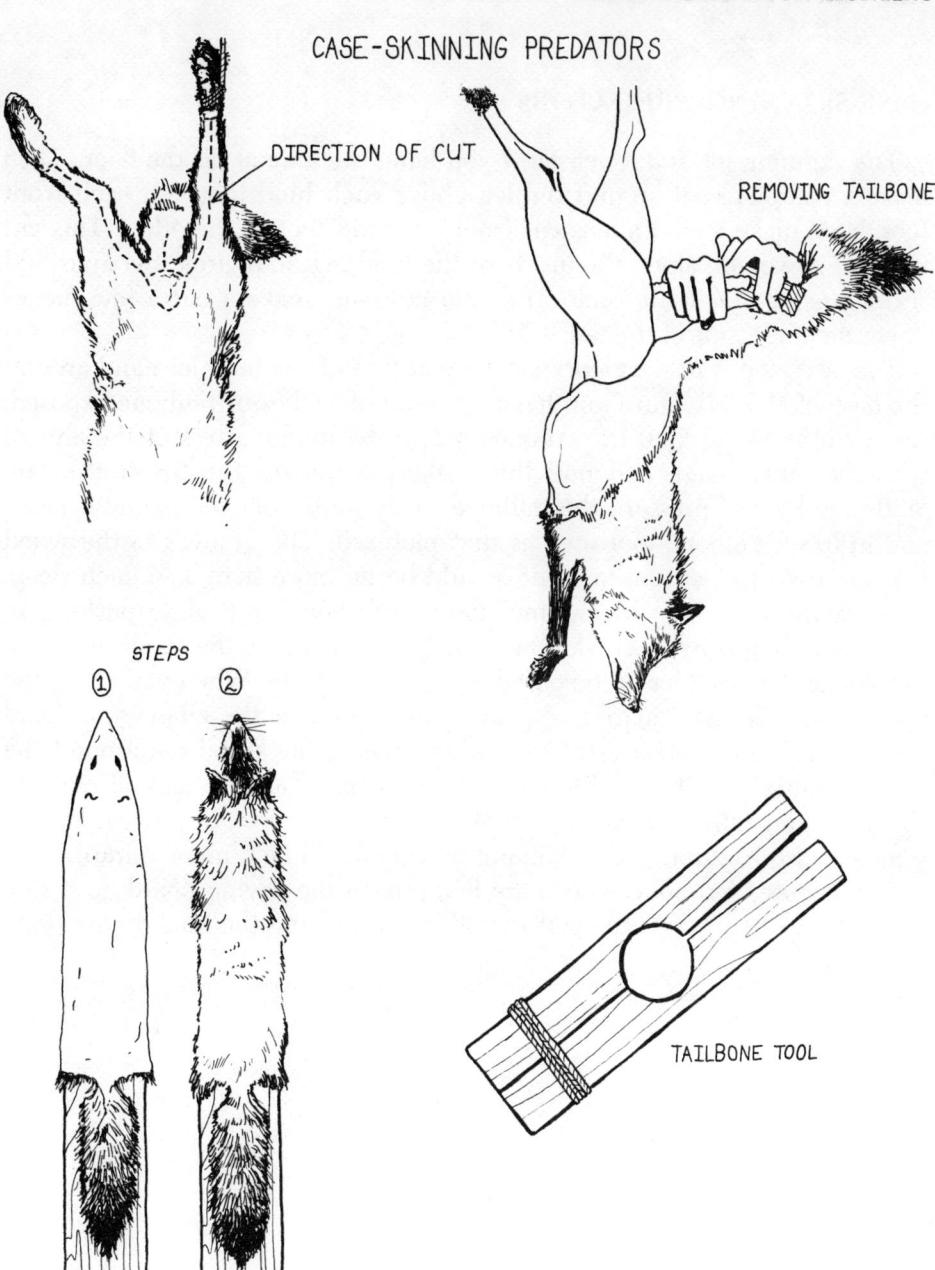

CASE-SKINNING PREDATORS

DIRECTION OF CUT

REMOVING TAILBONE

STEPS
① ②

TAILBONE TOOL

CASE-SKINNING PREDATORS

The skinning job is a lot easier if you hang the animal off the floor. Then make a complete cut around the leg above each hind foot and each front foot. Next make a continuous cut from one hind foot to the other. This cut will run down and along the inside of the hind legs and circle the anus and sex organs. To facilitate removal of the tailbone, make a cut a few inches down the underside of the tail.

The next step is to start working the pelt free of the hind legs and around the base of the tail. Once you have a couple of inches of tailbone exposed, slip a clothespin around the tailbone, grasp the hindquarters of the animal with the other hand, and pull the clothespin toward the tip of the tail. With any kind of pressure the tailbone easily pulls out. You can also make and utilize a tailbone tool such as that pictured. The grooves in the wood that are used to grip the tailbone should be no more than a ¼ inch deep.

Work the pelt loose by pulling down with one hand while pushing in with your thumb between skin and carcass. Sometimes the tissue between the skin and carcass has to be pared away with a knife. When you reach the front legs, it is just a matter of peeling the skin over the elbow joints and pulling the leg free. Use great care when freeing the skin from around the head. A knife must be used to work the skin free. Cut the ears off close to the skull and take care not to cut the eyelids and lips. If you can watch someone else go through the skinning process it will help immeasurably.

Fox, coyote, and bobcat pelts are first put on the drying board flesh side out. After 24 hours or so the pelt should be turned and the final drying done fur side out.

20
WINTER CAMPING

Late-fall and winter camping has dire connotations for many. They remember the times when bitter cold mornings made getting out of the sack nothing short of brutal. They remember malfunctioning oil and gas stoves, inadequate heaters, smoke-filled tents, and nights spent in shivering discomfort. It doesn't have to be that way.

TENTS AND STOVES

The secret of camping in comfort is a roomy tent—a tent you can actually get up and move around in—and lots of heat. Quite frankly, none of the modern gadgets such as catalytic heaters is going to do a bit of good when it comes to heating a roomy tent in winter. What you need is a dependable woodburning stove. Within minutes a sheetmetal stove with a good fire going will raise the temperature from an icy subzero reading to the upper 80s. You can sit around in shorts and T-shirt while just beyond those thin canvas walls the trees and lake ice are snapping and popping.

The tent shown in the illustration is a 10 × 13-foot model. A Coleman tent, a model no longer made, it was designed for summer use. There are many similar models available today. This is probably the largest size

A WARM INEXPENSIVE WINTER CAMP

you should use if mobility is a consideration. You can easily set up the tent alone. For two people, a 10 × 13-foot model is plenty spacious.

If you have in mind a semi-permanent camp such as a regular spot where you go once a year to hunt deer, elk, or moose you might consider an even larger model such as those used by Western outfitters, say 12 × 16 feet. These are usually available in white canvas that gives a lighter, brighter look to the interior. This style of tent normally comes without a floor or poles. You must build a framework of poles. In some Western hunting camps you can see very elaborate frameworks. Some look like partially built log cabins with canvas roofs. Because they come without a floor and other accessories, these large tents are surprisingly inexpensive. You can find them advertized in catalogs and magazines that cater to Western readers. Whatever tent you use, be sure the fabric is flame-resistant.

A good cheap stove to use is the lightweight style commonly called an airtight. These are sold in hardware stores in many of the northern states and Canada. The kind illustrated is manufactured by Jackes-Evans Manufacturing Company, 11737 Administration Road, St. Louis, Mo. 63141. This company's airtight stoves come in three sizes. The middle size is about right. This size will handle limbs up to 20 inches long. It is approximately 2 feet high with the detachable legs in place. It is 21 inches long by 15

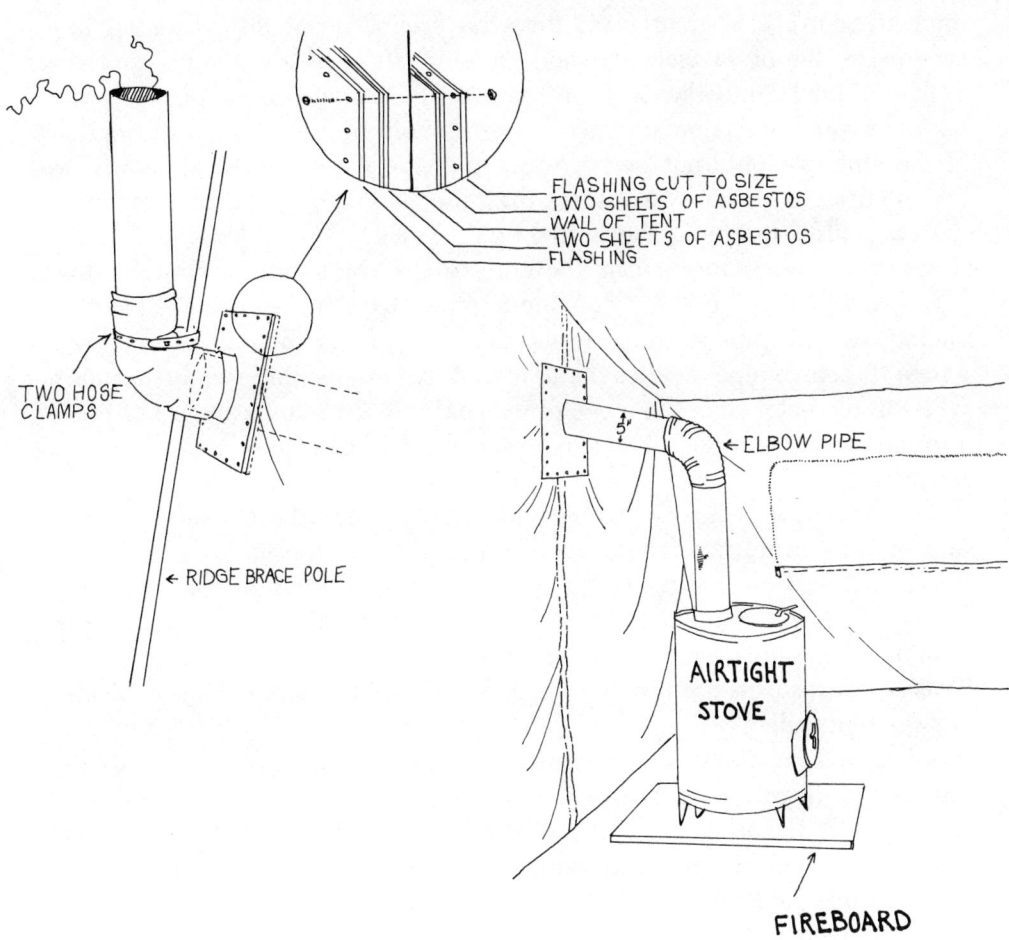

FLASHING CUT TO SIZE
TWO SHEETS OF ASBESTOS
WALL OF TENT
TWO SHEETS OF ASBESTOS
FLASHING

TWO HOSE
CLAMPS

← RIDGE BRACE POLE

← ELBOW PIPE

AIRTIGHT
STOVE

FIREBOARD

inches wide and weighs only 8 pounds. The stove cost only $11 in 1973; the price has doubtless risen.

The airtight works well because of its thin metal. It gives almost immediate radiant heat. The stove should be set on an asbestos, sheet metal covered fireboard. For greater stability the fireboard should be nailed to a cut-to-size slab of ¾-inch plywood paneling. It's not a bad idea to screw L-shaped hooks into the fireboard to hold the stove legs in place. A fireboard or something similar is necessary to avoid burning a hole in the floor of the tent. It would not be necessary with an earth floor. Fireboards are commonly sold in hardware stores that also handle woodburning stoves.

Here is just a brief guide to setting up the stove:

Set your stove in the tent on the fireboard, add a length of straight stove pipe, an elbow pipe (or two elbow pipes for increased height), then another straight pipe angling toward the back wall of the tent. At the point where this stove pipe touches the tent wall, cut an opening roughly 4 inches wider in diameter than the stove pipe. That will give you 2 inches of clearance all the way around. The stove pipe should be roughly 18 inches from the peak.

The parts used over this opening are four pieces of asbestos and two flashings of the correct size for the stove pipe. Actually the flashing on the inside is just a piece of sheet metal cut to size with a hole for the stove pipe cut in the center. The flashing used on the outside of the tent is a regular flashing. The four sheets of asbestos are cut to the same size as the flashings. Two asbestos sheets are used on each side of the tent between the flashing and the tent wall.

Asbestos is available in different thickness. If you have rolled asbestos handle it with care as it is fragile and tears easily. When making holes for screws, place the asbestos sheets between the two sheet-metal flashings and punch holes every three inches with a heavy nail or spike. About $\frac{3}{8} \times \frac{5}{8}$-inch machine bolts are used with washers and nuts. Corresponding holes must be punched through the tent canvas.

The middle-size airtight stove is designed for 6-inch pipe. This can be reduced to 5 inches, but do not make it any smaller than this; 3-inch pipe is a lot easier to handle but is a disaster with a stove of this size because the draft is inadequate.

Outside the tent, attach an elbow pipe to the flashing. To this, add a length of straight stove pipe. The top of the stove pipe should be a foot or more above the tent. By adding yet another length of stove pipe you can increase the safety margin and also increase the draft.

The outside stove pipe is clamped to the tent pole with hose clamps, available at hardware and auto-parts stores. You'll have to use two of these clamps together in order to go around the 5-inch or 6-inch stove pipe and the tent pole. Clamping the outside stove pipe to the tent pole is very important. This holds the stove pipe rigidly in place in high winds.

On summer campouts, when the stove is not in use, stuff a rag in the stovepipe opening to keep out insects and moisture.

Avoid pitching your tent in an open spot that can easily become wind-swept during a storm. Buffeting winds can cause the inner stove pipe to pull loose from the wall and fill the tent with smoke. The greatest hazard is the tent collapsing during a storm while there is a fire in the stove.

Never overload the stove with wood. Airtight stoves can suddenly get red-hot. The heat can drive you out of the tent, and it can be dangerous. Your flue should be wide open to get a fire started, then close down the draft as much as possible without extinguishing the fire. A portable fire extinguisher can add to your safety and your peace of mind.

It is wise to bring some dry wood from home. Once you have a good fire going with dry wood you can burn wet or green wood. On a prolonged campout of a week or more, dismantle the pipes at least once and knock out any creosote build-up. This is especially wise if you've been burning wet, green, or pine wood.

Old hardwood flooring makes excellent homemade tent pegs. Insert is cut from ½-inch dowel.

COTS AND SLEEPING BAGS

In a tent of the size shown there is easily room for two cots and a small table. The army-style cot is preferable to the very low cots being sold nowadays. It is high enough to sit on comfortably and extra gear can be stored under it. A cot can be made doubly warm and comfortable by topping it with 4-inch-thick foam rubber. Once you get away from having to squat on the floor, camping becomes a far more pleasant experience.

A quality goose-down sleeping bag is very desirable for winter camping but it is not always necessary. If you have a good supply of wood, you can get by with a summer sleeping bag.

A tent is almost as easy to heat with a wood stove as a cabin of equal size. There is one important difference: a cabin will hold heat for a time after the fire is out, while a tent loses its heat almost immediately. Nevertheless, even in midwinter it is possible occasionally to let the fire go out at night and sleep comfortably. You can start a new fire in minutes if you keep dry kindling ready.

Other ways to avoid discomfort are putting one summer sleeping bag into another, and wearing a wool stocking cap, wool socks, and insulated underwear when retiring. These should be clean and reserved for night wear.

The square-end sleeping bag is more comfortable and less claustrophobic than the mummy style. But in cold weather or winter camping there is a great heat loss. You can prevent this by wearing the hooded portion of a pullover sweatshirt over your head, with the body part of the sweatshirt pulled down over the outside of your sleeping bag. This does not cause a confined feeling yet it will retain body heat.

SLEEPING BAG MODIFICATION

HOODED SWEATSHIRT

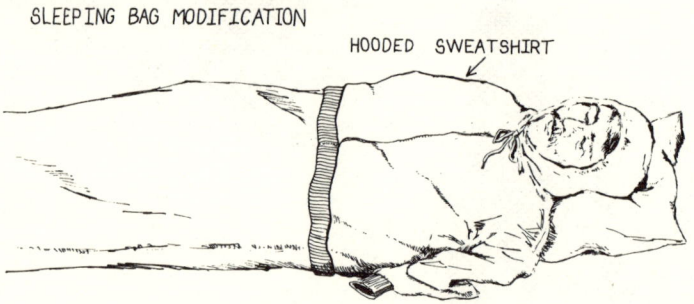

21
YOUR OWN HUNTING SHACK

Few hunters have not dreamed of having their own hunting shack, and of all the styles there are to choose from, none is quite so romantic as the log cabin. Unfortunately, few see their dream of a log cabin come true. Unless you have suitable trees in sufficient number growing near the building site, it is probably wiser, and considerably cheaper, to build a shack of plywood and lumber.

I know of one good cheap hunting shack that was built in 1975 in northern Minnesota by two hunters. The dimensions were 24 feet long by 20 feet wide. The framework was built entirely of used lumber, and the siding of 4 × 8-foot plywood paneling was also purchased used from a country lumber store. Even the nails were used and bought at a garage sale. The secondhand barrel stove that warms the shack during midwinter bobcat hunts cost only $5. Refurbished kitchen cabinets line one wall and gleam with a coat of clean white paint that was bought for pennies at another garage sale. Bunk beds are built of native cedar trees. The exterior of the shack was treated with a deep redwood stain from yet another garage sale. Total cost, less than $500. By 1977, however, the cost would have been double even with the same careful shopping, because of the sharp rise in lumber and other building materials.

This shack was built on a site leased from a logging company in northern Minnesota. The two hunters own no actual property, but the miles of logging-company property surrounding their shack are open to public hunting. Companies such as Weyerhaeuser grow timber and produce forest products—pulp, plywood, paper, etc.—and usually welcome hunters on their lands, although they're not necessarily willing to grant cabin sites.

The Algoma Central Railway, which was incorporated back in 1899 and which operates 296 miles of line between Sault Ste. Marie and Hearst in Ontario, has had a policy of leasing its land for decades. If you're interested, write to Mr. W. Leonard Oliphant, R.P.F., Manager, Lands & Forests Division, Algoma Central Railway, P. O. Box 7000, Sault Ste. Marie, Ontario P6A 5P6.

If you're set on building your own dream log cabin, here's some advice:

The best trees to use will depend on where you plan to build and what is available. Listing the most desirable first, in the eastern sections of the country use white pine, Norway pine, spruce, hemlock, tamarack, balsam, or northern white cedar. In the West use redwood, spruce, lodgepole pine, balsam, hemlock, red cedar, or tamarack. All these are evergreens, but surprisingly, a lot of log cabins have been built using aspen trees (poplar). While not the most desirable, it is a very common tree throughout much of the country and has little real commercial value except as pulp.

Ideally, trees should be cut in winter and piled on skids and left until spring when they will be easy to peel. The best place to peel logs is in a clearing where they can dry out quickly.

A good foundation will add years to your cabin's life. In soft ground you will need concrete piers or posts extending down to solid earth, below the frostline. A wood preservative should be used on these posts. The posts should be made from white cedar or locust, if available. The best and most permanent is a full cement foundation. However, if the ground is solid, you may get by with rock supports at the corners and at intervals of about 8 feet. Two flat stones can be used, one on top of the other.

Once you have laid the first round of logs and squared them up, they can be notched for floor joists. Some builders prefer to lay extra logs next to and inside the bottom ones. The floor joists can then be laid on top and nailed to these logs.

The saddle-notch type of corner is widely used. In the saddle-notch corner the logs protrude out about 6 to 8 inches from the actual corner.

Concrete piers that extend below the frostline will add years to a cabin's life.

The cuts can be made with an ax alone, although if you're working with very large-diameter logs a chain saw can be utilized to some extent.

When the walls are high enough, you can notch in the ceiling joists. Allow from 4 to 6 inches for settling when you're determining the height of the ceiling.

All log buildings should be pegged or have drift pins driven in around the areas where the door and window openings are to be cut out. If you're cutting out doors and windows and fear the logs are not pinned securely enough, you can put poles or 2 × 4s on both sides of the wall, and then wire them securely together through the cracks.

If you're using cement for chinking, allow the logs to settle completely first. It is advisable to drive nails into the cracks about every 6 inches and bend them over to help hold the cement.

Fiberglass insulation is very easy to use for chinking. It will last indefinitely without further fuss. However, small poles usually must be nailed over this chinking to hold it in place.

There is considerable work involved in building a log cabin, but the construction is relatively simple. And once you're finished there is considerable satisfaction. Calvin Rutstrum's *The Wilderness Cabin* is an excellent how-to building manual.

The location of your hunting shack is all-important. Most will build their shack in an area they have hunted in for years and know contains wildlife.

Saddle-notch corners.

Long threaded bolts with nuts on the end can be used to hold logs in place where the door and window openings are to be cut.

Starting on the roof.

The hard part is done; note construction features.

197

If you seek a new area, do not be seduced by the sigh of murmuring pines. Woodlands composed entirely of conifers such as pine, spruce, and fir are of relatively little value to wildlife. Look for acreage which is composed largely of hardwood and softwood deciduous trees—aspen-birch if possible, perhaps some maple, oak and ash—even if these trees lack some of the conifer's romantic charm.

Ideal acreage has aspen-birch stands of various ages. This is usually the result of logging or fires that have occurred at intervals over the years. Aspen is just about perfect for management purposes, and other plants associated with its growth stages provide food and cover for the greatest numbers of wildlife. This is especially true throughout the northern forested states and Canada.

There are several places you can look to for advice on where to find property most suitable for wildlife, or management for wildlife. State-employed professional foresters can be helpful. Locate the man in charge of the area in which you have an interest. Or if you have no area preferences, contact several or all of the extension foresters in outstate districts. Try to determine what the primary forest type in such areas is, and inquire about

"Stove kit" in place on a discarded 55-gallon drum. Barrel stoves have long been popular in hunting camps.

past and present logging operations, age of most forest stands, and related information.

For specific local information, county agricultural agents may have the information you seek. Your local representative of the Agricultural Stabilization and Conservation Service may also be of some help. Aerial photos are available from federal farm conservation program offices if you wish to really know the land before going out and looking at it.

You can supplement your hunting shack's wood supply with logs made of old newspapers. It really works. Roll the newspapers, beginning at the bottom, until you have a roll at least 6 inches in diameter. (A big Sunday edition or several daily issues should do the trick). To keep the log from unrolling, roll it diagonally across two sheets of newspaper, spread out completely. As you roll, tuck in each end of the covering pieces.

Your paper log will burn slowly, as surprising as that may seem. And it stretches out a wood supply. It is also a great way to get rid of that pile of old newspapers in the basement.

You can prolong the life of a barrel stove or sheet-metal stove by lining the bottom of the stove with 2 inches of dry sand. If sand is not available, dirt will do. In either case, dry the insulating material in a pan over a fire before putting it in the stove, to prevent rusting.

INDEX

ABOUT THE AUTHOR

Bob Gilsvik is an accomplished outdoorsman and a member of the Outdoor Writers Association of America. A frequent contributor to *Field & Stream, Sports Afield, Outdoor Life, American Hunter, True's Hunting Yearbook, Hunting, American Rifleman, Garcia Hunting Annual, Gun World,* and *Fur-Fish-Game,* he is also the author of *The Complete Book of Trapping* and *All Season Hunting.* He lives in Grand Rapids, Minnesota.

1. Start with the preferred side of the paper facing up.

2. Fold and then unfold your square in half diagonally.

3. Fold and then unfold your square in half on the other diagonal. Flip your paper.

4. Fold and then unfold your square in half horizontally.

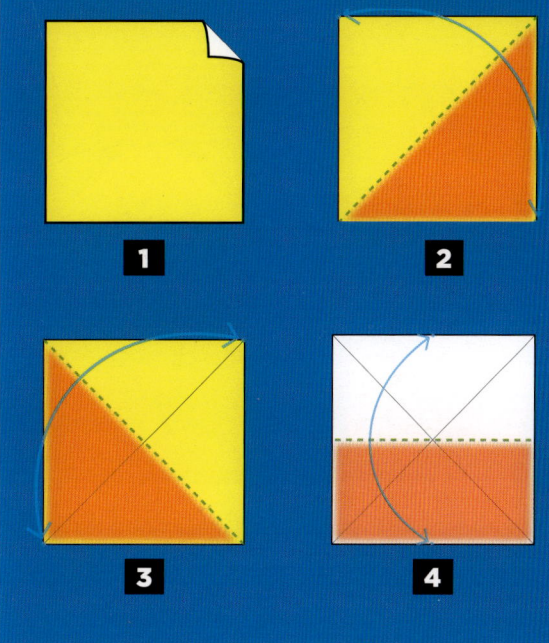

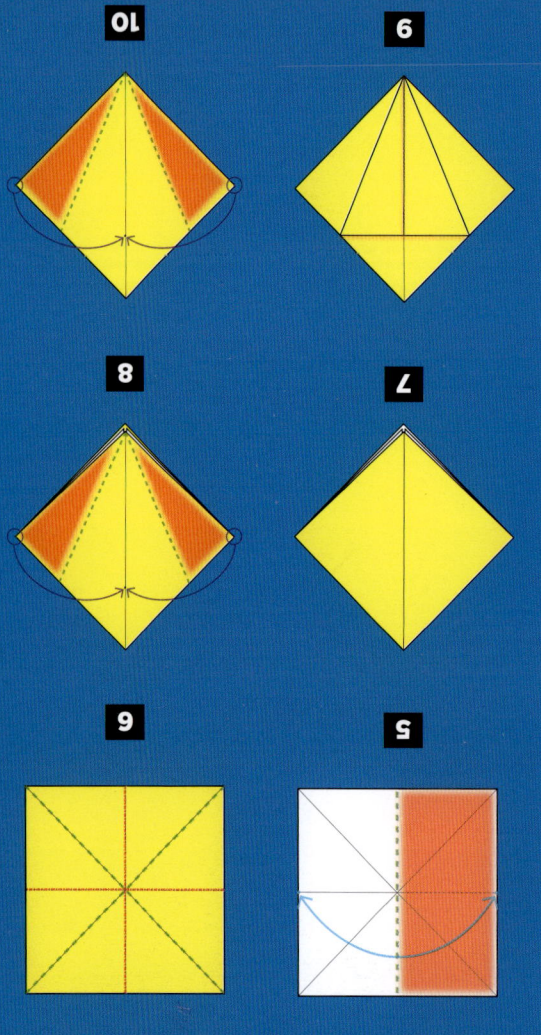

5. Fold and then unfold your square vertically. Flip your paper.

6. Your paper should look like this. The diagonals (green) are valley folds and the horizontals and verticals (red) are mountain folds.

7. Perform a collapse fold into a square so your paper looks like this.

8. With the open area of the collapsed square at the bottom, fold both the left and right corners of the top pleat of paper to the center.

9. Your model should look like this. Flip it.

10. Fold the left and right corners to the center just as you did in Step 8.

11. The model has the correct shape; however, all the loose flaps (four, two on each side) must be moved to the inside. The method for doing this is explained in Step 14.

12. When you unfold your model, the folding pattern will look like this. Make sure the preferred side of the square is facing up.

13. This diagram shows the direction of the folds at this point. Reorient your paper so it matches.

14. Reverse all the folds indicated. Just remember that all the shorter folds will become valley folds, and the goal is to tuck the sides inside the shape shown in Step 11.

15. Your square should look like this after you have reversed the folds in Step 14. The last step is to collapse the square into the basic form.

16. The completed basic form model.

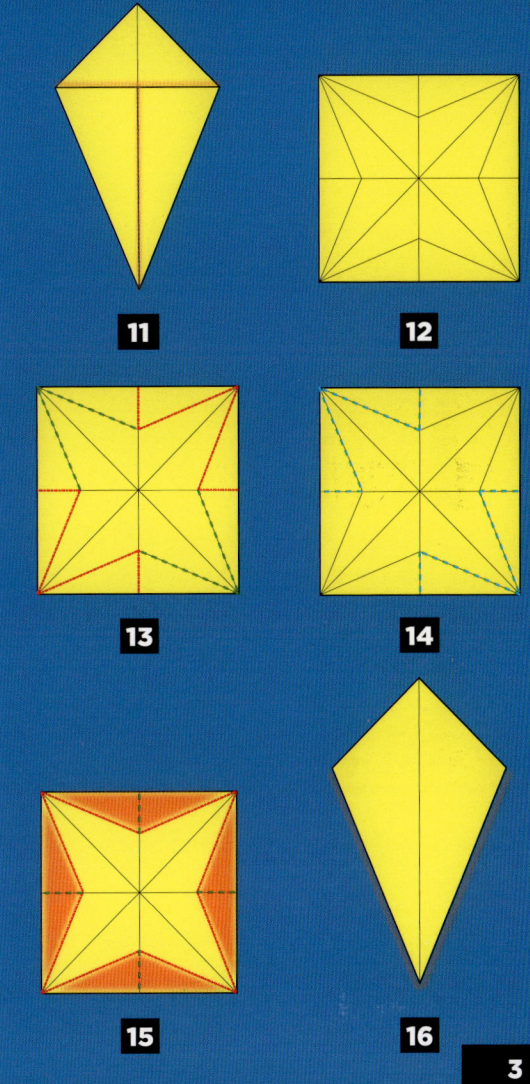

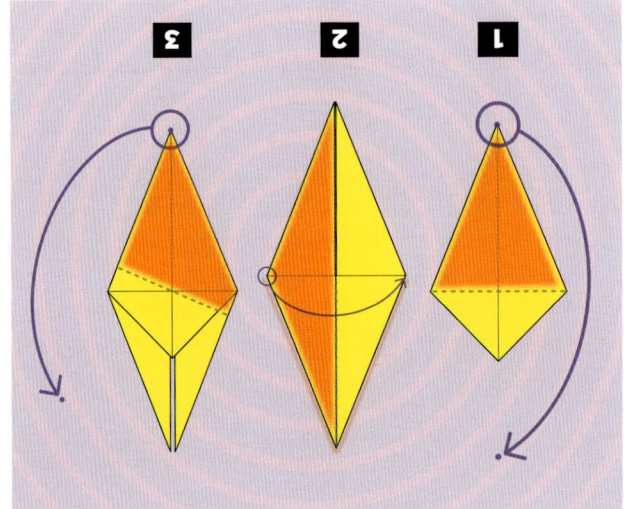

1. Begin with the basic form (page 1). Fold the bottom corner up to the top as shown. Flip your model and repeat this fold on the other side.

2. Book fold both sides of your model.

3. Fold the bottom corner of the top layer up and to the right, as shown, on both sides of your model.

THE FLYING CRANE

4. Pull the tips out and down, as shown, and then pinch as indicated to secure them. Notice that the upper edge of the left tip (in the next diagram) aligns with the fold line visible toward the bottom of the model.

5. Your model should look like this. Fold the left corner down to form the head.

6. Inside reverse fold the fold you made in Step 5.

7. Fold the wings down on both sides of your model. This fold line should be roughly perpendicular to the upper edge of the tail.

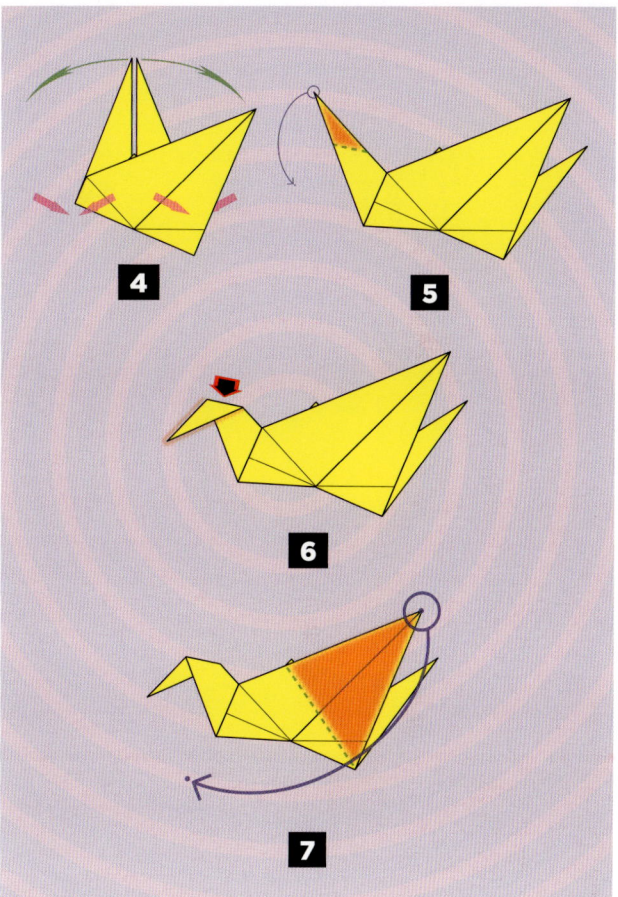

THE SITTING CRANE

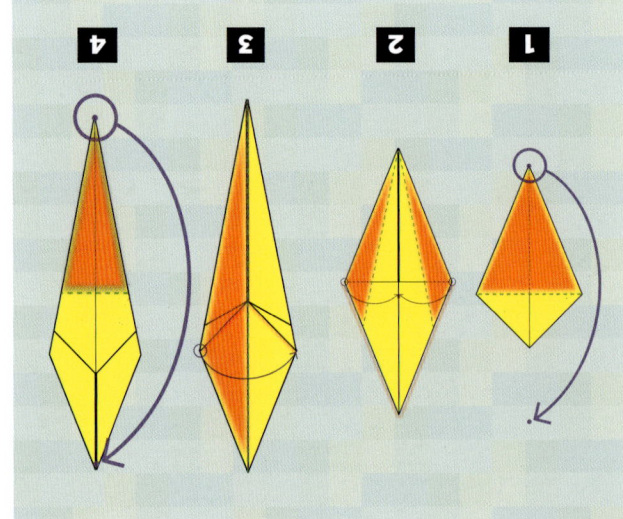

1. Begin with the basic form (page 1). Fold the bottom corner up to the top as shown. Flip your model and repeat this fold on the other side.

2. Fold the left and right corners of the top layer to the center. Flip your model and repeat on the opposite side.

3. Book fold one layer on each side of your model.

4. Fold the bottom corner of the upper layer to the top of your model. Flip it and repeat the fold on the other side.

5. Your model should look like this. Book fold one layer on each side.

6. Fold the top corner of the upper layer down, and then flip your model and do the same on the other side.

7. Pull the left narrow tip down and toward the left, and then pinch in the area indicated to secure it. Do the same with the tip on the right.

8. Fold one of the tips down, as shown, to form the head.

9. Inside reverse fold the fold you made in Step 8.

10. Lift the wings up a bit on both sides.

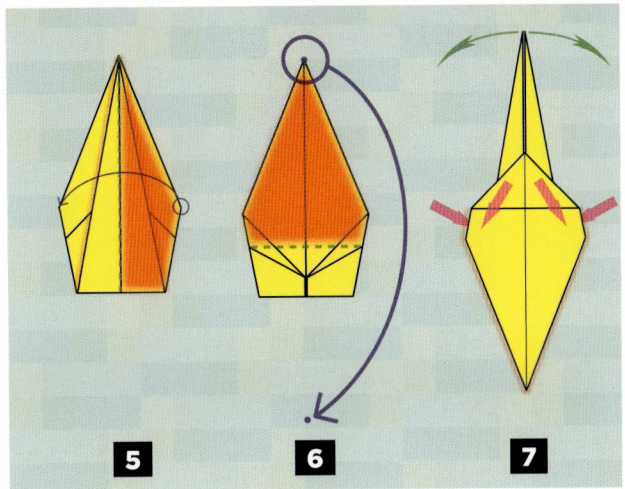

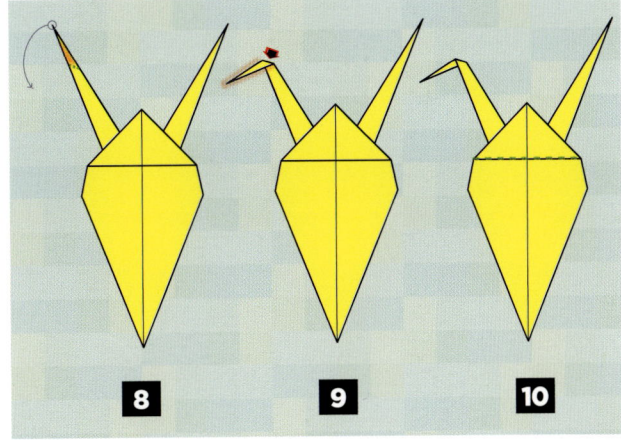

THE OLD CROW

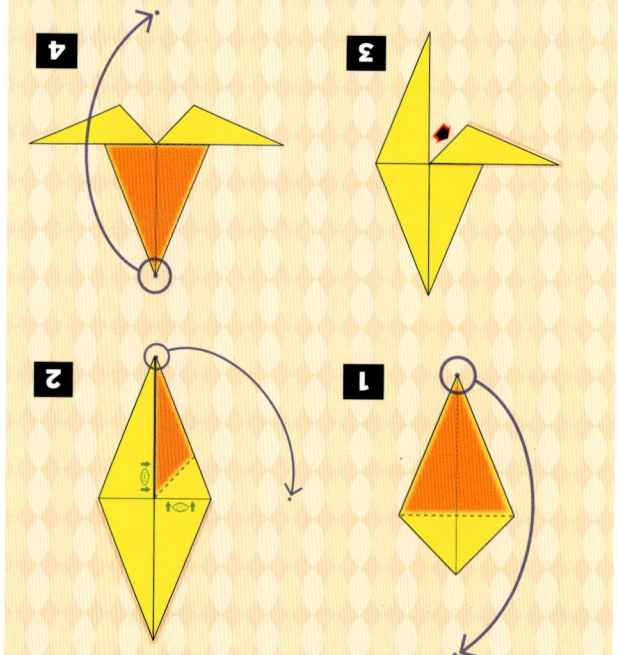

1. Begin with the basic form (page 1). Fold the bottom corner up to the top as shown. Flip your model and repeat this fold on the other side.

2. Fold the left bottom tip up and to the left.

3. Inside reverse fold the fold you made in Step 2.

4. Repeat Steps 2 and 3 on the right side of your model. Your model will look like this. Fold the top corner of the upper layer down to the bottom on the pre-existing fold.

5. Your model should look like this. Flip it.

6. Fold your model in half vertically.

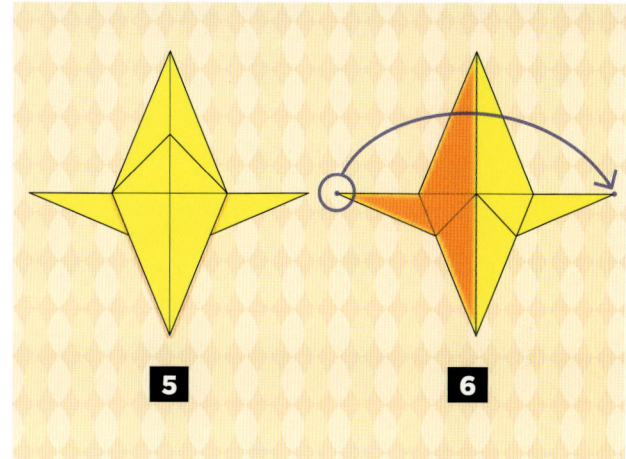

7. Your model should look like this. Fold the top corner down and to the right to form the head.

8. Inside reverse fold the fold you made in Step 7.

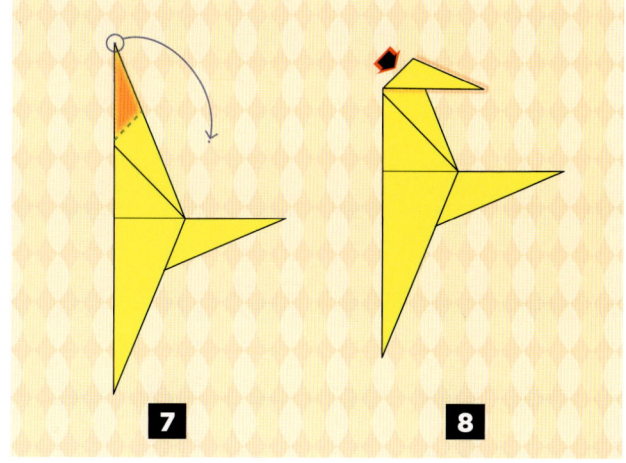

THE SEA LION

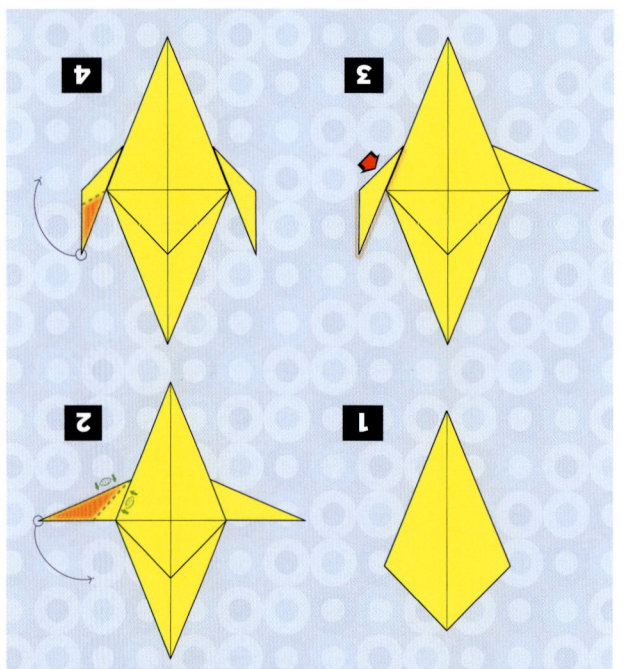

1. Begin by folding the basic form (page 1).

2. Fold the old crow (page 8) through Step 5. Fold the right tip up and to the left using the edges as shown for alignment.

3. Outside reverse fold the fold you made in Step 2. Repeat Steps 2 and 3 on the left tip, and your model should look like this.

4. Fold the upper right tip down and to the right as shown.

5. Outside reverse fold the fold you made in Step 4.

6. Repeat Steps 4 and 5 on the left tip, and your model should look like this. Fold it in half vertically.

7. Fold the top tip down and to the left, using the edge and horizontal fold, as shown, for alignment. This fold will encompass all the layers beneath it, so it will be a bit of a challenge on your first attempt.

8. Outside reverse fold the fold you made in Step 7. Look at the next diagram for clarification.

9. Fold the bottom tip up and to the right to form the body of the sea lion. This fold is roughly parallel to the paper edge above it, but the distance from that edge is up to you. Fold it farther from the edge to create a larger body, closer to create a smaller one.

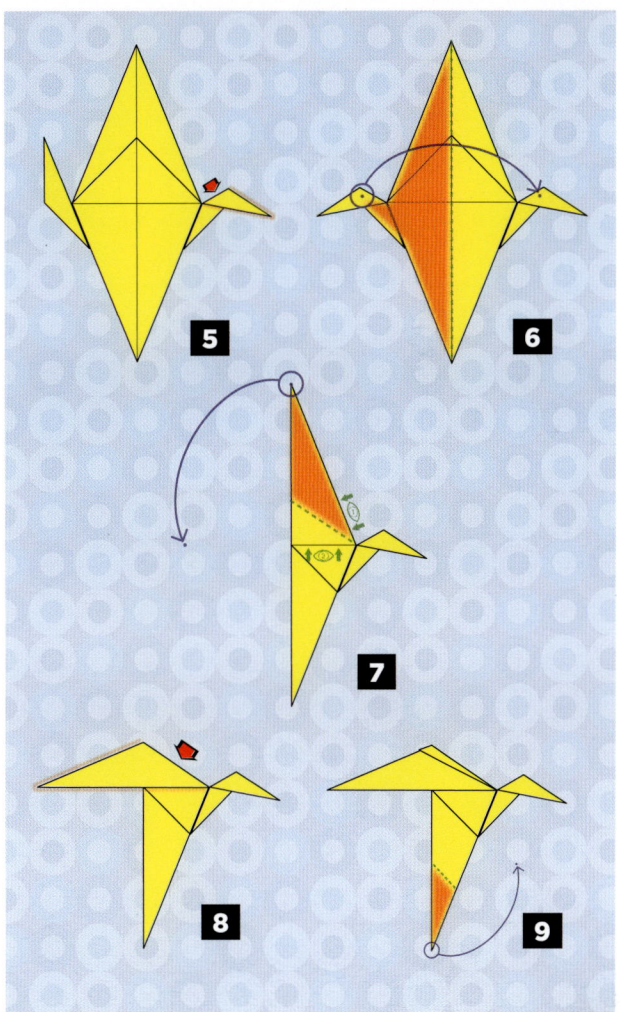

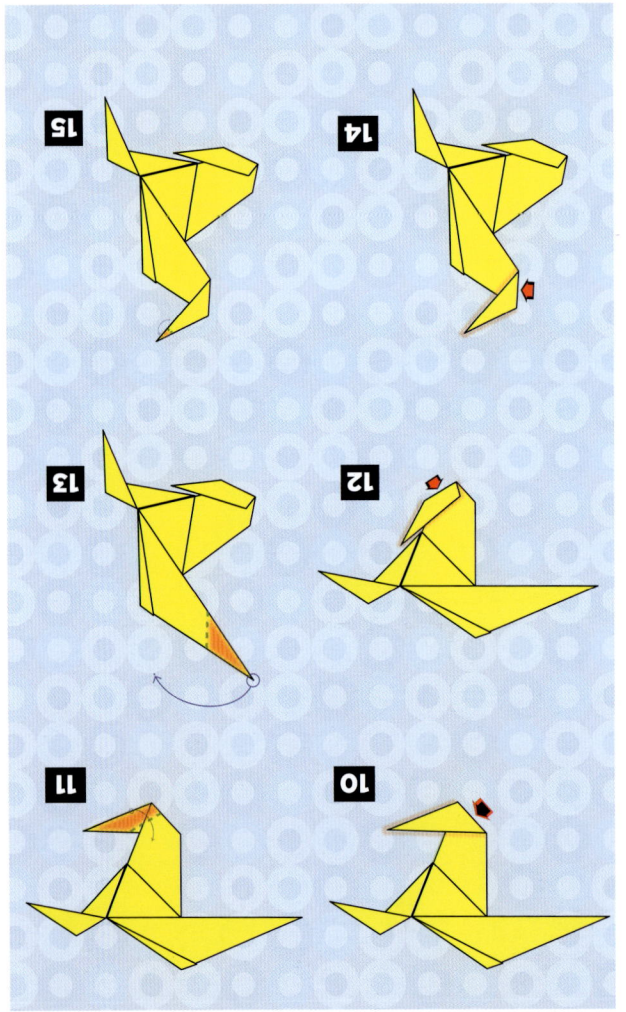

10. Inside reverse fold the fold you made in Step 9.

11. Fold all the layers up and to the left, as shown, to form a rear flipper.

12. Outside reverse fold the fold you made in Step 11. Reorient your model so it looks like the next diagram.

13. Fold the top tip to the right as shown.

14. Outside reverse fold the fold you made in Step 13.

15. Tuck the tip of the nose underneath to form a seal. You can spread its front flippers to obtain a more natural look.

THE ROOSTER

1. Begin by folding the basic form (page 1).

2. Fold the old crow (page 8) through Step 5.

3. Fold the sea lion (page 10) through Step 3. Fold the outer tips down and toward the center of the model.

4. Inside reverse fold the folds you made in Step 3.

5. Your model should look like this. Fold it in half vertically.

6. Fold the top tip down and to the left, using the outer edge and existing fold line to align it.

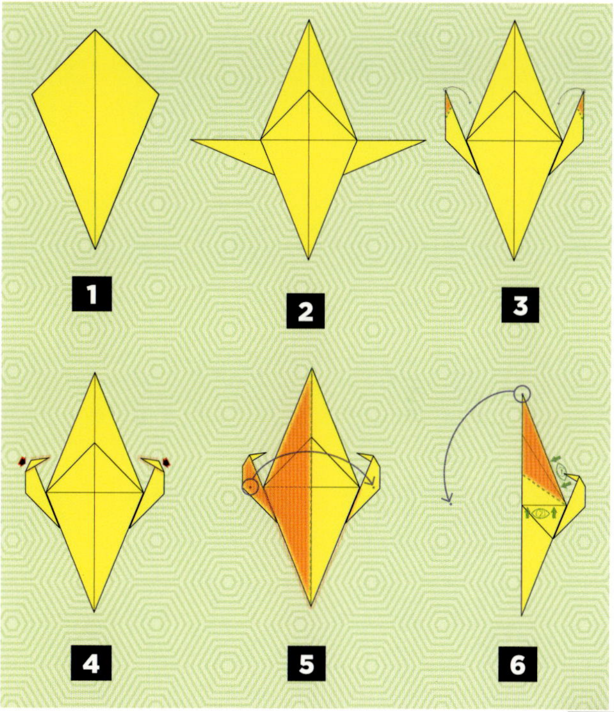

1

2

3

4

5

6

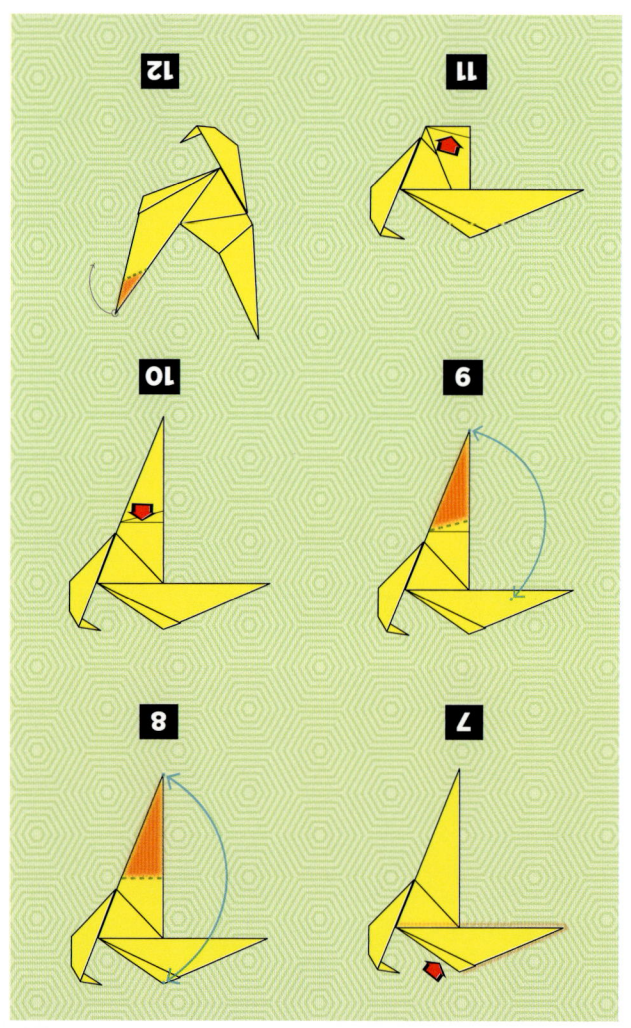

7. Outside reverse fold the fold you made in Step 8.

8. Fold and then unfold the bottom corner up to the top as shown.

9. Fold and then unfold the bottom corner up and to the left as shown.

10. Outside reverse fold the fold you made in Step 8. The bottom tip will end up inside the top area created in Step 9.

11. Outside reverse fold the fold you made in Step 9. Reorient your model so it looks like the next diagram. If you have trouble completing this fold, try doing Steps 10 and 11 at the same time.

12. Fold the right tip down and to the right to form the rooster's head.

13. Outside reverse fold the fold you made in Step 12.

14. To create a beak, fold the tip of the head back (underneath) and then forward again, leaving a small gap.

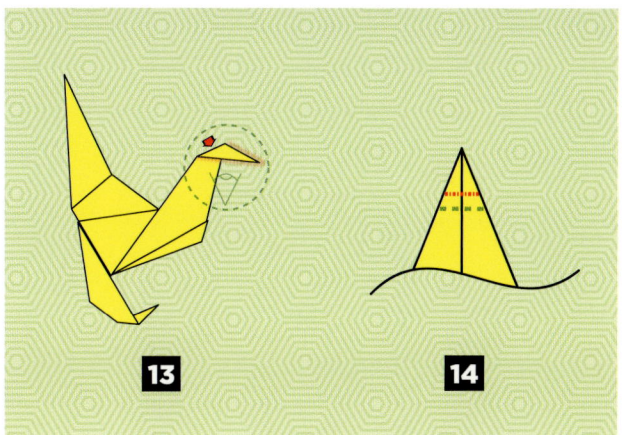

TIP

You can curl your rooster's tail if you so desire. The rooster doesn't have much surface area on his feet, so making him stand on his own can be a challenge. One solution is to flatten the feet or make them larger in Step 3 (perform the folds a bit lower).

THE FLAMINGO

1. Begin by folding the basic form (page 1).

2. Fold the old crow (page 8) through Step 5 and then flip it.

3. Fold the left and right edges of the top layer as shown. Notice that the fold lines don't extend all the way to the bottom corner of the areas. Small pockets form at the bottom of each fold which you...

4. ...crush fold into place.

5. Fold the top layer of the left side up as shown.

6. Fold the top and bottom edges of the left side to the center as shown. This will create a narrow leg.

7. Close the flap you opened in Step 5.

8. Repeat Steps 5, 6, and 7 on the right side of your model. Your model should then look like this. Fold the bottom tip up and toward the center as shown.

9. Fold your model in half vertically.

10. Fold the bottom left corner up and to the right as shown.

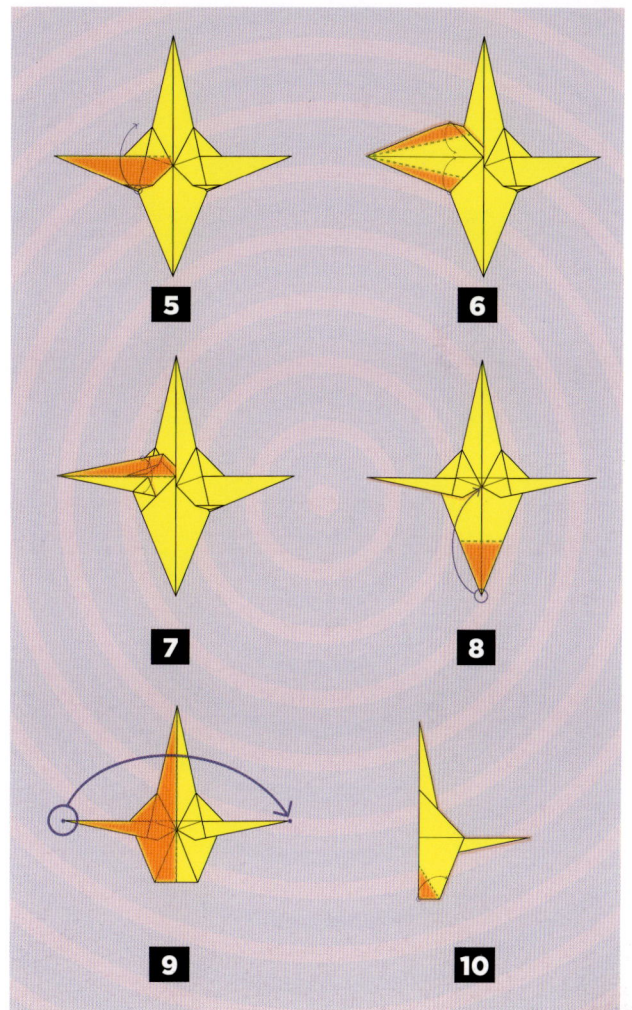

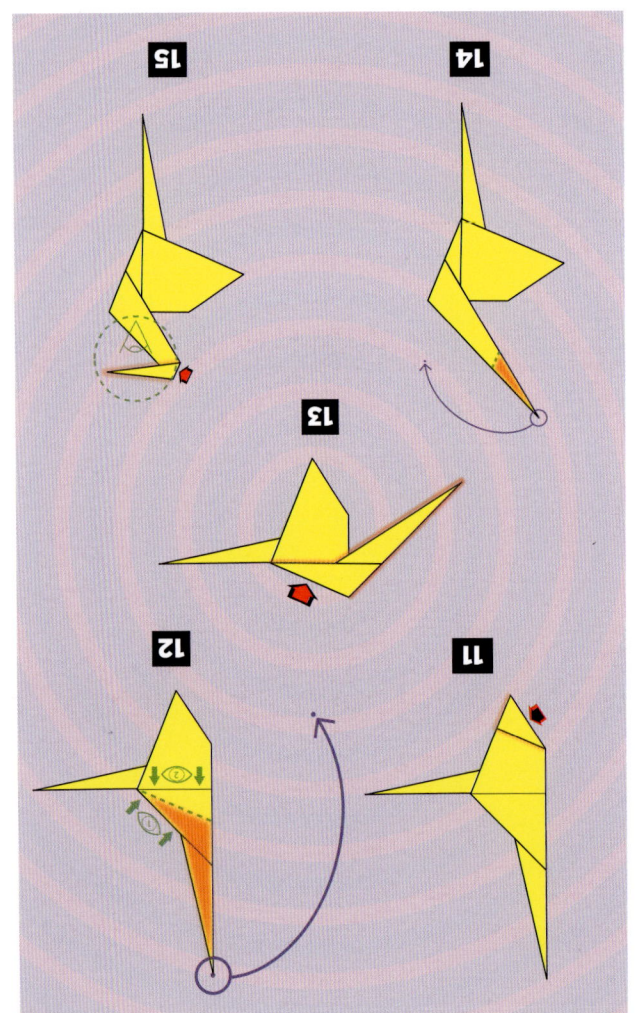

11. Inside reverse fold the fold you made in Step 10.

12. Fold all layers down and toward the left, as shown, using the upper edge and the fold line for alignment.

13. Outside reverse fold the fold you made in Step 12. Reorient your model so it looks like the next diagram.

14. Fold the top tip down and to the right to form the head.

15. Outside reverse fold the fold you made in Step 14.

16. Make a mountain and valley fold to create the flamingo's head, leaving as much room as possible for the beak.

17. Fold the bottom tip up and to the right, as shown, on both sides of your model.

18. Outside reverse fold the folds you made in Step 17.

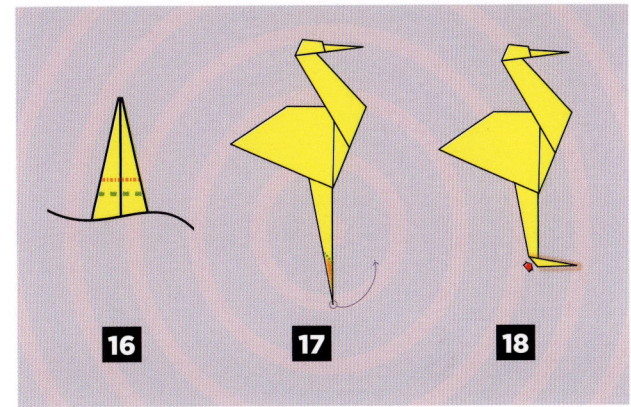

TIP

You can curve the beak by pinching it. Flattening the feet will make it easier for your model to stand on its own.

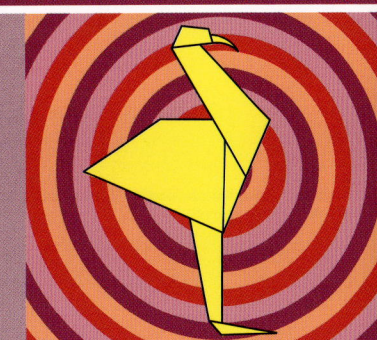

THE HUMMINGBIRD

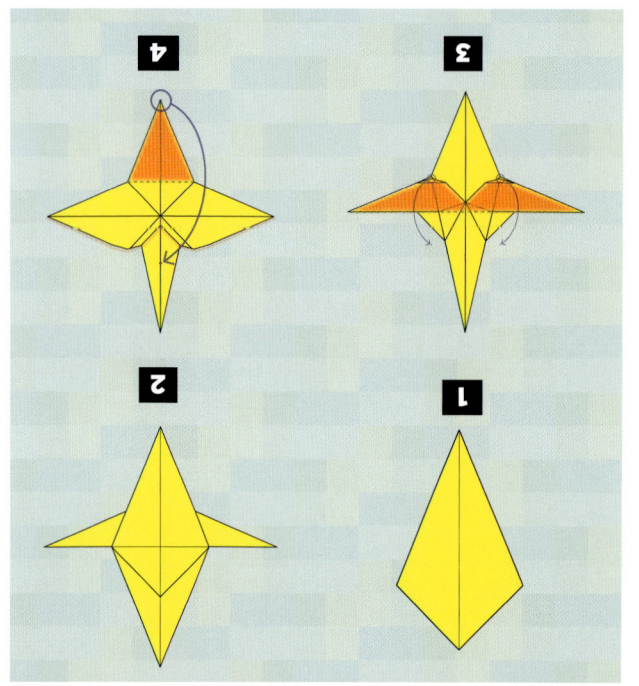

1. Begin by folding the basic form (page 1).

2. Fold the old crow (page 8) through Step 5.

3. Fold the flamingo (page 16) through Step 4. Open the left and right flaps as shown.

4. Fold the bottom tip up as shown.

5. Fold the flap back down, leaving a small gap.

6. Your model should look like this. Fold the bottom tip up again, leaving a gap about four times the size of the gap you left in Step 5; then fold it back down, leaving a gap similar to the one you left in Step 5. Repeat these folds on the flap until you run out of space.

7. Your model should look similar to this. Flip it.

8. Fold the outer corners of the top flap down and toward the center of the model as shown.

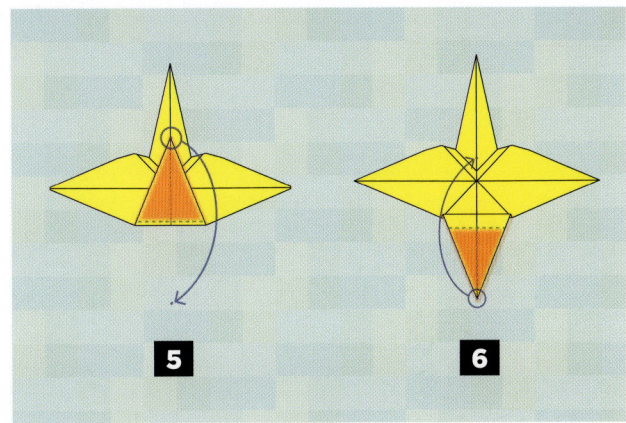

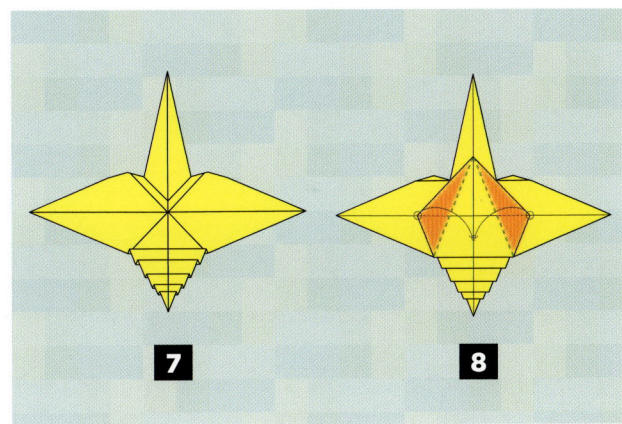

9. Fold your model in half vertically and reorient it so it looks like the following diagram.

10. Pull each pleat down and to the right, and then pinch it to secure it in position. See the next diagram for a clearer explanation.

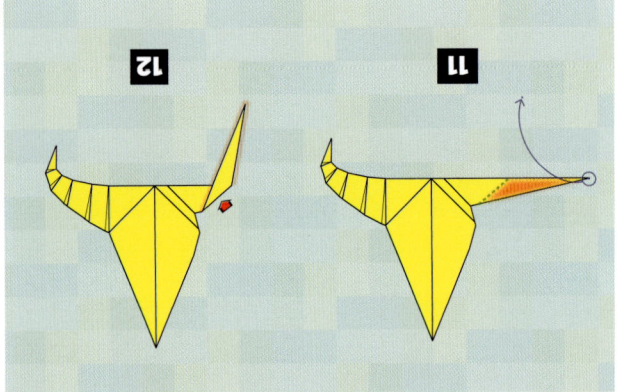

11. Fold the left tip down and to the right. This fold is made just ahead of the thickest layers of paper, so you can feel where it belongs.

12. Outside reverse fold the fold you made in Step 11. Your completed humming-bird should look like this.

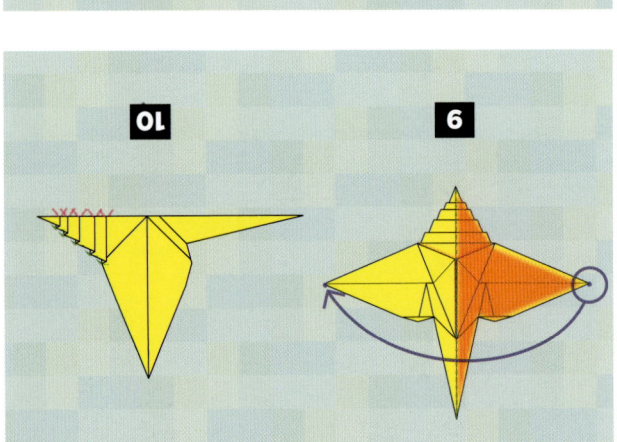

THE SEA GULL

1. Begin by folding the basic form (page 1).

2. Fold the old crow (page 8) through Step 5. Fold the outside tips up and toward the center as shown.

3. Outside reverse fold the folds you made in Step 2.

4. Fold the top two layers of paper up (on the existing fold), as shown, on both the left and right sides of your model. Allow the tips you folded in Step 2 to rotate freely.

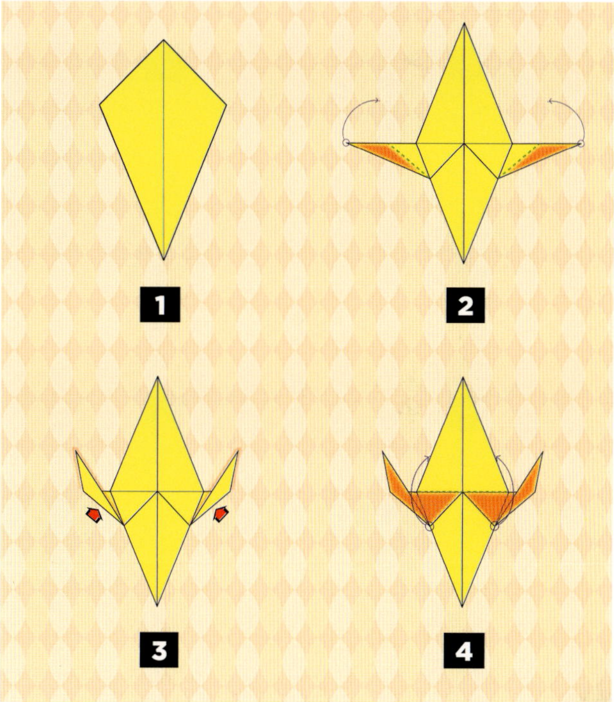

1

2

3

4

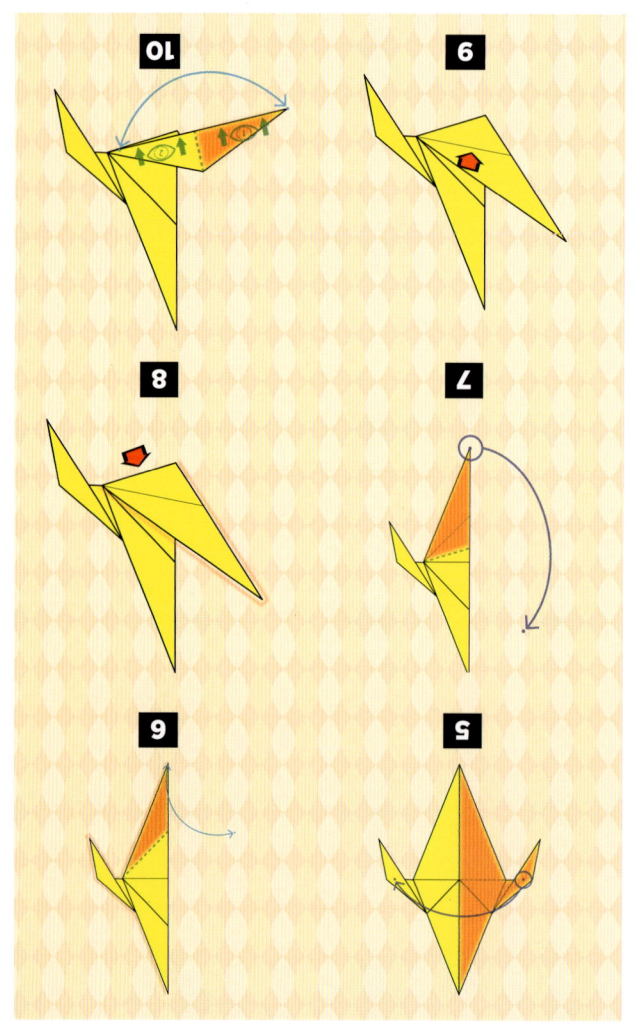

5. Your model should look like this. Fold it in half vertically.

6. Fold and then unfold the bottom corner up and to the left.

7. Fold the bottom corner up and to the left as shown.

8. Outside reverse fold the fold you made in Step 7.

9. Outside reverse fold the fold you made in Step 6.

10. Fold and then unfold the left tip to the right. Use the bottom edge for alignment.

11. Fold and then unfold the left tip down, using the top edge and the fold you made in Step 10 for alignment.

12. T-fold the folds you made in Steps 10 and 11.

13. Your model should look like this. Open the T-fold and…

14. …fold a valley and mountain fold to create a beak. Close the T-fold.

15. Reorient your model so it looks like this. Fold and then unfold both the bottom tips up.

16. Open the bottom tips and pinch the folds you made in Step 15 to form what look like webbed feet. Your completed sea gull should look like this.

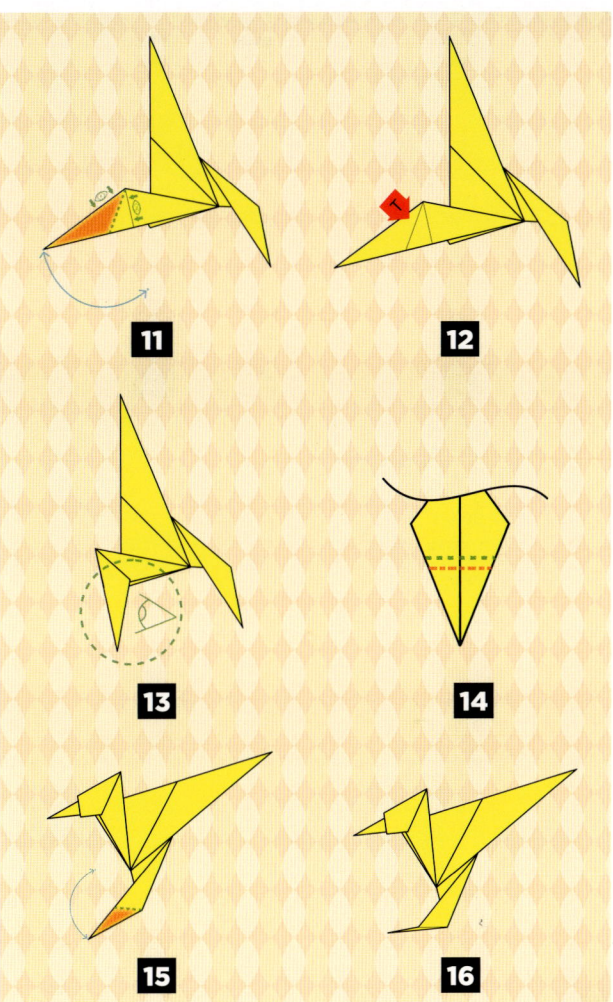

THE FLYING DRAGON

1. Begin by folding the basic form (page 1).

2. Fold the old crow (page 8) through Step 4.

3. Fold the flamingo (page 16) through Step 5 and then flip it.

4. Fold the top layer of the bottom tip up to the top.

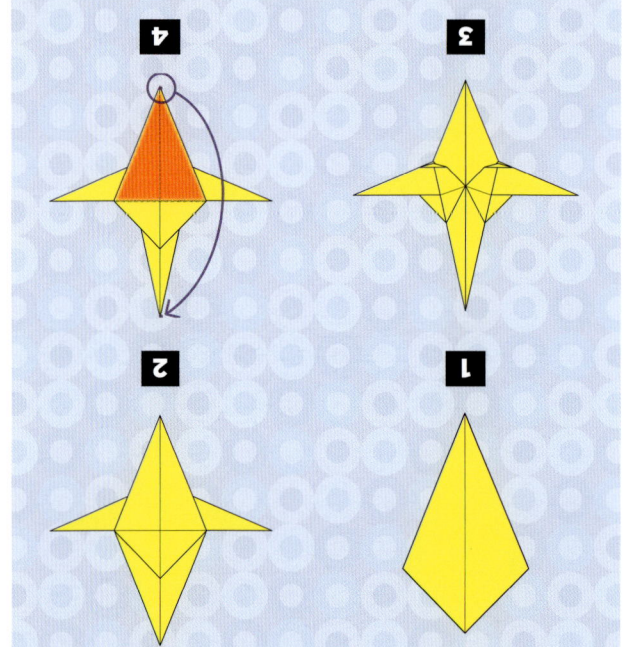

5. Narrow the top tips by folding the edges to the center as shown. Notice that the fold line does not extend all the way to the bottom edge of your paper. This is because you will have to…

6. …crush fold the flaps at the bottom.

7. Fold the top layer of paper down as shown.

8. Fold the small flap down and then flip your model.

9. Fold the top layer of paper up on both the left and right sides of your model.

10. Fold your model in half vertically.

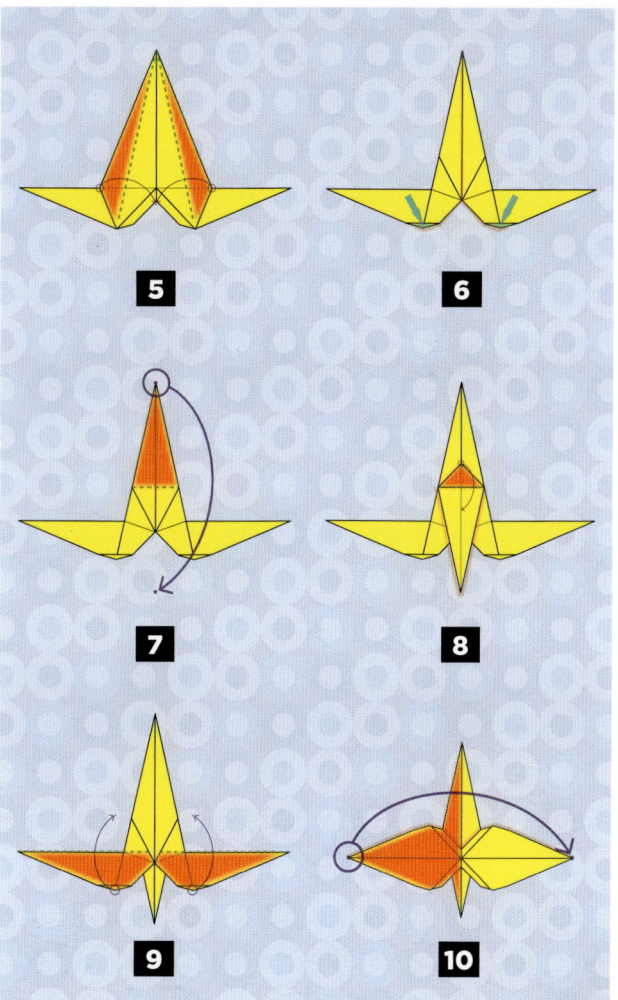

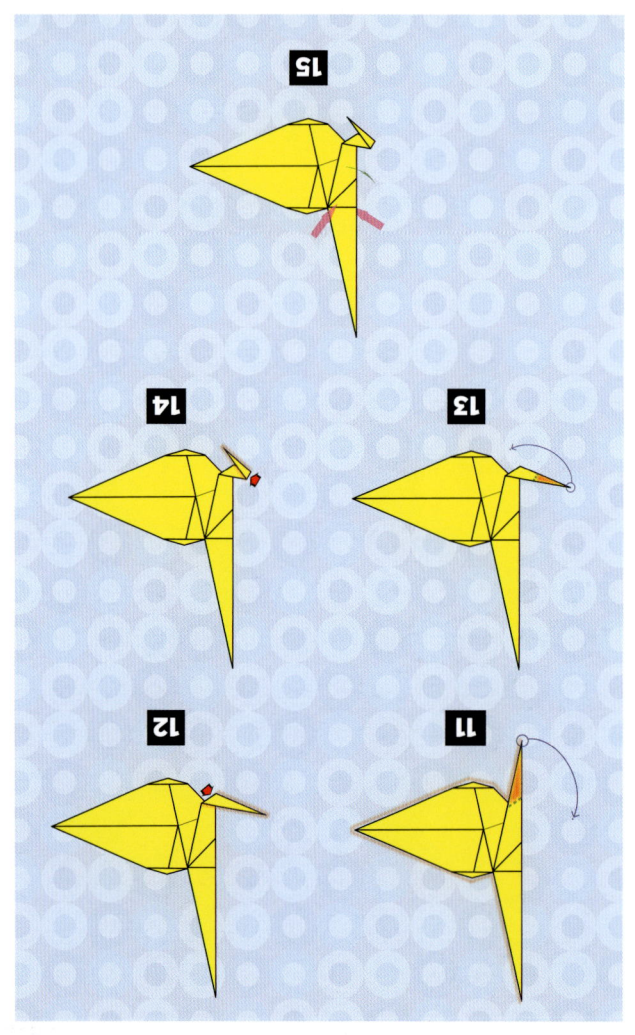

11. Fold the bottom tip up and toward the left.

12. Outside reverse fold the fold you made in Step 11.

13. Fold the narrow tip to the right and slightly down.

14. Outside reverse fold the fold you made in Step 13.

15. Pull the flap you folded in Step 8 toward the outside of the model, and then pinch in the area shown to secure it.

THE T-REX

1. Begin by folding the basic form (page 1).

2. Fold the old crow (page 8) through Step 4. Fold the outside tips down and toward the center.

3. Inside reverse fold the folds you made in Step 2.

4. Fold your model in half vertically.

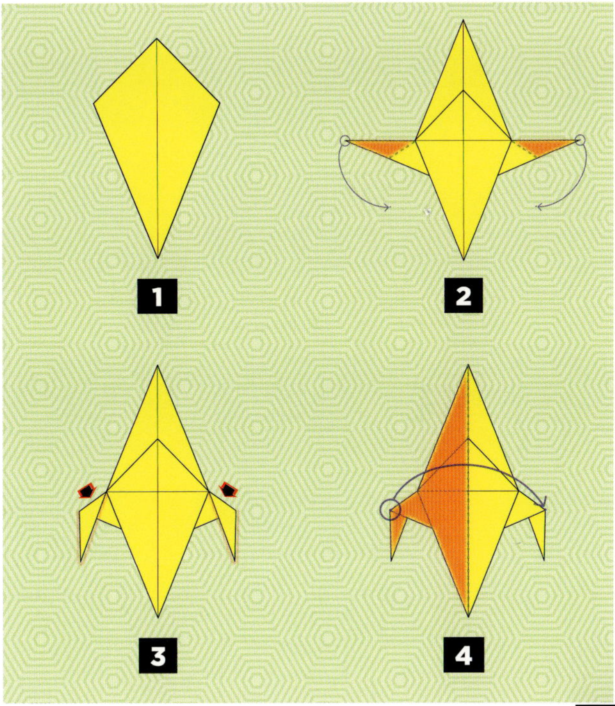

1

2

3

4

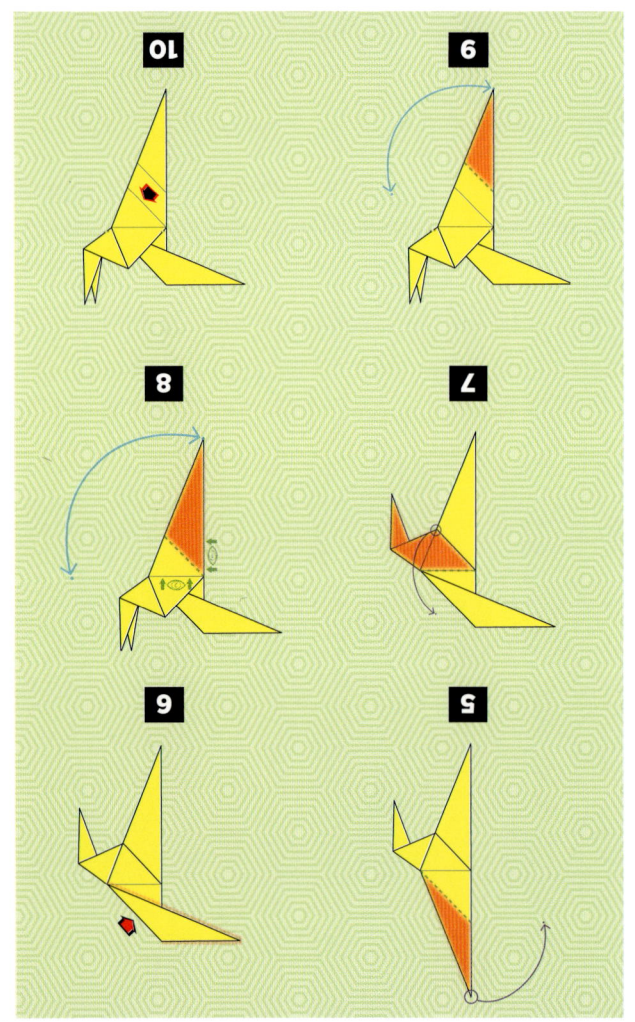

5. Fold the top tip down and to the left. This fold is made just ahead of the thickest area of paper, so you can feel where the fold line should be.

6. Outside reverse fold the fold you made in Step 5.

7. Fold the top two layers of paper up on the existing fold on both sides of your model.

8. Fold and then unfold the bottom tip up and to the right, aligning the left edge to the fold as shown.

9. Fold and then unfold the bottom corner again, parallel to the fold you made in Step 8 but a bit farther down.

10. Inside reverse fold the fold you made in Step 8.

11. Inside reverse fold the fold you made in Step 9.

12. Your model should look like this. Fold the left tip up and to the right to form the head of the dinosaur.

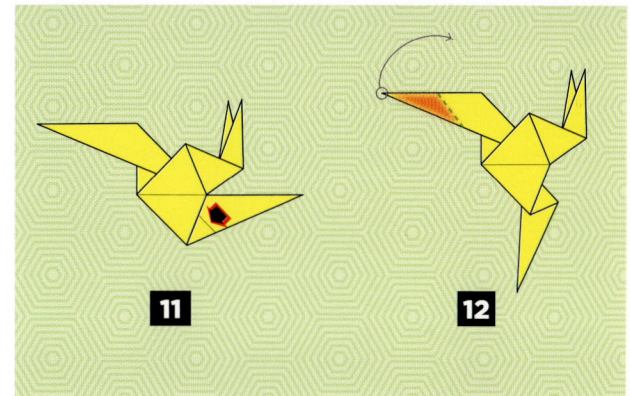

13. Outside reverse fold the fold you made in Step 12, and then reorient your model so it looks like the next diagram.

14. Fold the tip of the head underneath to form a nose and then pull the flap inside the neck down, pinch it, then pull it back up to form a tiny appendage.

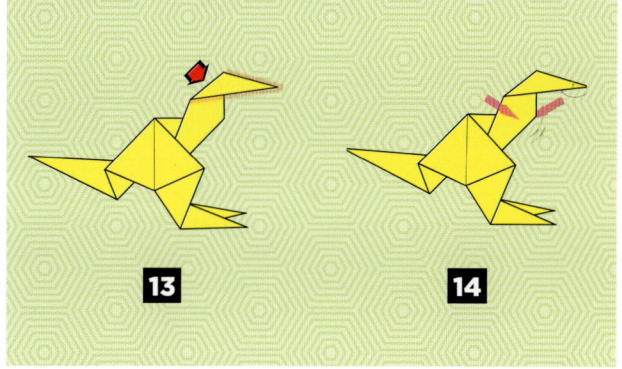

SYMBOLS INDEX

Fold: this symbol shows where to fold and in which direction

Fold and then unfold: this symbol indicates where to fold and unfold; there is also dashes indicating where the fold is on the paper

Alignment: this symbol is showing the alignment

Crush Fold: this a blue arrow indicated where to crush and fold paper

Zoom to a View: this symbol indicates zoom here

Pinch Fold: this symbol is a pink arrow that shows the direction of where to pinch

Pull and Pinch: this symbol uses arrows to show the direction of the pinch fold, and a green arrow to indicate the direction of the pull (most photos have a double green arrow)

Inside Reverse Fold
Sharpen the fold the arrow is pointing at. Unfold your previous fold. Determine the layers of paper the inside reverse fold affects. Position your middle fingers under the folds you want to make mountain folds and push the paper down. Fold in half and pinch to secure them.

Outside Reverse Fold
Sharpen the fold the arrow is pointing at. Unfold your previous fold. Lift the paper up and put your fingers under the fold to be reversed. Bend the fold over your middle finger. Once the fold becomes a mountain, remove fingers and pinch the fold closed.